Additional Praise for *Suddenly Hybrid*

"The old way of leading teams is now a thing of the past. The future of work is hybrid. *Suddenly Hybrid* is an excellent fact-based playbook with best practices that will inspire more engaged and satisfied employees.

—Sarah Johnston, award-winning career branding expert and founder of Briefcase Coach

"How can managers balance employee demands for flexibility with organization objectives? Reed and Allen answer that question in spades. *Suddenly Hybrid* is a critical, evidence-based book that has arrived at the perfect time."

—Phil Simon, author of *Reimagining Collaboration: Slack, Microsoft Teams, Zoom, and the Post-COVID World of Work*

"Who knew a meeting scientist and an on-camera coach would become so essential for leaders and employees in just about every office-based industry? Evidently, Karin and Joe did. This book is chock full of great guidance and actionable tips for both leaders and employees who want to perform at their best as individuals and teams!"

—Hoby Darling, human performance expert and executive at Logitech, Liminal Collective, Skullcandy, and Nike

SUDDENLY HYBRID

SUDDENLY HYBRID

Managing the Modern Meeting

KARIN M. REED
JOSEPH A. ALLEN

WILEY

Published by John Wiley & Sons, Inc., Hoboken, New Jersey.
Published simultaneously in Canada.

For general information on our other products and services or for technical support, please contact our Customer Care Department within the United States at (800) 762-2974, outside the United States at (317) 572-3993 or fax (317) 572-4002.

Wiley also publishes its books in a variety of electronic formats. Some content that appears in print may not be available in electronic formats. For more information about Wiley products, visit our web site at www.wiley.com.

Library of Congress Cataloging-in-Publication Data

Names: Reed, Karin M., author. | Allen, Joseph A., 1981- author.
Title: Suddenly hybrid : managing the modern meeting / Karin M. Reed, Joseph A. Allen.
Description: Hoboken, New Jersey : Wiley, [2022] | Includes index.
Identifiers: LCCN 2021045693 (print) | LCCN 2021045694 (ebook) | ISBN 9781119831082 (cloth) | ISBN 9781119831105 (adobe pdf) | ISBN 9781119831099 (epub)
Subjects: LCSH: Meetings. | Flexible work arrangements.
Classification: LCC HF5549.5.C6 R45 2022 (print) | LCC HF5549.5.C6 (ebook) | DDC 658.3—dc23
LC record available at https://lccn.loc.gov/2021045693
LC ebook record available at https://lccn.loc.gov/2021045694

COVER DESIGN: PAUL McCARTHY
COVER ART: © GETTY IMAGES | DIGITALVISION VECTORS / PAUL McCARTHY
AUTHOR PHOTOS: COURTESY OF THE AUTHORS

SKY10031937_121021

Writing a book in a year is no small feat. Writing two books in a year borders on insanity. This book is dedicated to our families, who made it possible and kept us grounded throughout the process.

Karin: For Shawn, Hayden, Jackson, and Mom

Joe: For Joy and Melva

Contents

Preface

Are your muscles still sore?

You know the ones we're talking about – the metaphorical muscles that we've been stretching more than ever before, the ones that allowed us to creatively and cautiously test out new ways of living, new ways of working necessitated by a global pandemic. The ones that allowed us to quickly go "suddenly virtual" – with almost all of our meetings in front of a webcam.

In many ways, COVID-19 was like a car accident. Most of us saw it coming too late to do little more than brace for impact. Some of the damage was revealed immediately as offices shut down and the world turned inward. Much of it was revealed over time with the heartbreaking loss of lives and livelihoods. Today, even with the initial crash in the rearview mirror, you may still be feeling the aches and pains from the whiplash we collectively suffered while constantly adjusting to the "new normal," a cliché that needs to be retired . . . but perhaps not yet, because we are entering a new phase of adaptation. In the midst of recovering from the whiplash of going fully virtual, those muscles will need to be stretched once again as companies respond to the workforce of today, which has totally different expectations than it did pre-pandemic.

The pandemic altered the paradigm for the world of work, forcing a grand experiment for knowledge workers across the globe: Can work from home actually . . . well . . . work? By certain measures, the answer was a resounding "yes," with nary a blip in productivity. Sure, there are exceptions to this glowing review, but by and large, it worked, at least at the enterprise level, with businesses maintaining or growing their bottom line. How well it worked for *individual* employees, though, depended on each person's circumstances, including personal and familial obligations as well as how easily one's home could accommodate it. (Is a closet really adequate space in which to get work done? At least it has a door. . . .)

For the mid-career executive with children old enough to look after themselves, work from home may have meant more time to exercise, get outside, and perhaps do some nagging projects around the house. Sounds pretty nice, right? But for employees trying to juggle their jobs with virtual school for their young children, the needs of their "quarantine puppy" and myriad other chores, work from home was an exercise in exhaustion. And we haven't even mentioned those who were just entering the workforce who hated the fact that their career path was paved with back-to-back virtual meetings, not in-person opportunities to start creating a network and building a professional identity. The stories of both the opportunities and challenges experienced by the suddenly remote workforce could fill volumes.

Perhaps one thing that is universal, though, is how the pandemic transformed our orientation toward health and well-being. We wash our hands more. We use more hand sanitizer. And it is understood that we should not go to the office when we are sick, and everyone is okay with this. The "good soldier" phenomenon of "I'm a big, strong person who can work while sick. Look how devoted I am" is gone. At least, we hope it is. "Keep your germs to yourself" is an appropriate takeaway from a year of relative isolation.

This combination of factors plays into the current workplace era, where flexibility is prioritized more than ever before and employees are given choices about how and where they want to work. For some employees, that means continuing to work from home. For others, that translates into a welcome return to the brick-and-mortar office. But for the largest proportion of knowledge workers surveyed time and again by various outlets and organizations, that involves a work-week where a few days are spent in the office and a few days are spent somewhere else, whether it be home, a local coffee shop, or a far-flung locale with decent Wi-Fi. The age of the hybrid workforce is upon us and at the center of getting business done is the hybrid meeting.

Prior to COVID-19, hybrid meetings were relatively rare and consisted of the majority of attendees being in-person with perhaps someone dialing in (and often forgotten about). The hybrid meeting of today has a totally different configuration and may involve a group of people gathered in one conference room, maybe another group of people gathered in a huddle room somewhere else, and a variety of folks showing up in their own individual boxes on screen via their personal webcams.

This relatively simple description undersells the complexity of a hybrid meeting in contrast to the meetings we are all more familiar with, where either everyone is gathered around a table or everyone is on their webcams. Managing the expectations, participation, and conversation flow for all of these different constituencies is fraught with challenges but presents opportunities as well. The leaders who lean into developing new skills and the attendees who figure out how to make their voices heard will emerge victorious in the evolving workplace meeting landscape, which can be more inclusive than ever before. But what do we need to learn, what skills do we need to develop in this hybrid meeting environment, and how do we know what actually works?

The Purpose of This Book

When we wrote our first book, *Suddenly Virtual: Making Remote Meetings Work*, it hit bookstore shelves at just about the right time – almost a year after the global stay-at-home orders were announced. At that point, many businesses were used to meeting virtually, but most did not feel like they were doing it well. They were also realizing that virtual meetings were not a Band-Aid, not simply a way to communicate with their teams and their customers in the short term until a return to face-to-face. Rather, virtual meetings were becoming an important part of the corporate communication DNA, and will likely remain so for years to come. *Suddenly Virtual* offered science-based insights into best practices, so businesses could be more strategic in their approach and get the most out of their virtual engagements, both internal and external. We are hoping *Suddenly Hybrid* will fill the same role.

Remember those muscles that we have been stretching seemingly nonstop since March 2020 as we have sought to respond to the changing face of the pandemic? So much of our energy has been focused on adapting to the primarily virtual way of working that it has actually constrained our ability to plan for the next normal – the inevitable hybrid modality. In late May 2021, a survey by McKinsey & Company found that a clear majority of organizations planned to go hybrid. However, only about a third of those organizations had developed a detailed plan to do so. More than two thirds of respondents said they did not have a plan in place (Alexander et al. 2021). Perhaps the planning process quickly accelerated after that mid-2021 survey, but with the arrival of virus variants, many organizations likely still lagged behind in formulating a solid return-to-office strategy. The good news is that wherever you are in hybrid work and the hybrid meeting transition, this book will serve as a key resource for both development of and revision of these plans.

The opportunity presented by this book is to learn how to optimize your hybrid meetings through a scientific approach, so the mistakes are minimized and the value of hybrid meetings is maximized – and there is a lot of value to be gained. We will share some initial data that points to the promise of hybrid meetings, and translate that into best practices to make your hybrid meetings as effective as possible – best practices based on the science of meetings that informs better management of multimodal meeting environments.

How to Use This Book

While theory is important, we believe practicality is critical, and that's why we include tools throughout this book that will help guide your implementation of hybrid meetings. We encourage you to not read this book passively but rather to actively engage with it by using its tools to assess yourself and your organization.

Checklists: In nearly every chapter, you will find a checklist that will help you apply the knowledge imparted. Sometimes the checklists involve a series of questions that will illuminate potential gaps in your hybrid meeting strategy. Sometimes they offer expert advice on what factors to consider on things like hardware, software or meeting room setup. While you can certainly check the boxes in the book itself, you can also access them on the book's website (www.wiley.com\go\reed-allen\hybrid), where you'll find all of the checklists available for you to fill out online or print out if you prefer putting pen to paper.

Chapter Takeaways: Each chapter is full of pertinent information for both those who are running and those who are attending a hybrid meeting, but we recognize the potential for information overload. That's why we include bulleted lists of key takeaways at the end of each chapter. Use these as a way to ensure that you have digested the most salient points, or return to them for quick reference at a later date.

Reflection Activity: At a minimum, we recommend going through the final exercise using something we call the Adaptive Improvement Model (AIM) framework. This reflection exercise will raise your awareness about where you are in your hybrid meeting transition and, most importantly, can reveal your next steps as you seek to make these meetings productive and satisfying for all.

Above all, we want you to gain confidence in your ability to conduct, manage, and take part in hybrid meetings. Reading this book is an excellent first step in accomplishing that goal.

Reference

Alexander, A., R. Cracknell, A. D. Smet, M. Langstaff, M. Mysore, and D. Ravid. 2021. "What executives are saying about the future of hybrid work." McKinsey & Company. https://www.mckinsey.com/business-functions/organization/our-insights/what-executives-are-saying-about-the-future-of-hybrid-work?utm_source=digg&utm_medium=email#

Acknowledgments

As with any book, we needed a team of great people supporting us to make this finished product possible. We are eternally grateful to Sheck Cho at John Wiley & Sons, who helped us to realize that an off-hand comment Joe made about how "we could write a book about all that has happened with hybrid meetings" truly *should* be a book. His encouragement allowed us to dive into the data to develop a roadmap for so many who have no clue how to even start the hybrid meeting journey.

When in the process of writing under deadline, it's easy to see only the chapter you are currently creating, which can pose a problem when you arrive at the conclusion to find that the narrative flow is all over the place. That's why we were incredibly fortunate to have Kristin Bair serve as our developmental editor throughout the process, applauding our efforts when deserved but, more importantly, pushing us to make revisions as we went along. If you find the book easy to digest, you can thank Kristin for making it so.

We are also grateful to three key members of Joe's team. First, we want to thank his research manager, Emilee Eden, for her assistance with identifying and sourcing references and citations. Additionally, Joe's research assistant, Katherine Castro, was truly essential in her efforts to help collect and analyze the new data shared in this volume. Lastly, our sincere thanks to Joy Allen, beta reader extraordinaire, whose insightful comments and ideas for enhancing the manuscript made the book so much better for our eventual readers.

Additional thanks to those who so willingly shared their expertise, insight, and anecdotes: Matt Abrahams, Tom Bridges, Shiraz Cupala, Dave Egloff, Dan Hawkins, Jay Hyett, Justin Mitchell, Darren Murph, Steve Santana, Rick Sems, Phil Simon, Elisabeth Steele-Hutchison, Lisette Sutherland, Eric Taylor, Kerry Troester, and Scott Wharton. By sharing your stories, you helped all of us to better understand our evolving meeting landscape and what the future may hold.

PART ONE

From Suddenly Virtual to Suddenly Hybrid

In March 2020, the world essentially shut down in response to the biggest global health disaster of the current century – COVID-19. The response to this deadly disease that has claimed the lives of so many was inconsistent across countries and even between states within the United States. However, nearly uniformly, organizations closed offices and sent their workers home, hoping they could figure out a way to get business done even though they were scattered to the winds.

The supply chain strained to the point of breaking as "suddenly virtual" workers scrambled to set up their home offices. There was a run on webcams, computers, office chairs, desks, and, oddly enough, toilet paper. Correspondingly, companies like Zoom, Microsoft, and Logitech saw massive growth in sales and usage, particularly of video-conferencing tools and platforms (Reed and Allen 2021).

While businesses accelerated the adoption of new tools and processes, leaders anticipated an inevitable dip in productivity . . . a dip that by and large did not occur. Much to nearly every leader's surprise, the data suggests that productivity in organizations during the pandemic remained stable (Gaskell 2021), at least for those industries that did not require face-to-face interactions. For those that rely almost entirely on people gathering together, like the hospitality industry, the pandemic caused tremendous suffering, forcing some businesses to close for good. Restaurants that had become institutions said goodbye to their patrons via social media posts. Still, for knowledge workers, the pandemic proved that fully remote work was possible and, in some cases, even preferable.

And then, this happened on Thursday, May 10, 2021 . . .

> If you are fully vaccinated, you can resume activities that you did prior to the pandemic. Fully vaccinated people can resume activities without wearing a mask or physically distancing, except where required by federal, state, local, tribal, or territorial laws, rules, and regulations, including local business and workplace guidance. If you haven't been vaccinated yet, find a vaccine. (Centers for Disease Control and Prevention [CDC] 2021)

The guidance from the CDC in the United States was applauded by most but met with apprehension by many. After a year of social distancing, COVID pods, and elasticized waistbands for work, the idea of navigating the nail-biting commute, throwing on the suit and tie or slingback heels, and heading back to the office was difficult to wrap our heads around. What did all of this relaxation of restrictions mean? Back to the office full-time? Would working from home simply end?

The answer to that final question, which hinted at the demise of remote work, is a resounding *no*. According to a multitude of surveys by many different interested parties, employees were not so ready to come back (e.g. Buchholz 2021). In fact, according to one of these surveys from the fall of 2020, as many as 65% of employees said they wanted to continue to work from home, with 35% indicating they'd be okay with a hybrid work arrangement. Perhaps the luster of working from home all the time started to wear off as the pandemic wore on, because results of a survey done in February 2021 found that about two-thirds of respondents considered a hybrid work environment their ideal work model, with only 15% expressing a desire to work from home full-time (Montgomery 2021).

As for employers, many found it harder to argue against what so many of their workers were desiring, especially when they looked at their key performance indicators. Not honoring those requests for flexible work options could easily become a retention issue. Employees could vote with their feet and leave for companies that offer them the opportunity to work the way they want to work – which, for many, is hybrid.

But what does "hybrid" mean, and what does it look like? And for the purposes of this book, what does it mean for meetings?

The events of 2020 precipitated the first major meeting disruption – a disruption ruled by necessity when virtual meetings became the predominant way to meet. However, a second major meeting disruption is underway – a move to hybrid meetings – and this one is being ruled by choice. If the majority of workers want to spend some of their time in the office and some of their time working outside of it, there still has to be a way for people to gather. Sure, teams can designate certain in-office days to meet, but ad hoc meetings happen and there's no guarantee that everyone will be available to be there in person.

Hybrid meetings provide the communication connective tissue for the hybrid workforce. They're flexible in how they are configured – flexible enough to allow in-office teammates to be in the same "room" with their remote colleagues. But flexible doesn't mean easy. In fact, making hybrid meetings work well requires planning, preparation, and know-how – but it's well worth your while, because this second major meeting disruption will likely stick.

But before we suggest a path forward, allow us to offer some perspective on the current state of meetings and provide some context that will inform how you approach hybrid meetings. In this part, we will take a look at the transition from being "suddenly virtual" to being "suddenly hybrid," as well as the drivers behind the shift to hybrid (Chapter 1). We will consider meeting modalities and present data that highlights the potential and challenge of each (Chapter 2). We will also highlight issues that came to light over the past year as meetings became mostly virtual (Chapter 3), paying particular attention to the prevalence of video call fatigue (Chapter 4). The lessons learned from our fully remote work life can and should be applied to our hybrid one, so we offer suggestions to ensure that we don't repeat the same mistakes in our hybrid (and virtual) meetings going forward.

References

Buchholz, K. 2021. "65% of remote workers do not want to return to the office – here's why." World Economic Forum, April 27. Retrieved July 9, 2021 from https://www.weforum.org/agenda/2021/04/survey-65-of-remote-workers-do-not-want-to-return-to-the-office/

Centers for Disease Control and Prevention (CDC). 2021. "When you've been fully vaccinated: How to protect yourself and others." Retrieved July 8, 2021 from https://www.cdc.gov/coronavirus/2019-ncov/vaccines/fully-vaccinated.html#vaccinated

Gaskell, A. 2021. "How productive have remote workers been during COVID?" Forbes, May 31. Retrieved July 8, 2021 from https://www.forbes.com/sites/adigaskell/2021/05/31/how-productive-have-remote-workers-been-during-covid/?sh=2ffa24e9639e

Montgomery, J. 2021. "New survey: What people really think about hybrid work." Zoom (blog), April 8. Retrieved from https://blog.zoom.us/new-survey-what-people-really-think-about-hybrid-work/

Reed, K. M., and J. A. Allen. 2021. Suddenly Virtual: Making Remote Meetings Work. Wiley.

Chapter 1

The Inevitability and Promise of Hybrid Meetings

The contrast on the screen could not have been more distinct.

In one Zoom box: Jay Hyett, who was bundled up appropriately, given the especially bitter day in Melbourne. In the other box: his coworker, who was basking in tropical sunshine on a beach in Thailand. Although Jay, a senior delivery coach for Envato, had perhaps a sprinkling of jealousy given his colleague's locale, he actually appreciated seeing the change of scenery: "It brings me joy as well. It does get me thinking that maybe my next holiday will be in Thailand."

What makes the Melbourne/Thailand scene truly unusual is that it is a snapshot from 2017 – pre-COVID-19, pre-pandemic, pre-work-from-home as a global norm. In other words, well before the world went suddenly virtual.

But this could be a snapshot of a virtual meeting on any given day at Envato, before, during, and certainly after the pandemic. Envato, an online marketplace where creatives can sell their digital assets, isn't a purely remote company. It has offices in Australia, the United States, and Mexico, but its founders built the company with a flexible workforce in mind. Personally, they prioritized the opportunity to travel, so they set up a policy that allows employees to work from anywhere for up to three months as long as the employee has a plan that is approved by the team. The Melbourne/Thailand scenario merely exemplified the "work from anywhere" ethos that has been ingrained into the company DNA.

Envato has been hybrid from the start and by all accounts it has worked quite well. Perhaps that's why it's been named one of the best places to work in Australia more than six times by the Great Places to Work Benchmark study (Scott 2019). That's not surprising when you consider occupational psychology research. Flexible work situations tend to motivate employees to be more committed to their organization, be more satisfied with their work, and enjoy a level of work–life balance that is uncommon among people who work the traditional 9-to-5 schedule (Allen, Johnson, Kiburz, and Shockley 2013).

With some surveys indicating that 9 out of 10 businesses are adopting a hybrid model, the success story of Envato will surely be heartening (Alexander et al. 2021). Hybrid work and hybrid meetings are uncharted territory for the vast majority of organizations. Many may feel like they are still recovering from their abrupt move to fully remote and want to avoid learning a whole new way of meeting. However, the trends toward flexible work can't be denied, and when done well, hybrid meetings get higher marks than every other meeting modality.

In this chapter, we will explore:

- What we mean by "hybrid work" and "hybrid meetings"
- Why it's worth the effort to make hybrid meetings work
- The powerful drivers behind the transition to hybrid meetings
- The changing perceptions of working remote

What We Mean by "Hybrid Work" and "Hybrid Meetings"

In order to define what we mean by "hybrid work," we must begin by understanding the nature of work in general. After all, the range of jobs people do entails various levels of interaction between workers as well as the different kinds of outcomes expected, like the number of widgets produced or words typed. Some workers are knowledge workers, much of whose time is spent on a computer, which may conjure up images of an employee confined to the cubicle, pecking away at a keyboard. Some workers labor with their hands, with little interaction with computers or even meetings – a materials handler in a factory, for example. Let's begin our conversation with what work is, how independent or interdependent it is, and how physical or virtual it is.

When people think of work, they often think of job tasks – what a person does, like typing a report or washing dishes. Some job tasks are independent. They don't require anyone else to provide information, instructions, guidance, ideas, or input. For example, a small farmer does not need anyone to assist them in planting their field. They gather their resources and plant the field. Now someone might say, "Well, who does the farmer get the resources, the seeds, and the fuel for the tractor from? Doesn't that mean they're dependent on others?" To be fair, it's hard to think of any job task that is not connected in some way to others. However, if the task can be done independent of others, then it's an individual noncollaborative task (i.e. it can be and often is better completed alone). If the task requires others' involvement, it's interdependent, so collaboration of some kind is needed. You can probably think of more examples of interdependent work than fully independent work.

Another significant differentiator for work is whether it's virtual or physical (Robey, Schwaig, and Jin 2003). "Virtual work" is work

7

that occurs in an online space. It may simulate or mirror physical work but it doesn't have to. For example, virtual work includes most knowledge work jobs, where someone works at a computer doing any number of tasks, like writing reports, running statistics, answering email, and so on. "Physical work" is work that requires engaging in tasks in the physical world and the deliverable is a tangible thing. For example, building cars, cutting lumber, or farming a field is physical work, not virtual work.

"Hybrid work" is generally synonymous with flexible work with a bit more specificity, and has components of both physical and virtual work. Hybrid work acknowledges the need for some standard in-office colocated work that is paired with the ability to work from home or anywhere else as needed. That means that all those benefits attributed to flexible work schedules generally apply to hybrid work, too. As soon as one person or team in an organization embraces hybrid work schedules, virtual and hybrid meetings become necessary – for them as well as for others who interact with them. And just as hybrid work has the potential to maintain productivity and improve well-being, hybrid meetings also hold that promise.

The Hybrid Meeting

As basic as this may seem, let's start with a definition of a meeting. A meeting is two or more people coming together to discuss a matter (Schwartzman 1986). It's usually more formal than a chat but less formal than a lecture. You are all probably painfully aware of what a meeting is, right? But there are different ways to *do* meetings. Historically, the fan favorite was the fully face-to-face meeting where everyone is in the same room. Then, there's the meeting de rigueur of 2020, the virtual meeting where everyone is logged in remotely. This one can have a couple of formats. Some virtual meetings include everyone on camera, everyone on audio, or some combination of the two. The latter is probably the most common because some people might not be "camera ready," whether it's due to a perceived "bad hair day" or a location that does not reflect the professionalism the meeting deserves. (Placing your laptop on the tile floor of the bathroom is not good video etiquette.)

So, what is a hybrid meeting? It's a meeting where some people are in the same room and some are linked in remotely (Saatçi, Rädle, Rintel, O'Hara, and Klokmose 2019). The result is that some people are face-to-face while others are connected via telephone, videoconference, or both.

Think about that a bit. What does this mean? Essentially it means that instead of one communication medium or network, we have the potential for multiple ones. In a face-to-face meeting, you have one network of people all using the same communication medium – the air that they collectively share in the room. In a purely virtual meeting, you have one network of people all represented on the screen using the same medium – the internet connection that conveys their audio and video. In a hybrid meeting, you can have multiple networks, all with different communication mediums.

This means that a hybrid meeting is much more complex in terms of how people are connected. Face-to-face, everyone's together. Virtual, everyone can join via videoconference or teleconference. Everyone is on the same wavelength, or at least communicating through roughly the same medium. Hybrid messes with that. For example, you could have three people together in a room, two dialed in on the conference line, and two more in their little video box on the videoconference screen. Or, perhaps you have two or three groups in different rooms all linked together through a videoconferencing platform. Regardless, now the environment includes paying attention to the people you're physically with, the people on the phone, and the people on camera. Accordingly, the cognitive load for these meetings can quickly become immense.

While hybrid meetings are a bit different and more complicated, they are not new (Reed and Allen 2021). They happened prior to 2020, but were pretty infrequent. In fact, our data from 2019 indicated that only 13% of meetings were hybrid. However, hybrid meetings are now on the rise and that means the need to master them is on the rise as well.

Much of what it takes to have a successful hybrid meeting parallels the elements of a successful virtual meeting. If you haven't quite mastered the virtual meeting, take heart. We will be revisiting many of the best practices throughout the book, as outlined in our previous book *Suddenly Virtual: Making Remote Meetings Work.*

But let's start with one important concept from our fully remote model that applies to hybrid as well: virtual meetings require more intentional participation and facilitation. For example, in virtual meetings, if two people talk at the same time, most people cannot understand either of them. That's partly a function of the technology, which limits concurrent audio tracks, and partly a result of a human's inability to comprehend two streams of information at the same time (Adams 2019). Therefore, the advice we give everyone in a virtual meeting is to foster a participative environment where turn-taking is established as a norm, and people are encouraged to use and reference the chat liberally during the flow of the conversation to ensure that ideas are not lost. In hybrid meetings, this emphasis on facilitated participation needs to remain and perhaps be emphasized even more. A free flow of communication can be hard in a hybrid meeting, especially if everyone is left to their own devices to determine when they want to talk. In fact, the communication challenges have prompted many facilitation and meeting experts to balk at even trying hybrid meetings. However, this would be a missed opportunity and one that is out of sync with the realities of our flexible world of work.

Why Should We Even Try to Make Hybrid Meetings Work?

Lisette Sutherland is one of the top thought leaders in the remote workspace as the director of Collaboration Superpowers, a consulting and training firm, based in the Netherlands. As such, it might be a little disconcerting to hear her say, "Hybrid is so painful inherently. In fact, when we used to teach the remote meetings master class, we would always say, avoid hybrid whenever possible." But even she acknowledges reality with a quick follow-up: "Now we are kind of changing our tune because it is clearly the way of the future."

Before we (Joe and Karin) dove into writing this book, we had an email exchange about this very issue. Is a hybrid meeting even worth the effort? Should we advocate simply sticking with virtual meetings, which we have at least gotten used to?

In that email Joe brought up three factors that may be holding us back from unlocking the potential of hybrid meetings, potential that the data supports and that we will share in Chapter 2. For now, we will take a look at what is influencing some of the pushback on hybrid meetings: Joe's initial thoughts coupled with some embellishments based upon our current thinking enlightened by our research for this book.

Factor 1: Hybrid Meetings Can Be Hard

First, as Lisette indicated, the recommendation for meetings to all be on video rather than hybrid has been a common refrain for some time. It was the standard suggestion from meeting consultants, because, frankly, hybrid is hard. It requires both leaders and attendees to deploy a slightly different set of skills within the meeting setting. Consultants sort of decided, at least temporarily, that rather than try to teach them how to make hybrid meetings work, they would suggest face-to-face or all virtual. But choosing the easiest path does not guarantee the best outcome. We argue that the effort you invest in running effective hybrid meetings is not only worth it but is acknowledging that the landscape has changed. People can learn new things . . . and fast. Heck, the pandemic certainly taught us that. But learning new things doesn't come without effort.

Factor 2: Virtual Meetings Seem to Be More Egalitarian

Early on, the data suggested that fully virtual meetings did create a level playing field as the norms of interpersonal interaction (e.g. who speaks first, who leads, and who sits in the corner) had not immediately migrated online. However, in recent months we have seen articles about women and minorities feeling marginalized online (e.g. Hansen 2021). The hierarchies and biases based on gender and race are starting to creep into virtual meetings. So, making meetings a level playing field takes more than changing their modality. To assume issues of diversity and inclusion are not problematic when virtual is to assume wrong. In a workplace that has been awakened to diversity, equity, and inclusion, virtual meetings are not a panacea.

Factor 3: Gathering Together Can Still Feel Uncomfortable After Our Period of Collective Distancing

Our pandemic pods were designed to create a personal safe space, and that prolonged cocooning had some lasting impacts. The angst over gathering is partly a function of "return-to-normal anxiety" (Chatterjee 2021). People can be afraid to gather in groups or get anxious when in groups. If this fear or anxiety creates unhealthy isolation, clinicians may even diagnose a person with context-specific agoraphobia (i.e. fear of places that incite panic attacks, such as large groups of people). Organizations and the teams within them are likely cognizant of that and want to avoid making anyone feel uncomfortable or even possibly triggering a panic attack. One avoidance tactic is to suggest sticking with virtual meetings for a while and then slowly transitioning to in-person.

In this regard, hybrid meetings can help. They allow people the flexibility they need to work where they are most comfortable, whether that is virtual or in-person. After-all, "return-to-normal anxiety" is just one of many reasons a person might need to work from home for a time but still need to interact effectively with those who are in the office.

The Biggest Reason Hybrid Meetings Are Worth It

There is one overarching reason for embracing hybrid, and it has roots in evolutionary theory. As much as Joe would like to do a deep dive into the work of Darwin and others, allow us to be direct. It is a known fact that humans like to be together and that if they ceased to be together, humanity would end. It's as simple as that. If you'd like a specific example, look no further than the penal system. There's a reason solitary confinement is the harshest form of incarceration. It's terribly difficult for humans to be alone.

While some poorly executed meetings might feel like you've been sentenced to attend them, most of them do have one redeeming quality: people like to be in the same room with others. It doesn't matter whether they are introverted or extroverted. They still want to be in the presence of others. And when they cannot be in the same room with others, for whatever reason, they want a way to feel connected by actually *being* connected, and technology allows us to do that now better than ever before. In fact, think about all the times you or others came to the office with a sniffle because you needed to be at a meeting. Now, you can comfortably keep your cold cooties out of the office by staying at home but still be present and a part of the in-office activities.

Hybrid meetings offer that opportunity, and make no mistake, they *are* an opportunity. Hybrid meetings are the "meeting of the future" and the future is *now*. In fact, it probably started a while ago, and you may be thinking, "I missed the boat." Don't worry! That's what this book is for. It provides answers to how to make these very complicated meeting environments work. Hybrid meetings are complex but not impossible. Read on.

The Drivers Behind the Transition to Hybrid Meetings

The anxiety about navigating hybrid meetings at every level of the enterprise across all verticals is understandable and practically universal for those who are entering uncharted organizational waters. We all just survived a colossal paradigm change in the way we meet, from face-to-face to virtual. Now we are expected to tackle another one? In short, the answer is "yes" because the vast majority of workers are asking for it and have demonstrated a "fight or flight" resolve.

Take the case of Catherine Merrill, the CEO and owner of Washingtonian Media. She made headlines herself after her essay touting the merits of working in the office was published. She even raised the possibility of turning those who chose to stay remote into independent contractors without benefits. The employee response? A work stoppage and a tweet:

> As members of the *Washingtonian* editorial staff, we want our CEO to understand the risks of not valuing our labor. We are dismayed by Cathy Merrill's public threat to our livelihoods. We will not be publishing today. (Flynn 2021)

Shortly thereafter, the staff was asked to form a committee to offer suggestions to management on a post-pandemic plan for the workforce. That was a very public "fight" response.

The "flight" response continues to play out across all industries as workers choose to walk rather than wait for their employers to be enlightened about the merits of flexible work. When push comes to shove, employees are choosing to quit and find a different job that offers them the hybrid or remote arrangement they desire, and they're even willing to take a pay cut to secure it (Melin and Egkolfopoulou 2021).

That's why even the experts who called hybrid meetings "inherently painful" know that the shift to hybrid is likely unavoidable. Flexible work is priority one and one of the key drivers for the move to hybrid meetings.

From Safety to Flexibility

The pandemic, for all of its horrors, did create an awakening of a sort. At first, the massive move to remote work was driven by a desire to be safe. Staying at home meant saving lives – of our families, our friends, our coworkers. As vaccination efforts ramped up and the pandemic's global grip began to loosen, the drivers of what work would look like started to shift. "Safety" started being replaced by words like "flexibility" for employees and "cost savings" for companies that were shocked by the meager line item that used to be the bloated travel budget.

Make no mistake, the publisher of the *Washingtonian* was not alone in pining for the days when everyone was back in the confines of the brick-and-mortar building. Many managers believed that employees were more productive in the office than elsewhere. They viewed flexible work arrangements with skepticism – how would they know someone was working if they couldn't see them? But the financial proof points were made by the pandemic and the productivity metrics were indisputable. According to a study quoted by Bloomberg, work-from-home lifted productivity in the U.S. economy by 5% (Curran 2021).

To meeting scientists, this came as no surprise. After more than 40 years of research on the topic of flexible work arrangements, the evidence is clear. People who are given flexible work arrangements are just as, if not more, productive than those in the office (Baltes, Briggs, Huff, Wright, and Neuman 1999; Hayman 2010). So, to those managers who are worried about work from home continuing, you needn't worry. In fact, further evidence suggests that flexible work schedules are also better for employees' overall well-being (Hayman 2010). The bottom line is that employees are as or more productive *and* they are healthier. (And with that, another potential cost savings – insurance premiums.)

For these reasons and more, the future of work is flexible and those who think otherwise will have a hard time making the case against it. "You can't go back and say it's not possible because clearly it was possible," says Lisette Sutherland, who has been evangelizing the merits of remote work and living it for nearly two decades as a German-born American living in the Netherlands and working remotely. "The flexibility and freedom are just too valuable. And now that they've had a taste . . . there's no way everyone is going to go back to the office full-time. I just can't see it."

Every survey conducted so far agrees. Microsoft's 2021 Work Trend Index found that 70% of workers want flexible remote work options. A significantly smaller proportion prefer either all remote or all in the office (Microsoft 2021). In other words, a one-size-fits-all approach is not the way to go. Organizations will need to strike the right balance between flexibility and bringing people together for their interdependent work activities.

One visible trend that indicates that companies are rethinking the need and desire to have everyone work in-person is that many have chosen to shrink their physical footprints and even to move their headquarters elsewhere. Not surprisingly, tech companies, often in the vanguard of work innovation, were some of the first to announce major changes to their corporate addresses. Snowflake, a cloud data analytics vendor, made quite a splash by shifting their corporate headquarters from San Mateo, California, to "No-Headquarters/Bozeman, Montana." In fact, the state of California saw a significant exodus of companies that then popped up in places like Colorado, Texas, and South Florida (Levy 2021). And many workers who were tired of paying astronomical rents and enduring relentless commutes were happy to follow, seeking a better quality of life at a much lower cost. The supply of homes, especially in suburbia, couldn't keep up with demand – an outcome of companies *reducing* office space and employees wanting *more* space. Remember Jay Hyett, the Melbourne-based senior delivery coach from our Part One introduction? At that time, he worked for Envato, an Australian company designed to be hybrid from the start. Jay is now working at Culture Amp, yet another highly distributed workforce with offices in San Francisco, New York, and London, but there are pockets of Culture Amp employees all around the world. As someone who valued his previous hybrid gig, Jay knew he'd feel right at home: "It's created this level playing field. It doesn't matter where you are. We are all there to get work done."

Work isn't where you go, it's what you do. Virtual meetings and now hybrid meetings are how we can coordinate the work, wherever we are.

The Diminishing Stigma of Remote Work

While the changes in location are certainly dramatic, they are not to be outdone by the significant shift in perceptions about those who choose to work from home. Did you have any coworkers who were remote prior to the pandemic? Chances are you might have fantasized about their daily work life. You were sure it involved maybe a few hours banging out a report or answering a couple of emails but was largely spent luxuriating over the morning paper with a cup of joe while deciding what sweatpants to pull on that day . . . or whether to just stick with the pajamas. Who would know?

Pre-Pandemic Perceptions

In fact, in a study from just before the pandemic, Tahrima Ferdous and colleagues (Ferdous, Ali, and French 2020) investigated whether the stigma associated with flexible work schedules impacted workers and in what way. That's right, "stigma." Using a sample of workers from Australia, their study showed that workers with a flexible work schedule felt stigmatized by their colleagues who were on a standard schedule and worked in the office. In fact, this stigma was related to lower well-being, thoughts of leaving the organization, and general reduction in the use of their flexible work arrangement. The old jokes (pre-2020) about "Yeah, Dave is just sitting at home in his sweatpants while we're here working" actually did hurt.

Additionally, this stigma had some very tangible manifestations, one of which could be described as the "promotion penalty." The promotion penalty refers to the fact that those who were in the office and had more face time experienced more opportunities to be assigned tasks that better prepared and positioned them for promotions. In a 2014 Stanford study of a large multinational based in China, work-from-home employees had a 50% lower rate of promotion within two years compared to their colleagues who worked in the office (Bloom, Liang, Roberts, and Ying 2015). In short, remote workers were often stigmatized as not "really working" because they didn't have the face time to prove that they were. Often, they were treated as second-class citizens by their coworkers and even their bosses, which led them to be overlooked and even undervalued. This contributed to a very slow adoption of flexible work arrangements in general, at least until March 2020.

Perception Shift During the Pandemic

The pandemic changed all that when everyone was abruptly placed in the very situation that they traditionally maligned . . . and found that the fantasy was just that. Remote work was indeed *work,* and, in reality, was much more challenging in many ways than being in the office, particularly since there was no delineated start and end to the day, which had an effect on work–life balance (which we'll address in Chapter 3).

Anecdotally, we were hearing about how the stigma attached to remote workers had faded away during the pandemic, but data from an early 2021 survey by the World Economic Forum of 5,000 workers in the UK confirmed it (Taneja, Mizen, and Bloom 2021). When asked "How have your perceptions about working from home changed?," more than three out of four respondents indicated that their perceptions had improved, with over half saying that their perceptions about working from home had either substantially or hugely improved (Taneja, Mizen, and Bloom 2021).

Prior to the pandemic, the associated remote work stigma kept many people from even considering it. The desire and the willingness to work from home, even for part of the time, would likely have been largely absent without this forced "learn by doing" exercise. By having no choice but to work remotely during the pandemic, most people discovered that remote work was actually better than expected, and attitudes adjusted accordingly. In fact, that same World Economic Forum survey found that 70% of respondents would embrace working from home two to three days a week even after the COVID-19 crisis passes.

Will the Stigma Return?

While the pandemic did open our eyes to new ways of working, how lasting the impact will be is unknown. As the reshuffling and transitioning continues, the stigmatization of remote work may creep back in. Will people be judged by the number of days they choose to be in the office? ("Oh, you're only coming in one day a week? I don't feel comfortable unless I'm in the office at least four days.") The metrics by which we measure performance will likely evolve as well, but will face time no longer be part of the equation? Will we see promotion penalties arise again?

Lisette Sutherland echoes that concern for those who opt to stay solely remote. "My biggest concern is that the remote people will totally get left behind. Connecting over a big plate of nachos and drinks with your coworkers . . . there's just no replacement for that online. You can connect through video. You can be a robot with telepresence, but you still won't be able to share that plate of nachos with your colleagues. You're simply at a disadvantage."

The Gender Gap

Who may be most often subject to the potential return of the stigma of remote work could be directly related to gender. In a survey by the *Harvard Business Review,* 30,000 men and women with young children were asked how often they would like to work from home after COVID-19. While nearly two-thirds of all respondents expressed a desire to work at least one day a week from home, women with young children wanted to work from home full-time almost 50% more than did fathers with young children (Bloom 2021).

Part of the motivation for women to want to work from home full-time is that childcare duties fall upon them more than they do for men. The research confirms that couples with small children do not equally share the responsibilities for caring for the children (Cohut 2017). In their free time, mothers tend to focus more on child-rearing and household duties while fathers engage in more leisure activities and hobbies. The fact that this is an unfair situation does not change the fact that for the majority of women, this is their reality. So, when asked if they want to work from home so they can more easily do their second job, the answer is more likely to be "sign me up" than it is for men.

That's why Nicholas Bloom, a professor of economics at Stanford University and one of the lead researchers for the survey, is voicing concern: "Single young men could all choose to come into the office five days a week and rocket up the firm, while employees with young children, particularly women, who choose to WFH [work from home] for several days each week are held back. This would be both a diversity loss and legal time bomb for companies" (Bloom 2021).

As organizations and team leaders plot out their hybrid path, Bloom suggests not allowing individuals to dictate how often they're in the office but instead have managers choose what days their team should work from home. That way, face time is equal across the team, and no one can feel like they will receive brownie points for putting in an extra day or two in the office.

Even with guardrails put up around potential inequities, organizations that are going all-in on hybrid work should monitor for any early warning signs that one group is being marginalized by the choices they have made on where they will work and when.

Conclusion

Hybrid meetings bring a level of complexity to the meeting environment that few have experienced before, but hybrid meetings can work well when done right. Leaning into learning how to conduct effective hybrid meetings echoes the call for greater flexibility from a workforce enlightened by the possibility of working remote while also acknowledging the human desire for in-person connection. Still not convinced? Let's look at the data next: it may surprise you.

Chapter Takeaways

- Hybrid meetings are those where attendees are showing up in person as well as virtually, whether that be via video or audio alone.

- What makes hybrid meetings especially challenging is the creation of multiple networks, which all need to communicate with each other.

- Some meeting consultants who previously recommended avoiding hybrid meetings have recognized the necessity of holding them to accommodate the hybrid work environment.

- During the pandemic, the main driver for remote work was safety. The post-pandemic push for hybrid work is being driven by a desire for flexibility that employees are prioritizing above all else.

- The stigma of flexible work schedules, like hybrid work, is lifting and, hopefully, will never return, but we're keeping our eye on it.

References

Adams, C. 2019. "Can people really multitask?" ThoughtCo. Retrieved July 9, 2021 from https://www.thoughtco.com/can-people-really-multitask-1206398

Alexander, A., R. Cracknell, A. D. Smet, M. Langstaff, M. Mysore, and D. Ravid. 2021. "What executives are saying about the future of hybrid work." McKinsey & Company. https://www.mckinsey.com/business-functions/organization/our-insights/what-executives-are-saying-about-the-future-of-hybrid-work?utm_source=digg&utm_medium=email#

Allen, T. D., R. C. Johnson, K. Kiburz, and K. M. Shockley. 2013. "Work–family conflict and flexible work arrangements: Deconstructing flexibility." *Personnel Psychology* 66 (2): 345–376.

Baltes, B. B., T. E. Briggs, J. W. Huff, J. A. Wright, and G. A. Neuman. 1999. "Flexible and compressed workweek schedules: A meta-analysis of their effects on work-related criteria." *Journal of Applied Psychology* 84 (4): 496.

Bloom, N. 2021. "Don't let employees pick their WFH days." *Harvard Business Review, May.* https://hbr.org/2021/05/dont-let-employees-pick-their-wfh-days

Bloom, N., J. Liang, J. Roberts, and Z. J. Ying. 2015. "Does working from home work? Evidence from a Chinese experiment." *The Quarterly Journal of Economics* 130 (1): 165–218.

Chatterjee, R. 2021. "As life begins to return to normal, psychologists say expect anxiety." NPR, May 25. Retrieved August 30, 2021 from https://www.npr.org/2021/05/25/1000043035/as-life-begins-to-return-to-normal-psychologists-say-expect-anxiety

Cohut, M. 2017. "Women 'spend more time on housework, childcare than men.'" *Medical News Today.* Retrieved from https://www.medicalnewstoday.com/articles/319687

Curran, E. 2021. Work from home to lift productivity by 5% in post-pandemic U.S. *Bloomberg.* Retrieved August 30, 2021 from https://www.bloomberg.com/news/articles/2021-04-22/yes-working-from-home-makes-you-more-productive-study-finds

Ferdous, T., M. Ali, and E. French. 2020. "Impact of flexibility stigma on outcomes: Role of flexible work practices usage." *Asia Pacific Journal of Human Resources.*

Flynn, K. 2021. "Washingtonian staffers protest CEO's 'public threat' to return to in-person work." *CNN Business*, May 7. Retrieved from https://www.cnn.com/2021/05/07/media/washingtonian-remote-work-culture/index.html

Hansen, A. 2021. "Is gender bias amplified in the virtual workplace?" *The Glass Hammer*, April 15. Retrieved August 30, 2021 from https://theglasshammer.com/2021/04/is-gender-bias-amplified-in-the-virtual-workplace/

Hayman, J. 2010. "Flexible work schedules and employee well-being." *New Zealand Journal of Employment Relations* 35 (2): 76–87.

Levy, A. 2021. "Snowflake relocates executive office from California to Bozeman, Montana, as company goes distributed." CNBC, April 26. Retrieved from https://www.cnbc.com/2021/05/26/snowflake-moves-executive-office-from-california-to-bozemanmontana.html? sourcesharebar%7Ctwitter&parsharebar

Melin, A., and M. Egkolfopoulou. 2021. "Employees are quitting instead of giving up working from home." Bloomberg Wealth, June 1. Retrieved from https://www.bloomberg.com/news/articles/2021-06-01/return-to-office-employees-are-quitting-instead-of-giving-up-work-from-home

Microsoft. 2021. *2021 Work Trend Index: Annual Report – The next great disruption is hybrid work – Are we ready?* Retrieved from https://www.microsoft.com/en-us/worklab/work-trend-index/hybrid-work

Reed, K. M., and J. A. Allen. 2021. *Suddenly Virtual: Making Remote Meetings Work.* Wiley.

Robey, D., K. S. Schwaig, and L. Jin. 2003. "Intertwining material and virtual work." *Information and Organization* 13 (2): 111–129.

23

The Inevitability and Promise of Hybrid Meetings

Schwartzman, H. B. 1986. "The meeting as a neglected social form in organizational studies." *Research in Organizational Behavior* 8, 233–258.

Saatçi, B., R. Rädle, S. Rintel, K. O'Hara, and C. N. Klokmose. 2019. "Hybrid meetings in the modern workplace: Stories of success and failure." In *International Conference on Collaboration and Technology*, 45–61. Cham: Springer.

Scott, D. 2019. "Great Place To Work results honour Envato's consistency." *Envato Blog*. Retrieved from https://envato.com/blog/great-place-to-work-results-honour-envatos-consistency/

Taneja, S., P. Mizen, and N. Bloom. 2021. "How has working from home impacted productivity? This UK survey has answers." World Economic Forum, March. https://www.weforum.org/agenda/2021/03/survey-what-are-uk-attitudes-to-working-from-home-in-the-new-normal/

Chapter 2

Considering Meeting Modalities

With hybrid meetings defined, it's time to consider the current meeting environment. That is, what is the current "state of play" for meetings as the world recovers from the COVID-19 pandemic? There are a lot of opinions out there about this, but we have something that you won't find anywhere else: actual data to help guide your decisions and actions as you adapt to the hybrid meeting. You should expect nothing less from a book cowritten by a meeting scientist.

Allow us to explain. By the fall of 2019, Joe had been studying meetings for more than a decade. However, he admittedly had not considered modality – virtual, face-to-face, hybrid, telephone – to a great degree, and when he did, the focus was on face-to-face meetings. After all, the face-to-face meeting was king in 2019, and pretty much forever before that. So, in September 2019, he decided to start studying virtual meetings, and a month later, he launched a survey of 1,000 knowledge workers across a broad range of organizations and industries in the United States.

It was terribly good timing, with an emphasis on the "terrible," considering the things that followed in 2020. The events of that year presented a veritable treasure trove of data-gathering opportunities to study the first major meeting disruption in modern history, and Joe took advantage of it. He already had the pre-COVID-19 data from that sample set of 1,000 people from the fall, so why not learn how they responded to the pandemic? In May 2020, he asked the same questions to the same people from the October 2019 survey, and used the keen insights from that data for our book, *Suddenly Virtual: Making Remote Meetings Work* (Reed and Allen 2021). Then, in June 2021, as the United States and the world began to recover from the pandemic (note, before the Delta variant of COVID-19 surged), Joe once again collected more data from mostly the same people. The chance to study the state of meetings before, during, and as we begin to recover from COVID-19 using the same participants was remarkable. Throughout this book, we will share all sorts of insights from the data collected across those three years.

In this chapter, we will explore:

- Where people are conducting meetings now
- The surprising benefits of hybrid meetings as shown in our data
- Six key insights that can only be found in our multi-time-point data from pre-, during-, and post(ish)-COVID-19

Where Are People Conducting Meetings?

There were many different perceptions and opinions about what common practices would be as organizations figured out how to operate as COVID-19 began to subside or at least be more effectively managed. Some believed we would return to business as usual, with everyone face-to-face and with meetings, in general, returning to that format as well. Others believed that the change would be permanent, that we would never fully return to 2019 "normal," and that most things would remain virtual. Still others, like us (Karin and Joe), felt that the reality would probably be more complicated and somewhere in between, with some organizations and individuals resuming operations in a face-to-face, almost pre-2020 manner, while others embraced a more hybrid style of work and meetings.

Rather than speculate, we decided to find out what was actually happening on the ground, via the survey data. Let's begin our journey through this data by focusing on the question about what would happen when COVID-19 subsided: Where are people conducting meetings post-pandemic, as opposed to pre- and mid-pandemic?

We decided to ask our sample of knowledge workers. Our survey from 2019, 2020, and 2021 included the question, "What was the format of your last meeting?" Response options included "face-to-face," "virtual," "telephone," and "hybrid," with hybrid being defined as some participants in the meeting being co-located in a conference room with some participants joining remotely. The following graph shows the results compared across all three time-points.

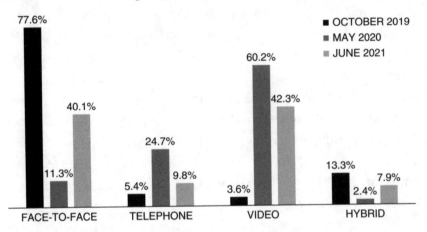

In October 2019, most people were meeting face-to-face. In May 2020 (the first disruption), most people were meeting virtually. In June 2021, another major disruption was well underway. Face-to-face was coming back, telephone was fading, video was holding on stronger than some had speculated, and hybrid rose a bit from mid-pandemic levels (i.e. May 2020). From an egghead scientist's perspective (Joe's words, not Karin's, for himself), these dynamic shifts are exciting and significant, because shifts of this proportion in how people meet just do not happen regularly. Usually it takes a major event, an equilibrium shift like a pandemic, to change people's behavior permanently. For example, think about how air travel was transformed for all of us after 9/11. But when shifts like these do happen, it's both remarkable and worth considering the reasons and implications.

With this data in mind, what does this mean from a practical standpoint? Well, based on these numbers, we'd recommend that people keep their webcams. In fact, our belief is that June 2021 was at the beginning of the transition, and hybrid meetings will actually start absorbing some of the video and telephone meetings moving forward. We'd also recommend that people be prepared for further transition, as neither Karin nor Joe believes this is the "end state." That is, many companies are continuing to transition from fully remote to some in-person/hybrid combination situation. The so-called "Future of Work" is hybrid, and that means hybrid meetings using a virtual meeting platform are not going away. People are now accustomed to more alternative forms of both communicating and working. Working from home is now normalized within a society that was not fully onboard with the idea pre-2020. Since hybrid meetings are going to be part of our lives, it is useful to study the experiences of the effective hybrid meetings in our sample in order to develop best practices.

Meeting Metrics by Modality – The Promise of Hybrid Meetings

Since hybrid meetings appear to be on the rise, we thought it would be helpful to take a deeper dive into the data we collected on hybrid meetings and to provide some insights that can guide best practices. However, the data also revealed some fascinating takeaways about all of the meeting modalities, which we want to share as well, including substantive differences and changes that have occurred over the three time-points collected before, during, and as we recover from the pandemic.

Insight 1: Early Users of Hybrid Meetings Are Seeing Substantial Benefits

Given the complexity and potential challenges of hybrid meetings that we mentioned in Chapter 1, we were surprised to see that early users of hybrid meetings are seeing some benefits that were not anticipated.

Meeting satisfaction is one metric that factors into the overall meeting experience. There is plentiful research that backs the assertion that people are reliable in evaluating their overall feeling of satisfaction with meetings (e.g. Rogelberg et al. 2010). According to our data, hybrid meetings appear to be just as satisfying as face-to-face meetings, and not far from video meetings. The following table provides the scores by format style for meeting satisfaction. The higher the score (out of 7), the more satisfactory the experience was, on average.

Meeting Satisfaction – June 2021

Format Style	Meeting Satisfaction
Video	4.94
Face-to-Face	4.84
Hybrid	4.82
Telephone	4.32

Because hybrid meetings are more complex and challenging than other formats, when Joe first saw this data, his reaction was, "How did *this* happen?" His initial thoughts? Maybe people are just so excited to be together with even part of their team in a room that they don't recognize the problems yet. Or, perhaps there's something wrong with the sample. But that doesn't make sense, given that the data from these same people from previous years has been extremely predictive of how things were and how they would become.

Then, it dawned on him. Given the time that this sample was taken, the people engaging in hybrid meetings might be best described as "early adopters." They may be people who have specifically chosen to be the vanguard of this particular format. What's special about early adopters? Early adopters tend to be well-informed about the new thing that they are trying, and often actually employ best practices, which produce better results and satisfaction.

Despite this encouraging news for those who have yet to dip their toes in the hybrid meeting pool, we cannot automatically assume that these high levels of satisfaction and participation will apply to later adopters of hybrid meetings. For example, we all know people who always have to have the hottest new tech release – they spout off all sorts of specs and know how to take advantage of every feature. In most cases, the rest of us later adopters will end up with the technology ourselves, but we probably won't have the same level of knowledge and enthusiasm. But still, the positive signs from these early adopters of hybrid meetings should not be dismissed.

Insight 2: When It Comes to Participation, Hybrid Meetings Come Out on Top

Now, you may be thinking, "I don't care how happy people are with the meeting so long as it works!" Fair point – so let's now look at meeting participation. This refers to the degree to which the meeting leader and attendees feel as though they were able to adequately contribute their ideas, opinions, and thoughts during the meeting (Yoerger, Crowe, and Allen 2015). The table here provides the scores by format style for participation, with higher scores (out of 7 this time) representing more participation. Yes, the differences may seem relatively small, but put the numbers within this context: they amount to a 15% difference from top to bottom. That is, hybrid meetings have 15% more participation than telephone meetings. In fact, this rate is higher than every other meeting modality's!

Meeting Participation – June 2021

Format Style	Meeting Participation
Hybrid	6.12
Video	5.61
Face-to-Face	5.56
Telephone	5.31

On its face, 15% higher participation in one meeting might not seem like it will make a huge difference, but think about how many meetings are on a manager's calendar, or across an organization. That 15% represents a huge opportunity for the exchange of ideas, for the buy-in of employees, and for the growth and improvement of the company at large. Plus, fostering a participatory and inclusive environment in meetings has a direct impact on the bottom line. Meeting science shows that it leads to better business outcomes, including increases in overall employee engagement and subsequent performance on the job. After all, research shows that a highly engaged team is 21% more profitable and 17% more productive than a more disengaged team (Przystanski 2021). And, good meetings with high participation absolutely engage employees (Allen and Rogelberg 2013).

Insight 3: Teleconferencing Still Stinks

Although Zoom fatigue has been much discussed by thought leaders, journalists, and even among you and your colleagues, our data points to one unmistakable fact: teleconferencing, not videoconferencing, ranks dead last with respect to overall meeting satisfaction and participation. This was true in October 2019, it remained true in May 2020, and it's still true in October 2021. Dare we say it's probably still true today? We do not dispute the truth of the fatigue that people feel after a long day of being on camera. In fact, check out Chapter 4, where we talk about the problems people are having with video meetings. However, the suggestion of opting out of video and proceeding with a meeting using audio alone is counterproductive. The data is clear in terms of overall meeting experiences and behavior in meetings, and that data tells us that teleconferencing is at the bottom of the meeting heap.

Insight 4: We're Seeing Less Bad Behavior in Hybrid Meetings

Counterproductive meeting behaviors are all those annoying behaviors that people do in meetings that really undermine what could be a good meeting (Allen, Yoerger, Lehmann-Willenbrock, and Jones 2015). For example, complaining, multitasking, running off-topic, monologuing, and nonessential conflict are all types of counterproductive meeting behaviors. In our data, counterproductive meeting behaviors were not considered individually, but as a composite of bad behavior in meetings. These were assessed on a five-point scale, with lower values representing less of these bad behaviors in the meeting. Take a look at the following table.

Counterproductive Meeting Behaviors – June 2021

Format Style	Counterproductive Meeting Behaviors
Hybrid	1.77
Face-to-Face	2.19
Video	2.27
Telephone	2.60

Take note of what receives the highest marks (represented here by the lowest number) yet again: hybrid meetings – which means that they had the least amount of counterproductive meeting behaviors by participants in our sample. This implies there are fewer complaining cycles, monologues, and multitasking on unrelated items in hybrid meetings compared to a similar meeting in any other format. (Not surprisingly, telephone meetings appear to have the most counterproductive meeting behaviors.)

While hybrid meetings seem to already have the potential for less counterproductive meeting behavior, we suggest you check out the list of these meeting roadblocks in our previous book, *Suddenly Virtual*. Having a heightened awareness of the behaviors will allow you to thwart their eruption in your own hybrid meetings.

Insight 5: In Hybrid Meetings, Participants Are Doing Less "Surface Acting"

One of the most damaging behaviors that undermines meeting effectiveness and satisfaction is surface acting, where employees fake the appropriate emotion required for their job. Think about "service with a smile," even when you'd rather smack the rude customer. Not smacking the customer is adaptive in the service sector, as pleasing the customer usually means more goods sold or more food purchased, not to mention a larger tip. However, the dissonance between smiling and how you might feel inside is draining and can be a real problem (Shumski, Olien, Allen, Rogelberg, and Kello 2018). Previous research on workplace meetings indicates that people tend to engage in surface acting in meetings, particularly when a high-ranking member of the organization is present. That is, we fake positivity for the boss, even if we don't feel that positive about whatever we're meeting with them about.

In the survey, surface acting was rated on a five-point scale, where higher scores indicate more faking of what is believed to be the appropriate emotion for the context.

Surface Acting – June 2021

Format Style	Surface Acting
Telephone	2.94
Video	2.79
Face-to-Face	2.44
Hybrid	2.08

Once again, hybrid meetings are coming out on top by being at the bottom of the list. Our data shows that people are engaging in less surface acting in hybrid meetings compared to all other types. Top to bottom, we see nearly a 30% reduction in this behavior. Once again, telephone comes in with the most surface acting, adding insult to injury considering that telephone was also ranked the worst in terms of satisfaction and participation. And now, we learn that people are faking what they think is the appropriate emotion when on the phone more than when they are in-person or on video.

Some might wonder why we should care so much about faking emotions. Good question. The reason this matters is because of the consistent research on surface acting's correlation to burnout (Brotheridge and Grandey 2002). Burnout is the feeling of being used up at the end of the day, being fatigued and emotionally exhausted to one's breaking point. People tend to get sick more frequently when they are burned out and they are more likely to develop serious long-term illnesses such as cardiovascular disease, obesity, diabetes, and chronic pain issues; thus, we want to avoid the contributing causes to burnout if we can (Maslach and Leiter 2006). In addition to lessening burnout, authentic emotions enable more appropriate participation, idea generation, and more employee engagement, always a desired outcome across any enterprise.

Insight 6: People Need Less "Meeting Recovery" after Hybrid Meetings

"Meeting recovery" refers to the time needed after a meeting to essentially be human – you know, things like going to the bathroom, grabbing something to eat or drink, or simply taking a moment to decompress cognitively and take a few deep breaths. We all need transition time between meetings in order to attend to our biological needs, but also to reset our brains. Meeting recovery becomes even more important when experiencing back-to-back meetings, a phenomenon that jumped in astronomical proportions during the pandemic. When this happened in our pre-COVID-19, colocated office world, we at least could walk from one conference room or office to another, find the bathroom on the way, and grab a water. With virtual meetings, this becomes more difficult, because the next meeting is still in the same chair, stool, or couch spot you've been sitting in all day. How can we expect people to come prepared to meetings if they have no time to even take a bathroom break? In short, we need to give them recovery time, but how *much* recovery time?

Joe delved into this topic with some recent research on meeting recovery (Knowles and Allen 2020). (Perhaps the onset of COVID-19 and back-to-back meetings on his calendar inspired him.) Mid-pandemic, using a sample of more than 500 working adults in the United States, he compared meetings that were rated as terrible and those that were rated as wonderful. What he found was fascinating and worth considering when you schedule any of your meetings. Looking at the data, he discovered that after a terrible meeting, employees need about 17 minutes to recover and transition. After a wonderful meeting, employees need about 5 minutes to recover and transition. That's right: you still need at least some recovery time after even a *good* meeting. That's because people still need to use the restroom from time to time and to take stretch breaks. But, more importantly, neuroscience confirms that people need between 5 and 7 minutes to cognitively switch between disparate complex topics.

Now that you understand the purpose and necessity of meeting recovery, let's take a look at our new data concerning recovery in workplace meetings by modality. Once again, we use a five-point scale, with higher values indicating a need for more meeting recovery.

Meeting Recovery – June 2021

Format Style	Meeting Recovery
Hybrid	2.70
Face-to-Face	3.52
Video	3.74
Telephone	3.89

Are you seeing a trend here? Once again, our data shows that these early adopters of hybrid meetings require the lowest amount of meeting recovery of all the meeting formats assessed. This may be, in part, due to hybrid meetings requiring less surface acting. In fact, those who are participating in hybrid meetings need 23% less meeting recovery time even compared to face-to-face, the next best on the list. Don't misinterpret the data here. This is not a green light to schedule less recovery time after a hybrid meeting than when holding other types of meetings; we all need time to switch tasks and to take care of basic biological needs. But this does suggest that perhaps good hybrid meetings just make things a bit easier on employees in general.

Conclusion

Hybrid work appears to be the desirable mode of working for the future, and the early data tells a compelling story. It turns out that the meeting room with both in-person and remote attendees can allow you to get the job done and yield higher rates of meeting satisfaction and participation. Additionally, the early adopters of hybrid meetings appear to be engaging in less surface acting, fewer counterproductive meeting behaviors, and need less recovery time after the meeting. In other words, the hybrid meeting looks like a very effective option for meetings, and when done well, may be even better than virtual or face-to-face. However, the success of hybrid meetings is not a given and requires an intentional approach. In the next chapter, we will start shaping that approach by discussing what we learned from our fully virtual experience and suggesting ways to apply those lessons to your hybrid meeting strategy.

Chapter Takeaways

- Our data suggests that hybrid meetings, when done well, can be very effective.
- Hybrid meetings are the most satisfying and inclusive, from a participation perspective, of all the modalities studied.
- People in hybrid meetings fake positivity less, engage in fewer monologues, complain less, and need to recover less after the meeting.

References

Allen, J. A., and S. G. Rogelberg. 2013. "Manager-led group meetings: A context for promoting employee engagement." *Group & Organization Management* 38 (5): 543–569.

Allen, J. A., M. A. Yoerger, N. Lehmann-Willenbrock, and J. Jones. 2015. "Would you please stop that!? The relationship between counterproductive meeting behaviors, employee voice, and trust." *Journal of Management Development* (October).

Brotheridge, C. M., and A. A. Grandey. 2002. "Emotional labor and burnout: Comparing two perspectives of 'people work.'" *Journal of Vocational Behavior* 60 (1): 17–39.

Knowles, S., and J. A. Allen. 2020. "Why am I so exhausted?: Exploring the Meeting Recovery Syndrome." Research accepted for the Interdisciplinary Network for Group Research's (INGRoup) 15th Annual Conference, July 30–August 1, 2020, Seattle, WA.

Maslach, C., and M. Leiter. 2006. "Burnout." *Stress and Quality of Working Life: Current Perspectives in Occupational Health* 37, 42–49.

Przystanski, A. 2021. "The ROI of employee engagement: 5 reasons it's worth the cost." *Lattice.* Retrieved August 30, 2021 from https://lattice.com/library/the-roi-of-employee-engagement-5-reasons-its-worth-the-cost

Reed, K. M., and J. A. Allen. 2021. *Suddenly Virtual: Making Remote Meetings Work.* Wiley.

Rogelberg, S. G., J. A. Allen, L. Shanock, C. Scott, and M. Shuffler. 2010. "Employee satisfaction with meetings: A contemporary facet of job satisfaction." *Human Resource Management: Published in Cooperation with the School of Business Administration, The University of Michigan and in alliance with the Society of Human Resources Management* 49 (2): 149–172.

Shumski, T. J., J. L. Olien, J. A. Allen, S. G. Rogelberg, and J. E. Kello. 2018. "Faking it for the higher-ups: Status and surface acting in workplace meetings." *Group & Organization Management* 43 (1): 72–100.

Yoerger, M., J. Crowe, and J. A. Allen. 2015. "Participate or else!: The effect of participation in decision-making in meetings on employee engagement." *Consulting Psychology Journal: Practice and Research* 67 (1): 65.

Chapter 3

Lessons Learned from Our "Suddenly Virtual" Work Life

"Hey, we're two weeks into summer break!" Joe quipped on his "Family Zoom call" with the extended Allen clan on March 29, 2020. It wasn't the first video call with his family, but it soon became standard practice for Joe's family as well as countless other folks who found video calls to be a lifeline for connecting with loved ones when face-to-face interactions were off-limits. Birthday parties, baby showers, practically every meaningful moment went virtual, and all of us made do. The real problems arose from spending both our personal and professional lives through a webcam, which led to a host of issues, including digital exhaustion, a lack of boundaries between work and home life, and a steep rise in mental health problems from anxiety to depression, just to name a few.

Hybrid meetings should help alleviate some of these woes, but only if we carefully consider how to avoid making the same mistakes we made when we were fully remote. The truth is that the work-from-home experiment taught us many things. During this time we (Joe and Karin), like so many others, worked from home, lived on our webcams, and tried to remain as productive as possible, but as a meeting scientist and communication expert, we also sought to make sense of the work-from-home situation, and accordingly, we learned quite a bit, which is the focus of this chapter.

In this chapter, we will explore:

- What happened to meetings when so many workers went home
- How an all-meeting culture evolved into a multitasking epidemic
- The issues and opportunities presented by the work–family interface
- The role of diversity, equity, and inclusion in meetings

What Happened When Work Went Home?

In Joe's home state of Utah, you could clearly see what happened when work went home . . . literally. Utah, sadly, is known for being home to a weather phenomenon called an inversion, where pollution is trapped in the valleys between the mountain ridges. These inversions can make breathing difficult for just about everyone, but in 2020, residents experienced a summer of the cleanest air quality in recent memory. For the first time in Joe's lifetime, you could hike up to the top of Ensign Peak on the border of Salt Lake and Davis Counties and see both valleys and their surrounding mountains and beyond with perfect clarity. Why? Because people were at home, not driving their cars or flying on airplanes. During this time, people literally breathed easier, amid the ambiguity and stress of the pandemic.

But more broadly, when people went home, they *really* got to work. Despite having to rely on their personal internet connections, productivity levels remained stable or even improved (Gaskell 2021). However, this came at a cost. According to Microsoft's 2021 Work Trend Index completed in February 2021, 54% of workers felt overworked and 39% said they were exhausted. Now imagine if every organization's climate survey (a snapshot of how things are going in the workplace environment in general) suddenly showed that half of its people were at risk for burning out and more than a third of its workers already *were* burned out. That's 93% of the workforce! It would set off alarm bells at the highest levels of the organization and elicit a swift response. First, every manager and C-level executive would likely spend some time breathing into a metaphorical paper bag to ward off hyperventilation – but then they would start asking this question to every person who might have a possible clue: "Why is everyone burning out?"

In the case of the Microsoft report, the answer might have seemed obvious. Duh, there was a pandemic, so some of the burnout and exhaustion was justifiable from the inherent stressful nature of the constant worry about oneself, family, and particularly older loved ones at highest risk. But no climate survey we know of was prescient enough to have questions that dove deeper into the root cause about such things as life stressors, whether they were experienced individually or by everyone. However, Microsoft's survey told us some meaningful things about the workplace itself that we can use to identify some cause and effect beyond COVID-19. We would like to highlight some of them specifically.

The Meeting Explosion

If you take a look at your online calendar for much of 2020 and at least the first part of 2021, this will come as no surprise: globally, our time in meetings doubled from February 2020 to February 2021. Without the luxury of popping into someone's office down the hall, even those quick check-ins seemed to require an official "meeting invite," often on a video collaboration platform. With many calendar apps defaulting to a set period of time, chunks of time were eaten up quickly and clogged many a calendar. What might have been a five-minute catch-up blossomed into a 30-minute placeholder.

Prior to 2020, meeting scientists were claiming we already had a meeting load epidemic in terms of the number of meetings and time spent in them, and here's the real rub. Previous research as early as

2006 showed that people's daily fatigue levels were affected by their meetings, particularly when those meetings interrupted their workflow (Rogelberg, Leach, Warr, and Burnfield 2006). So the more meetings you are in, the more tired you are likely to be at the end of the day. The pandemic put that into overdrive by taking everyone's meeting burden and doubling it.

So, how did that affect people? It was not healthy across the board, but it was more problematic for workers in certain roles than for others. For example, managers were used to their days being heavily populated by meetings, but those whose roles required them to think deeply and innovate – think designers, coders, copywriters, and the like – found the interruptions to their idea creation time untenable. How can someone get into the flow when they're constantly being pulled out of it and being pulled into meetings?

Some organizations course-corrected as the detrimental effects became more and more apparent, and instituted things like "No Meeting Mondays" or allowed employees to designate "think hours" on their calendars. Culture Amp found that having calendar transparency across the entire organization makes people be more intentional before simply shooting off a calendar invite. "People are really upfront in blocking off time and saying, 'This is my time to focus. No meetings for me at this time,'" said Jay Hyett. "What this does as a meeting organizer is that you can see, 'Ah, the team's got a lot of focus time here.' Don't just book stuff right over top of that." Still, maintaining the sanctity of "think time" or "focus time" becomes tougher and tougher when the calendar gets more crowded.

Meeting Creep

Along with a dramatic increase in the number of meetings we were having, we also saw their time extended. No one has ever bemoaned a meeting that ends early, but everyone despises a meeting that ends late. The move to virtual meetings exacerbated the latter. Not only was the average meeting 10 minutes longer in February 2021 than in February 2020, but most meetings also overstayed their welcome . . . often by a lot. Instead of a 30-minute meeting that ran five minutes long, people started having 30-minute meetings that ran 15 minutes long.

Once again, managers recognized the problem and tried to implement solutions. A popular one was blocking out even more time for the meeting, so what was anticipated to be a 30-minute meeting became a 45-minute meeting to avoid running over. But that created a whole set of new problems. Longer meetings required more time being "on" – listening, participating, and contributing to the decisions being made – against the backdrop of the seemingly constant distractions that we were all fighting while trying to work from a place that was likely not designed to be where we should be working. It's no wonder many people started discovering virtual meeting fatigue as a new and nearly constant source of drain.

Pop-Up Meetings

So far, we've talked about the meetings that were scheduled that were more numerous and often longer than intended, but we haven't even mentioned another major issue that cropped up: a rise in unplanned, or "pop-up," meetings. According to the February 2021 survey, 62% of calls and meetings on Microsoft Teams were unscheduled or ad hoc. So, picture this: your calendar is already chock-full of scheduled meetings, the ones that you know you are expected to attend or lead. Then you are tasked with wedging in a significant number of meetings that simply crop up as a result of an immediate but unforeseen business need. How on earth do people fit twice as many scheduled meetings into their eight-hour workday and then sandwich in 62% more impromptu meetings that just pop up but do not populate the official calendar? The answer is . . . they don't. Instead, people extended their workday in both directions. That's right – people dealt with the additional meeting burden by working longer, starting earlier and ending later.

The extension of the workday was seen by another research study conducted during the same timeframe as the one done by Microsoft. Researchers from Harvard and New York Universities at the National Bureau of Economic Research found that the average workday was 48 minutes longer during the pandemic than before (Green 2020). That means, in a given week, workers added four more hours to their regular work schedule. Now this might not seem so alarming, except when you consider this: in many cases, workers were already exceeding 40 hours a week, with some pushing 60 or more hours per week in 2019.

How did they do this? Let's help you visualize it through one of Joe's favorite pandemic "dad jokes." On many a day and certainly well beyond the time his kids found it funny, Joe would grab a glass of water and his iPad to go down to his office in the basement, while announcing, "I'm starting my commute." His commute used to be about 30 minutes each way. Now it amounted to 15 to 20 steps. What did he do with the extra time? Well, mostly he spent it staring into his webcam during scheduled and unscheduled meetings, along with simply working in general.

Sure, replacing one's commute with more work doesn't sound so bad. Think of all you can get done! However, that commuting time has value. It's often used to decompress, listen to an audio book in the car, read a book or the news on your phone while sitting on the bus, or simply listen to some tunes while trying not to use a rude gesture at the idiots on the freeway. Psychology research confirms that people often see their commute as their own personal, sacred time, when no one can bother them, and they can just relax from a long day's work (Wilhoit 2017). This transition time was lost for many during the pandemic, and what did we fill it with? Work.

A little discomfort for four more hours of productive work time may be a tradeoff you are willing to make, and some managers and leaders in organizations are likely okay with it, if not in favor of it. But, there's another more problematic driver of the expanding work day: work-from-home paranoia (Wilding 2021).

Work-from-Home Paranoia – Making Your Presence Known

When colocated in the office, we are able to get continuous feedback. We can ask quick questions and can get a feel for how people are reacting to our work. When isolated on the sofa at home, how our work is being evaluated can be more difficult to ascertain. That longer feedback loop, or sometimes even an absence of one, can create a black hole in our perceptions of how our contributions are valued, and too often we fill that void with negative thoughts. This is "work-from-home paranoia," the state of fear in which a person misinterprets ambiguous situations, seeing falsely negative meanings and potential threats when no such thing exists.

When we were all remote, we lacked those in-person touch-points, so employees tried to get a sense of where they stood with their managers and colleagues by reading the tone of emails or the vocal and nonverbal cues on video calls. That's a heavy lift in the best of circumstances, and with all the other stressors of that time, the uncertainty of whether their contributions were considered up to snuff put people into hyperdrive. They responded by working even harder and longer than might have been reasonable, and the lack of commute made that possible by giving employees extra hours in their days that they could fill with job-justifying work – at least four hours more per week.

Lesson Learned When Fully Virtual

Meetings grew in number and length, adding to the exhaustion of all and the frustration of those who were constantly interrupted from their asynchronous creation work.

Policies to Apply When Hybrid

To mitigate this, try to:

- Right-size the meeting by blocking out only the calendar time needed for the planned agenda. Don't let the calendar app dictate length.

- Encourage space on everyone's calendar for focus time and don't override it.

- Offer more frequent feedback on the contributions of remote employees who might be more susceptible to work-from-home paranoia, leading them to overwork and burnout.

Working more wasn't the only by-product of the meeting explosion that occurred during the pandemic. There was also a normalization of a meeting behavior that would have been considered the height of rudeness during an in-person meeting. Let's take a closer look.

The Rise of the Multitasking Epidemic

Imagine you are attending a meeting with everyone gathered around the same conference table. No one is remote; everyone is in-person. The purpose of the meeting is mission-critical and the stakes are high with very real impacts on the business's bottom line. The leader of the meeting is working her way through the agenda, but then you notice out of the corner of your eye something a bit odd. One of your colleagues is very visibly answering emails and loudly plucking away on her keyboard. Then you start scanning the other attendees. Some are actively listening to the leader and even participating by offering input. However, there are more than a few who are on their own laptops, or scrolling through their phones, or simply zoning out. What is going on? Don't these attendees, who are obviously not paying attention, know how disrespectful and rude this is? And that's not even considering how much is lost by their lack of contribution to the discussion.

When a meeting is held in person and everyone can easily see what each person is doing, multitasking is nearly impossible to pull off without being called out, but during the pandemic when almost all meetings were virtual, multitasking was a coping mechanism that was green-lighted almost out of desperation. People first just tried to expand their workday to compensate for meetings exploding onto their calendars, but it wasn't enough. The to-do lists were getting longer and the time available to accomplish those tasks was shrinking. So, people tried something even more difficult to pull off in a truly effective way . . . multitasking. That's right, people tried to do more than one thing at a time, which we have known for many years is really a myth. People actually cannot do two things at once effectively or with true focus. There's a reason why we joke about walking and chewing gum at the same time. While on a Zoom call with their team, they managed the kids' online schooling, banged out a few emails, and secured a grocery pickup time slot. The problem with this effort toward efficiency may have come to light later that day, perhaps in the form of an email from their boss, asking where the report was that they were supposed to have completed and submitted by lunchtime. They were given the assignment during that earlier meeting, but somewhere in all that multitasking, that assignment got lost.

Lessons Learned from Our "Suddenly Virtual" Work Life

Here's the thing: even with countless cautionary tales such as these, people still believe that multitasking can work. For example, in a *WIRED* article (Johnson 2021), Microsoft's chief scientist, Jaime Teevan, stated, "There's an opportunity with remote meetings to just 'sort-of' attend a meeting." We've probably all successfully "sort-of" attended a meeting, where others talked, decisions were made, none of them mattered to our work, and we were on video typing away at our email, with no one saying a word about it or expecting our participation. However, in our view, this is not a meeting success story. Instead, this is a prime example of a bad meeting, or at least one you should not have had to attend. If it wasn't relevant to you and your participation was not expected or required, why were you there in the first place? A meeting you can "sort-of" attend is likely a meeting you should have been given a pass to miss.

Going a bit further, though, Jaime stated, "You can skip a meeting and watch it at double-speed if it was recorded. You can have it playing in the background while you do other things and listen for important points." This is an intriguing concept, but there's still a problem here. Listening for important points while a meeting is "playing in the background" also requires us to do two things at the same time. Our brains will not effectively allow us to separate the noise from the key takeaways if we are doing something else that is requiring our attention. You'll more than likely cost yourself even more time and effort because you will have to surrender to actually watching it again, this time without distraction.

We cannot endorse multitasking because the science is clear. Multitasking is a myth (Rosen 2008). People actually cannot pay attention to more than one thing at a time. That's a fact of sensation and perception research and is taught to every student who takes a Psychology 101 class (Crenshaw 2008). That's why the idea of "sort-of" attending a meeting might sound good . . . but only in theory.

You may *think* you are doing two things at one time, but you aren't. You are simply giving attention to other tasks while the meeting carries on. You may have seen this play out in meetings you've attended. Someone is called on who clearly has been multitasking. They might try to cover it up by saying, "What's that? You were cutting out. My internet has been choppy today. What was the question?" The person is then brought up to speed on what they missed, wasting valuable meeting time due to their multitasking behavior. What's worse, the offender typically answers the question and then resumes their "sort-of" attending behavior.

It probably comes as no surprise that a study from Microsoft found that more multitasking occurs in larger and longer meetings than it does in recurring meetings (Johnson 2021). There are a few reasons for this. First, people feel more anonymous in larger meetings. Responsibility is diffused in these larger settings, so people feel they can check out and get some real work done. Second, longer meetings start to make people anxious because of their ever-increasing inbox "to-read" list. They feel like they have to check their email and get back to those seemingly urgent requests, even at the expense of contributing in the meeting. Third, recurring meetings are usually with longer-standing teams. These meetings tend to include people that matter the most to them in a professional sense. So in those meetings, they pay more attention because they don't want their direct boss or their colleagues to think less of them.

But it doesn't stop there. According to Microsoft's data (Johnson 2021), morning meetings have higher rates of multitasking. That's probably because the inbox is fresh from the overnight emailing that people in other time zones sent, or from people who couldn't sleep. And the longer the meeting goes on, the more likely people will multitask. Multitasking happens six times more often in video meetings lasting more than 80 minutes compared with video meetings that are 20 minutes or less.

Lesson Learned When Fully Virtual

Multitasking increased substantially as a product of the meeting explosion that happened during the epidemic.

Policies to Apply When Hybrid

To stop this counterproductive behavior, try to:

- Cut down on the number of meetings.
- Keep the meetings brief and purpose-driven.
- Include only the people who need to be there. If the meeting is not relevant for them, they don't need to be there.
- Include everyone in the discussion. When people are "seen," it's harder to multitask and easier to contribute meaningful ideas.
- If you see someone multitasking, try to get them to stop by calling on them to provide input. Their initial embarrassment at being "caught" will hopefully help break a bad habit that is counterproductive for all.

Discovering and Managing the Work–Family Interface

Prior to the pandemic, organizational scientists studied something often referred to as the "work–family interface" (Major and Burke 2013). This area refers to how work interferes with or enriches family life. More common terms used in the literature for this concept include "work–family conflict" and "work–life balance." In general, this all refers to how a person's work and employment as well as their personal life interact in both positive and negative ways (Greenhaus, Allen, and Spector 2006). For example, many have experienced times they had to work late, and that interfered with evening plans with family, friends, or loved ones. Alternatively, many have had the experience of receiving a sizable raise at work or a promotion that resulted in more resources being available at home. Joe recalls getting a sizable increase in his salary and feeling a significant weight lifted, knowing that it would be easier to pay for all of those dance classes for his four daughters. That's work–family enrichment at its finest.

The work–family interface came to the fore during the pandemic, as the stay-at-home mandates blurred the boundary between work and home like never before. People who typically worked in an office now worked at home with no commute to buffer the good or bad from work spilling over at home. No longer was there some distance, if any at all, between the small children at home and the video-conference call. Now the kids made cameo appearances, or the cat decided to type an email, or the dog needed attention, and it was all within view of co-workers and customers. Home and work, work and home, were now colocated for a vast majority of people.

Sure, some employees had dealt with this before. Prior to the pandemic, some had even sought alternative work schedules that actually allowed for more working-from-home situations. However, no one had experienced the expanding workday and the explosion of scheduled and unscheduled meetings that occurred during COVID-19. Suddenly, the flexibility dreamed about or even stigmatized in 2019 was had by just about everyone, and it wasn't all it was cracked up to be. Keeping work at work and home at home was nearly impossible and work–family balance became out-of-whack.

Some of the solutions people found for regaining balance were simple enough to employ. Locks were put on de facto office doors, as were signs that said things like, "I'm in a meeting. Do not interrupt unless bleeding." (That only worked for those whose children were able to read, of course.) There were also daily negotiations on who could gobble up the bandwidth at what times. When the kids had a synchronous Zoom class, the parents tried to keep that time slot free of video calls to ensure that the classroom experience was not compromised. The list of these ad hoc solutions goes on and on, with reports of varied results.

But are there some overall strategies that we can use to better define our work life and our home life when both take place in the same physical space? We'll focus on a few common problems and offer some solutions that have proven successful in creating boundaries when we live where we work and work where we live.

Be Aware of Time Zone Differences

As a meeting leader, you can play a pivotal role in providing separation by being mindful of when you schedule meetings. For example, if your team's typical schedule is from 9 a.m. to 5 p.m., you can make sure to not schedule any meetings outside that timeframe. That's a relatively light lift if your team resides in the same time zone, but becomes a bit more challenging if your team is scattered across several. For those who have a team that crosses time zones, you need to be mindful of what time it is for everyone. Remember, a 4 p.m. meeting in California is a 7 p.m. meeting in New York. Scheduling gets even trickier when teams are international in nature and, say, the North Carolina folks need to meet with the Germany folks.

Lisette Sutherland from Collaboration Superpowers offers these tips for working with multiple time zones:

- *Make it fair.* Don't always opt for the same time for a meeting with global teams where one or two people always end up doing the late night or the very early morning shift. Lisette says, "Everyone should feel and share the pain of time zones when you're working on a team."

- *Make a shared calendar.* It's easy to make mistakes when scheduling across time zones, but if you have a shared team calendar, you can spot those more easily when everyone inputs their working hours into one calendar. Many calendar apps automatically include time zone conversions.
- *Record meetings.* We touched on the value of asynchronous video earlier but when managing meetings across time zones, it really shines. As Lisette explains, "On global teams, not everybody can make every single meeting. Recording allows the people who have missed it to feel like they're equally valued."

What about if you are not the organizer of your meetings? If you are not the organizer of meetings that are infringing upon your family and nonwork time, speak up! That is, don't be afraid to let those who are scheduling those meetings know that they're impacting your home life. Perhaps that sounds difficult. How do you tell your boss, "Hey, you're killing me here with these dinnertime meetings?" Try raising their awareness by putting it in an in-person context. You might mention that before the pandemic, we wouldn't schedule a face-to-face meeting in the office at this time. Is there a way we can avoid doing it when we meet virtually or hybrid, too?

Science supports the decision to keep work to predefined business hours. Specifically, there is strong evidence that longer work hours, especially when they include before- or after-hours meetings, are related to higher levels of stress, anxiety, depression, and general poor health (Schonfeld and Chang 2017). Let's put that in a lifelike framework. People who work longer hours and have meetings when they should be vegging in front of the TV or even when they ought to be asleep get sick more often and even have greater risk of cardiovascular disease (Smith, Folkard, Tucker, and Evans 2011). Clocking in and out at reasonable times is essential for a healthy mind and body.

Rethinking Your Commute

Another thing that can be done to mitigate or help eliminate the impact of work–family conflict is to create a virtual commute. In mid-2020 this became a popular go-to idea for helping create the cognitive separation between work and home (MacLellan 2021). This virtual commute could be taking the dog for a walk, or listening to your favorite tunes on a drive in the neighborhood, or any number of other things. Think of it as a "me meeting" that is just for you and is all about helping you get in the right mindset at home.

For those opting to work hybrid or fully remote, the daily commute might look different than it had in the past, but the science that supports its value still holds true. Part of what keeps work from spilling over into home is that time to decompress, make some decisions, think through the annoying behavior of a colleague, or whatever else is still lingering on your mind while commuting (Greenhaus and Allen 2011). Carving out that commuting time, whether real or virtual, is critical.

The Silver Lining of the Blurred Work/Life Line

The sudden influx of virtual meetings and some of the infringing on personal time wasn't all bad. It did create a sense of camaraderie that we likely would not have found were it not for the joint work-from-home experience. We were all in it together, right? Jared Spataro, corporate vice president (CVP) at Microsoft, stated, "The shared vulnerability of this time has given us a huge opportunity to bring real authenticity to company culture and transform work for the better" (Microsoft 2021). In fact, according to their Work Trend Index survey, 39% of employees said they were more likely to bring their full, authentic selves to work and 31% of employees were less likely to feel embarrassed or ashamed when home life shows up at work. In other words, our shared work-from-home experience has introduced a little bit of humanity into our lives as employees in organizations. We are seen not just as our roles but as whole people.

It also offered an opportunity to create connections that would not have happened without the portal into the personal lives of our coworkers. Jay Hyett of Culture Amp recalls a delightful discovery he made on a video call with some colleagues: "I was in a meeting just the other day and someone had a massive collection of LEGOs in their background. Straight after the meeting, I was on Slack going, 'My God . . . I just saw your LEGO collection. Can we talk about that?'"

Lesson Learned When Fully Virtual

Some blurring of the work/life line may be okay, but finding the perfect balance was and will continue to be an ongoing battle.

Policies to Apply When Hybrid

Here are some strategies to get you started:

- Keep meetings within business hours, and be aware of the time zone disparities.
- Create a shared calendar to avoid scheduling mistakes that place undue burden on those who are outside of the majority's time zone.
- Record meetings to be viewed at a later time by those who can't reasonably attend live.
- Consider introducing the virtual commute – a "me meeting" for you to decompress from the day's work-from-home experience.

Flexible Work and Its Impact on Diversity and Inclusion

The context through which we view our coworkers has been immeasurably impacted and often positively enhanced by our virtual meetings, which were both distant and intimate at the same time, but there is one important caveat that should be highlighted. In the Microsoft survey, Black and Latino workers in the United States reported they were less likely than the year before to bring their authentic selves to work than the broader population was (26% and 24%, respectively, compared to the national average of 17% who felt *less* likely to be authentic in their interactions with co-workers). While the boxes on a Zoom call might all be equal, giving a feel that everyone is showing up in a more egalitarian manner, not everyone in the boxes may feel the same sense of equality and inclusiveness. Efforts always need to be made to ensure that meeting interactions, whether virtual or hybrid, encourage authenticity for all.

Incorporating Diversity, Equity, and Inclusion into Hybrid

The return to the office, whether it's one day a week, three days a week, or even once a month, is also full of subtext. One dimension of this subtext concerns the racial reckoning that swept the United States in the midst of the pandemic. In response to the calls for change, many companies invested time and resources into developing robust diversity, equity, and inclusion (DEI) initiatives. Through that lens, leaders can be thoughtful in their approach to hybrid meetings that support and incorporate DEI in ways large and small.

Consider the work of Elisabeth Steele Hutchison. She is director of admissions at the William S. Richardson School of Law at the University of Hawai'i at Manoa, arguably one of the most diverse law schools in the country. However, much of her time since the start of the pandemic has been geared toward helping lawyers and law school professors to be polished and professional on Zoom.

"We are so hyper-focused on what people look like, and we make judgments incredibly quickly," she says. "The way that I am presenting myself may be as important as what I'm saying."

As a woman of color, she's also aware of the additional burden the virtual environment created. She often kicks off her workshops with an image of a white commentator who is "Zooming" in front of a messy background and jokes, "This is Zooming with white privilege. I'm just going to show up. I'm smart. They're just going to know. And that's something that Black folks just have never been able to do."

That extra level of attention to production value – curating a non-distracting background, ensuring adequate lighting, selecting attire befitting the situation – isn't by chance. Rather she sees it as a reflection of what has traditionally been the case, but has been revamped for the virtual window: "We [Black people] are used to having to be really thoughtful in how we present and having that added burden."

Even the webcams used for hybrid and virtual meetings can pose problems for those with darker complexions. For example, Elisabeth has had to battle with her webcam photo sensors that attempt to whiten her skin. She's come up with workarounds, but she says it's important to keep this in mind: "There are some people where the technology that we are using for a hybrid meeting or a virtual meeting suits them perfectly. But actually, that is not a given."

Even the ubiquitous icebreakers that have become a common kickoff to many a meeting can be fraught with problems. Often, they are designed for homogeneous groups and only serve to marginalize those who are not in the majority. ("Okay everyone, please submit a baby photo and we are going to guess who each person is. Guess who . . .?") Good intentions can still lead to uncomfortable scenarios.

But we don't know what we don't know, and that's why Elisabeth is a strong advocate for soliciting anonymous feedback after every meeting. However, it's equally important to let participants know that feedback is not just going to be stuffed into a suggestion box, never to be read. Elisabeth kicks off each meeting by reporting on the feedback she received about the previous one. It can spark discussion or give you a chance to explain how you plan to or already have responded to it. The iterative feedback loop shows that you are indeed listening and acting upon suggestions and comments. Attending to the voice of one can benefit all.

Elisabeth likens it to accessibility efforts made for those with disabilities. "When we added captioning to websites, we did it to help those with limited vision. However, we found out we all benefited from it. When we built ramps, we were thinking about people who were wheelchair-bound, but it turned out to help people who had baby carriages, people who had shopping carts, people who had rolling luggage. So being really thoughtful and intentional in the way we set up meetings in the same way, it's going to help everybody."

Lesson Learned When Fully Virtual

What we perceived to be an inclusive way of meeting may not have been as inclusive as we thought.

Policies to Apply When Hybrid

In order to create an equitable meeting culture:

- Solicit anonymous feedback to uncover any blind spots that you might have about approaches or processes that may be marginalizing others.

- Give careful consideration to icebreakers. What you might think is all in good fun could be very uncomfortable for others.

- Explore ways to incorporate DEI initiatives into the new workflows you create for hybrid meetings that lead to an inclusive space for all.

Conclusion

As we transition to hybrid work situations, we need to fix the problems that fully virtual meetings caused. The extra-long workday and the ever-expanding numbers of meetings cannot continue, or the burnout will carry on unrestrained, literally killing the workforce. Also, we must be cautious in the rollout of hybrid work as there may be unintended consequences for diversity, equity, and inclusion. An additional problem that we need to address is a result of a solution we touted in our first book, *Suddenly Virtual*. We made the case for turning the camera on in virtual meetings, but we learned some lessons about this as well. While we are not shying away from that strong assertion, we need to provide some guardrails. In the next chapter, we will take a look at when video is imperative, and, just as importantly, when it's not.

Chapter Takeaways

- Working from home led to an explosion and expansion of meetings.

- Work-from-home paranoia helped elongate the workweek, which was already overburdened.

- Multitasking became necessary and even normalized despite its scientifically proven negative effect.

- Work–life balance became harder to manage when we worked and lived in the same place.

- The shared vulnerability and collective experience allowed employees to bring their authentic selves to work.

- The hybrid world of work is taking shape not just post-pandemic but also post–racial reckoning. To create an inclusive environment, DEI initiatives need to be considered within the context of hybrid meetings to avoid unintended consequences.

References

Crenshaw, D. 2008. *The Myth of Multitasking: How "Doing It All" Gets Nothing Done*. Wiley.

Gaskell, A. 2021. "How productive have remote workers been during Covid?" *Forbes*, May 31. Retrieved from https://www.forbes.com/sites/adigaskell/2021/05/31/how-productive-have-remote-workers-been-during-covid/?sh=b5ebf97639e4

Green, J. 2020. "The pandemic workday is 48 minutes longer and has more meetings." *Bloomberg*, August 3. Retrieved July 9, 2021 from https://www.bloomberg.com/news/articles/2020-08-03/the-pandemic-workday-is-48-minutes-longer-and-has-more-meetings

Greenhaus, J. H., and T. D. Allen. 2011. "Work–family balance: A review and extension of the literature." In J. C. E. Quick and L. E. Tetrick. 2011. *Handbook of Occupational Health Psychology*, 165–183. American Psychological Association.

Greenhaus, J. H., T. D. Allen, and P. E. Spector. 2006. "Health consequences of work–family conflict: The dark side of the work–family interface." In *Employee Health, Coping and Methodologies*. Emerald Group Publishing.

Johnson, K. 2021. "It's true. Everyone is multitasking in video meetings." *Wired*. Retrieved from https://www-wired-com.cdn.ampproject.org/c/s/www.wired.com/story/stop-looking-your-email-youre-video/amp

MacLellan, L. 2021. "Separate work from life with a "virtual commute" that energizes you." *Quartz at Work*. https://qz.com/work/1909901/how-to-design-virtual-commute-rituals-that-energize-you/

Major, D. A., and R. J. Burke. 2013. *Handbook of Work–Life Integration Among Professionals: Challenges and Opportunities*. Edward Elgar.

Microsoft. 2021. *2021 Work Trend Index: Annual Report – The next great disruption is hybrid work – Are we ready?* Retrieved from https://www.microsoft.com/en-us/worklab/work-trend-index/hybrid-work

Rogelberg, S. G., D. J. Leach, P. B. Warr, and J. L. Burnfield. 2006. "'Not another meeting!' Are meeting time demands related to employee well-being?" *Journal of Applied Psychology* 91 (1): 83.

Rosen, C. 2008. "The myth of multitasking." *The New Atlantis* 20: 105–110.

Schonfeld, I. S., and C.-H. Chang. 2017. *Occupational Health Psychology.* Springer.

Smith, C. S., S. Folkard, P. Tucker, and M. S. Evans. 2011. "Work schedules, health, and safety." In J. C. E. Quick and L. E. Tetrick (Eds.), *Handbook of Occupational Health Psychology*, 185–204. American Psychological Association.

Wilding, M. 2021. "Managing your WFH paranoia." *Harvard Business Review.* Retrieved from https://hbr.org/2021/04/managing-your-wfh-paranoia?utm_medium=email&utm_source=newsletter_daily&utm_campaign=mtod_notactsubs

Wilhoit, E. D. 2017. "My drive is my sacred time": Commuting as routine liminality. *Culture and Organization* 23 (4): 263–276.

Chapter 4

New Insights: A Recalibration of Video Use

Our soapbox was relatively short in stature, maybe an inch and half when resting flat but growing to over nine inches when standing on end. Still, we hoped the message delivered in our book *Suddenly Virtual: Making Remote Meetings Work* would penetrate the collective psyche of the corporate world. In Chapter 7 of the book, we even put it in bold print just in case:

The Case for Making Every Virtual Meeting a *Video* Meeting

Presumably it did have impact; at least it caught the attention of folks at prestigious places like McKinsey & Company, who featured it on their best-selling business books list and even talked to Karin about the importance of effectively using a webcam during a virtual meeting (McKinsey & Company 2021). So the title of this chapter might seem very confusing to you. What do we mean by "A Recalibration of Video Use"? Wasn't the data presented in *Suddenly Virtual* all about how video is as good as face-to-face and better than telephone? Wasn't that what we were evangelizing about even before the pandemic? While we recognize and understand your disorientation, we also have to acknowledge and explain how our original advice was applied within the context of our "suddenly virtual" world. When we strongly asserted the need for using video in addition to audio alone in virtual meetings, we had no idea that we were about to experience an explosion of meetings. Who knew that in addition to being suddenly virtual, we'd also double the number of meetings on people's calendars (see Chapter 3). The "meetingization" of our work lives meant that if you followed our advice to the letter, you were spending your entire day on a webcam, spending hours and hours watching yourself along with your colleagues and customers on a screen.

The ensuing exhaustion from that experience became commonly known as "Zoom fatigue," even though the drain was felt by those using any and all of the video collaboration platforms. Video call fatigue is real (Fosslien and Duffy 2020), but the explanation for why it is happening is where we humbly diverge from the opinions put forth by a bevy of scientists, technologists, and business folks. We feel strongly enough about it that we will give it the same treatment as we did our headline about video in our previous book:

Video Call Fatigue Is Not the Fault of the Technology; It's Due to Operator Error

You may be wondering why we are spending so much time focusing on a major issue in *virtual* meetings in a book about *hybrid* meetings. Consider this: a hybrid meeting by design will include virtual participants and they will likely be joining via video. (Yes, some people may still insist on dialing in, but hopefully the data from Chapter 2 will dissuade them.) Concerns over video call fatigue will not disappear in a hybrid environment; they will remain an issue that will require mitigation. Thankfully, our time spent battling the fatigue during our fully virtual work life can better inform how we handle it when we are hybrid, so first, we look back at the root causes and then look forward to solutions.

In this chapter, we will explore:

- How an overreliance on live video calls leads to video call exhaustion
- Strategies to combat video call fatigue
- When using video is imperative in a virtual or hybrid meeting and when it is not

Let's Hop on Zoom

You might be tempted to feel badly for Zoom seeing that their company name has been linked with what became one of the most bemoaned by-products of the pandemic, but, as Kleenex is to tissues and Band-Aids are to bandages, Zoom is to videoconferencing platforms. The company found substantial product/market fit as a result of COVID-19 and it shows in their user numbers. In December 2019, they reported a total of 10 million daily meeting participants. By April 2020, just a month into the global lockdown, they had 300 million daily users (Zoom 2020). At the time of this writing, Microsoft Teams was in second place with 75 million active users every day, but Zoom was clearly the giant in the room, dominating the market in 44 countries, where it garners more than 50% of the market share (Brandl 2021). In fact, Zoom leads the way in critical countries like the United States, the UK, and Japan. So, don't feel too bad for Zoom, even if many people will continue to disparage their name with "Zoom fatigue" complaints. They'll take the market saturation that comes with it. Other platforms also saw meteoric rises in their user numbers with one exception: Skype, which used to be synonymous with video calling, actually lost nearly 26% of its market share.

Figure 4.1 was put together by Email ToolTester, which studied the global usage of 16 of the most popular videoconferencing platforms across 122 countries (Brandl 2021).

The rapid adoption of video collaboration and conferencing tools during the global lockdowns was not surprising, considering how they seemed to be as close an approximation of the face-to-face interactions as you could get at that time (Reed and Allen 2021). However, what was not anticipated was how nearly every human touchpoint became a video call. All of the usual in-person meetings became video meetings (or at least held the possibility of being video meetings if people agreed to turn on their webcams). However, lower-level interactions also went digital. A quick phone call was often replaced with a video chat that likely went longer than the phone call ever would have. Heck, even our happy hours with our colleagues, designed to build team cohesion, were hosted on Zoom. In a world where we felt isolated and starved for human connection, video calls became a panacea of a sort to soothe those cravings for simply *seeing* people's faces. Humans are social creatures and video calls became our source for social connection.

"The main change that I've seen and in talking with IT leaders around the world is that I think most people before the pandemic said, '*Aah*, video . . . I don't really need it.' The conventional wisdom was, 'Maybe I'll use it in an executive meeting,'" observed Scott Wharton, the vice president and general manager of the Video Collaboration Group at Logitech. "Most people now will say that's not true. Video is better. It works. We all know empirically it allowed us to keep being productive, so I think the whole notion that video doesn't work or is not helpful is just gone."

But every virtue has the potential to be a vice. Too much of good thing can be bad . . . ergo, video call fatigue. What did we expect,

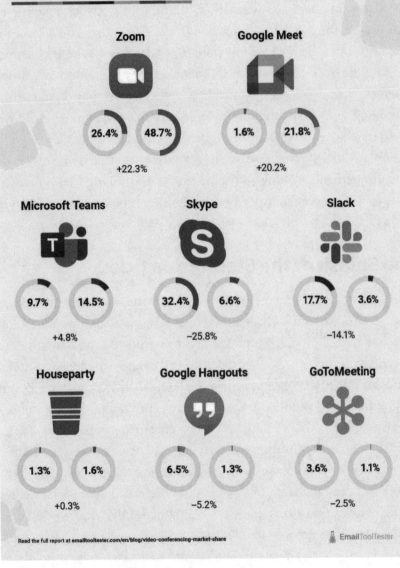

Figure 4.1 Email ToolTester 2021
Source: Robert Brandl 2021 / Tooltester Network

New Insights: A Recalibration of Video Use

though, from a work style that meant staying rooted in one spot for hours on end? Here's Scott Wharton again: "I guarantee if you were sitting in a conference room and you didn't move all day, you would be fatigued. It's just tiring, thinking all day and being in meetings. I think what's happening is we are just working more because you can stack up 10 meetings together." When meetings are back to back for hours at a time, and they are video meetings, when do you go to the restroom? When can you grab lunch without being under the uncomfortable eye of colleagues? And we wonder what's causing the fatigue? Yes, being on camera all the time plays a big part, and we'll get into that. But ignoring basic human needs, like going to the restroom and taking lunch breaks, is also a key contributor that made the "always-on" workstyle unsustainable.

The Splash of the Stanford Article

In February 2021, an article published in the journal *Technology, Mind and Behavior* by Dr. Jeremy Bailenson, founding director of the Stanford Virtual Human Interaction Lab, purported to have answers as to why nonstop video calls lead to fatigue (Bailenson 2021). Professor Bailenson said his article "systematically deconstructs Zoom fatigue from a psychological perspective" and identified four consequences of our hours spent on video chats (Ramachandran 2021). He also made suggestions for interface changes as well as adjustments users can make on how they are using the platforms to help combat Zoom fatigue. While we can wholeheartedly endorse many of the recommendations, there's a real concern that many people in the general population will cite this article as an excuse to turn their video off for good. This would be a costly mistake. Allow us to share the suggested causes of Zoom fatigue mentioned in the article and offer our own take on how best to respond to them.

Stanford Reason 1: Seeing Yourself Constantly During Video Chats in Real Time Is Fatiguing

On this suggested reason for video call fatigue, we couldn't agree more. Video collaboration platforms put us in a highly unusual communication scenario. For the first time, many of us were seeing ourselves communicate in real time. Seeing our image on the screen was fascinating and perhaps frightening, distracting and possibly disconcerting. *Is that* really *how I look when I speak? Do I always tilt my head to the side like that? And what is up with my hands flitting around my face?*

Video meetings made us hyperaware of something we are never aware of when we are speaking in person with someone . . . how we look when we talk to other people. After all, it's not as if we walk around with a mirror held up to our faces – but on a video chat platform, that in essence is what we are doing. Seeing ourselves on-screen allowed us to monitor our performance by watching ourselves converse, but this threw our communication focus completely off.

Typically, we focus much of our attention on our conversation partner in an attempt to read their responses to what we are saying. Are they nodding, a sign of approval or agreement? Are they frowning, an overt display of just the opposite? Are they not making eye contact, an indication they are uncomfortable with your message? During video meetings, though, the gravitational pull of gazing at ourselves was incredibly strong. This fixation on our own faces was likely more pronounced at the beginning of the pandemic when our visage on the screen was relatively new. However, as someone who trains thousands of people in proper eye contact during a virtual meeting or presentation, Karin still sees many people who can't stop looking at themselves. That disruption in the typical conversation dynamic puts everyone at a disadvantage. The speaker who can't avert their eyes from their own image can easily miss out on nonverbal cues from their conversation partner (or partners). Plus, the very act of monitoring your own performance automatically undercuts your authenticity. In other words, you lose part of your genuine self simply by watching yourself "perform." The result is a lack of authenticity that is exaggerated by the camera lens and will come across as fake to those receiving your message.

Stanford Proposed Solution 1

Bailenson proposes a tweak to the Zoom interface that other platforms should also heed: don't make people see their own images by default. Zoom does allow you to take yourself off the screen. The simplest way to do so is by hovering over your own video box, clicking on the three dots in the upper right-hand corner, and selecting "Hide Self View" from the menu. You will immediately disappear from the screen and will just see the other people on your call, which puts you into a more natural conversation dynamic. Unfortunately, many other platforms do not have that feature, tempting you to sneak a peek or even stare at yourself during a call because you cannot hide that view.

Our Proposed Solution 1

We would also recommend hiding your own image on the screen when possible, but if that's not an option, follow these best practices for eye contact:

- In order to speak with impact, you want to primarily look at the camera lens, not at the people on the screen. This will go against all of your natural human impulses because you will want to look people in the eye, and your people are staring out from the boxes on the screen. However, because the camera lens is not embedded into the screen, it will look to your conversation partner(s) like you are not looking at them at all but rather somewhere else.

For example, if you are using the webcam embedded in your laptop, typically the camera lens is in the bezel at the top of the screen. If you look at the faces on the gallery view while you speak, you will appear to be looking down.

By looking at the lens while you are speaking, you can't see your conversation partners as well, but you also can't see *your* image, either. Therefore, you won't be fixated on monitoring your performance, a performance that will be much more authentic than if you were watching yourself deliver in real time.

Before you start to complain about how it's fundamentally necessary to be able to read the nonverbals of your audience, allow us to underscore the word "primarily." When speaking, you want to interact with the camera the way you would with someone face to face. We naturally look away all the time when speaking to someone in person because staring at someone's face without breaking our gaze makes them feel uncomfortable. The same holds true when speaking through a webcam. Don't stare at the camera lens. Quick glances away from the webcam can allow you to not only come across as more genuine but also allow you to read the body language of your conversation partner(s). It takes less than a second to see if someone is nodding . . . or nodding off.

- If you are not speaking, feel free to look at the person who is. It will allow you to focus on reading their body language. So much of how we convey a message is through our facial expressions and other nonverbals. By watching the speaker on-screen, you will be able to better understand the intent of their message.

Stanford Reason 2: Excessive Amounts of Close-Up Eye Contact Is Highly Intense

Professor Bailenson astutely observes that video calls often violate societal norms related to eye contact and interpersonal proximity. When interacting with colleagues or others not in our inner circle of close friends or family, we typically maintain a comfortable distance from them to avoid invading their personal space. However, Bailenson notes, "On Zoom, behavior ordinarily reserved for close relationships – such as long stretches of direct eye gaze and faces seen close up – has suddenly become the way we interact with casual acquaintances, coworkers, and even strangers" (Bailenson 2021). He draws a parallel to behavior on an elevator. People are forced to stand close together (pre-COVID-19, of course) and as a result, usually avert their gaze from each other. (If you really want to freak people out, enter an elevator and don't turn around to face the door. Simply stare at the people who are along with you for the ride.)

The conversation space created on a video call is very intimate. You are as close to your conversation partner as your eyes are to your webcam and their screen is to their eyes, and sometimes that distance feels inappropriate for the people you are meeting with. Have you ever encountered a "close talker" in person? As they were inching ever nearer, you likely felt a strong urge to push them away. We can be close talkers on video calls too but we don't have those in-person social cues from our conversation partner to indicate we've crossed a boundary for personal proximity.

Bailenson also points out a problem with the gallery view on the screen, where all the attendees appear to be staring straight ahead and almost at you for a prolonged period of time, which simulates eye contact. He cited research showing that being stared at while speaking causes physiological arousal, even when the faces are virtual, and being on video calls with a slew of participants creates significant stress for the speaker.

Stanford Proposed Solution 2

To deal with the intense eye contact issue, Bailenson recommends taking the video call window out of full-screen mode and reducing it to minimize face size. He also suggests using an external keyboard "to allow an increase in the personal space bubble between oneself and the grid" (Ramachandran 2021). We at least partially agree with his advice.

Our Proposed Solution 2

Before we present our proposed solution, let's take a closer look at Bailenson's suggestion. No doubt, when you are on a video call, you can feel like you are under the microscope if you have a whole screen full of faces staring back at you. However, there are benefits of having those heads appearing on-screen, too.

One of the biggest complaints we often hear is that when presenting virtually, it can feel like you are talking to no one. There's no laughter after you crack a joke because people are told to keep themselves on mute, lest an errant dog bark interrupt the audio for everyone. If people have kept their cameras off, there's not even a head nod or smile to offer encouragement to the speaker as they are moving through their presentation. Perhaps all of those eyeballs looking out from the boxes can be a bit unnerving, but they also remind you that you are indeed speaking to an audience, and they provide critical feedback to help you deliver at your best.

Professional speakers and comics refer to responding to the non-verbal communication of the audience as "reading the room" or "playing to the room." The best speakers and stand-up comedians are more adept at it than typical people. This is because they likely have innate ability and have developed skills around situational awareness and impression management (Leary and Kowalski 1990; Abrahams 2016), which allows them to react to the feedback they are receiving from their audience and adjust their delivery accordingly. Every person has a level of both situational awareness and impression management, and in a virtual or hybrid meeting when an audience is visible, we use these abilities and skills to help us communicate more effectively. If cameras are off, there is a reduction in the feedback system needed to play to the room.

Bailenson's suggestion to minimize the size of the faces on the screen has a similar effect to turning cameras off: it minimizes the size of the nonverbals you as a speaker can use to help you present well. We are already at a disadvantage in reading the room because we are limited by the size of the boxes and the way people are situated in them. Making those boxes even smaller seems counterintuitive.

Although Bailenson doesn't address this in his work, it's worth noting that the issue with minimizing opportunities to read nonverbal cues becomes even more pronounced when you are sharing content like slides. Most platforms prioritize showing the slides and show only a limited number of participants or no attendees at all. Gauging the way your message is resonating is nearly impossible without any nonverbal cues.

Instead of minimizing the entire window, try these techniques instead:

- *Leverage the faces but limit them*. If you are presenting to a larger group (beyond, say, 10 people), consider asking a few people to be designated "camera-on" people. You can use their body language to assess how well you are communicating your message and adjust your delivery accordingly. That representative sample allows you to present with more confidence and get a better sense of your impact while minimizing the number of eyes staring at you.

Try rotating the role around the group to ensure that the attention burden is equally shared. When you are a "camera-on" person, you may find you get more out of the presentation anyway because it forces you to stay tuned in.

Use those faces on the screen as a way to connect and even personalize the experience. If you see someone offer an approving nod after you make a comment, acknowledge that by saying, "I see, Bob, that you're in agreement with me on that." That helps to create a communal experience where it's not you presenting to an endless sea of faces but rather to individuals who are part of a larger conversation.

- *Pick the proper framing.* The way you frame yourself, meaning how much of you can be seen on-screen, establishes the distance between you and your conversation partner. The less they can see of you, the closer you will seem to the people on the other side. For example, if they can only see you from the neck up, that's emulating a very close conversation that most would consider inappropriate. With that in mind, be aware of how framing will impact how you are perceived. There are two options that work well:

1. A medium shot, where you are seen from approximately the waist up, which creates a conversation space with several feet between you and the attendee.

2. A tight shot, where you are seen from about mid-chest up, which simulates a close but still appropriate professional conversation space. If you appear from just the neck up, it will feel too close, as if you are invading the personal space of the person on the other side.

No matter which you choose, aim to have a few inches between the top of your head and the top of the screen and an equal amount of space from each shoulder to the edge of the frame. If you need a point of reference, try stacking three fingers on top of your head. That's the amount of distance you should have between your crown and the top of the frame.

Source: Courtesy of Karin M. Reed.

An additional layer of flexibility for framing can be provided by Bailenson's idea of using an external keyboard. Sometimes it can be difficult to achieve a shot that provides enough distance because you need to reach your keyboard on your laptop. An external keyboard or wireless mouse offers you the freedom to create the proper spacing while manipulating the content on the screen.

The problem of being too close for comfort when appearing on the screen is an easy one to fix as long as you are aware of what framing works best.

Stanford Reason 3: The Cognitive Load Is Much Higher in Video Chats

When having a conversation face to face, the interaction's complexity is solely dependent on the complexity of the topic being discussed. A discussion a boss has with a subordinate over poor performance requires a higher level of brain power than a chat with a friend about what you had for dinner last night. But take either of these scenarios and put them on a videoconferencing platform and it becomes infinitely more complicated. Bailenson supposes that the energy and effort required for any conversation via video is much higher given the challenges of interpreting and emitting nonverbal cues as well as navigating the technology itself.

Take, for example, the exaggerated hand wave that many of us have adopted as a greeting and as an official sign-off. We wouldn't do this in face-to-face conversation, especially one that is as close as the one we are emulating on video calls, but we somehow feel it's necessary to go above and beyond with our body language to clearly communicate the beginning and end of our conversation. This is one example of what Bailenson would consider our propensity to send extra cues when on video calls. Not only do we try to amplify our body language, we also amplify our voice. Research shows we speak 15% louder on video calls than we do when meeting face to face (Croes, Antheunis, Schouten, and Krahmer 2018).

Bailenson also notes the possibility of misreading nonverbal cues and jumping to wrong conclusions. The cognitive load is increased by our efforts to interpret the extra nonverbal cues. He speaks of the way a sidelong glance in an in-person meeting might be read accurately when those in the room look in the same direction and see someone walk through the doorway. That same glance committed by someone in a Zoom box might be misinterpreted as boredom or inattention when it might be a reaction to a child entering someone's office.

Stanford Proposed Solution 3

Bailenson offers this suggestion: "Make 'audio only' Zoom meetings the default." He also praises the merits of "audio only" breaks, where body language isn't available to be delivered or received. He elaborates by saying, "This is not simply you turning off your camera to take a break from having to be nonverbally active, but also turning your body away from the screen." In fact, he says the nonverbals, while limited in nature on video, are what he calls "perceptually realistic but socially meaningless." Here is where we must disagree.

Our Proposed Solution 3

Can you imagine going back to the days of the spider phone on the conference room table as the default way of meeting? Why would you use only half of the capabilities of a videoconferencing platform by default?

The value of video has been proven time and time again, and is largely based in "media richness theory." The richer the medium used to deliver the message, the more easily you can convey it in full. The more complex the message, the richer the medium required. The data we presented in *Suddenly Virtual* showed this to be true as teleconference meetings – the most lean medium (besides text-only) – were rated the worst. Meanwhile, video was perceived to be just as effective as face to face. Therefore, when doing a hybrid meeting, it's important to match the richness of the medium with the optimal potential effectiveness of the meeting. In other words, using video and face-to-face for your hybrid meeting will generally be better than using face-to-face with virtual attendees using audio only. The reason media richness matters is that it levels the "communication cue" playing field. Video and face-to-face attendees have the potential to deliver all the verbal and nonverbal cues, whereas audio-only attendees offer just what you can hear.

Rather than defaulting to an audio-only version of a video call, a version of throwing the baby out with the bathwater, consider doing this instead:

- Ask yourself whether that meeting needs to be a meeting at all. If it's only information sharing, think about recording the presentation and posting it on a Microsoft Teams or Slack channel.

- If it is a meeting that calls for collaboration, discussion, and dialogue, by all means turn those cameras on so you can communicate in full. We speak not just with our words and our tone of voice; we speak with our whole bodies. If video is off, that body language is silent. To us, that black hole of nuance is more dangerous than an overload of nonverbals.

- Do give yourself some "audio only" breaks during a meeting if the need for your active participation is not imminent. Say there are three agenda items for the meeting and item two only tangentially relates to you. Allow yourself to turn off your video during this discussion as a cognitive break, but let your fellow attendees know what you are doing. Your sudden disappearance from the screen might be interpreted as you ducking out of the meeting. Instead, put in chat that you've been on video calls nonstop, and you need a bit of break from being on-screen. However, as soon as the attendees start talking about something where your input is not just valued but expected, turn your camera back on.

A client of Karin's learned how our body language on camera can be misinterpreted when she was interviewing for a job during the pandemic. The hiring process was totally virtual, with all

79

interviews conducted over Zoom. During the final interview, the hiring manager spent the entire time looking down and to the side. He barely even glanced at the camera. Karin's client assumed that she was totally bombing the interview. Lo and behold, she actually landed the job, and a few months later, she told her now boss about her impression of how her final interview went. Her boss was shocked. He explained that he wasn't looking at the camera because he was too busy writing down all of the fantastic answers she was giving. Same meeting – two very different versions of how that meeting went.

Context is everything and too often when we are virtual, context is what we lack. That does require you to be more aware of the signals you might be sending with your body language or even your actions on camera. You might be turning off your camera so you can eat your lunch without grossing out your colleagues, but your teammates might assume you are simply not all that invested. If you explain what they're seeing on their screens, you remove all doubt.

Stanford Reason 4: Video Chats Dramatically Reduce Our Usual Mobility

Have you ever been on a video call with someone who decides to change location right in the middle of the meeting? They pick up their laptop and take you on what feels like an amusement park simulator ride. There's the ceiling. Whoa, we almost hit the wall. Spin, spin, spin. Stop.

Video meetings are inherently stationary and as we just illustrated, really should be. Movement on camera should be limited to gestures, not laps around a track. But staying within the conical view of the webcam can hurt our performance, according to Professor Bailenson, who says, "There's growing research now that says when people are moving, they're performing better cognitively."

Bailenson points out that being stuck in one place doesn't happen as much during an in-person meeting where people can get up to stretch, grab a glass of water, or write on a whiteboard. Sure, you can leave your chair when on a video call, but your absence will be noticed. It is up to you to explain the reason why you left your post.

Stanford Proposed Solution 4

To combat this reduction or even loss of mobility, Bailenson reiterates the possibility of reducing the number of meetings and/or opting for a different way of interacting when possible, optimizing the use of asynchronous forms of communication like recorded videos. Once again, he endorses the audio-only option but this time in the form of good, old-fashioned phone calls, which he says, "have driven productivity and social connection for many decades, and only a minority of calls require staring at another person's face to successfully communicate."

We were with you all the way, Professor Bailenson, until that last part about the minority of calls requiring video, which takes us to our suggestions on this topic.

Our Proposed Solution 4

We are true video evangelists and believe that for many meetings it is indeed essential for effective communication, but it is worth taking some time to discuss when it is imperative to have video on and when it is not.

Some companies have mandated that employees show up on camera for every single meeting that is held. While we might have initially applauded that move, we acknowledge that video call fatigue and the explosion of meetings in this last year call for a more nuanced approach and, therefore, we recommend setting up some guidelines for video usage. Here are our suggestions for video use on the enterprise level:

- For team meetings that are discussion-based (i.e. decisions will be made) and involve only a handful of participants, turn your video *on*. The benefits of body language go both ways. When speaking, your body language will allow you to better communicate the intent of your message. As a listener, your nonverbals provide valuable clues for the speaker, who will be able to better gauge the impact of their message on you.

- For larger meetings involving more than 10 people, it is less essential that everyone be on camera. In general, for more collaborative meetings, five to seven people is the ideal size (Littlepage and Silbiger 1992). In larger, more presentation-oriented meetings, allow those who are not directly participating to keep their cameras off. Designate a few people to be "camera on" attendees who can provide nonverbal feedback to the speakers. Rotate that role throughout the organization.

- For meetings with external stakeholders, consider the purpose of the interaction. Ask yourself if you would normally be meeting with them face to face for this particular kind of meeting (an introductory call or a negotiation). If the answer is yes, turn your video on. If it's a quick check-in, feel free to keep the video off. A phone call might even suffice unless you would like to share content from your screen.

- Consider how well you know the people you are about to meet with. If this is a team of folks you have worked with for years or have met with many times before, you probably know how they react to your jokes, what they look like when they agree, and what they sound like when they disagree. In other words, you do not need the richer medium to understand what is happening. In that case, consider turning off the cameras and giving yourselves a video break.

To help with people in their decision making about whether to use video in their meetings, we've provided a checklist at the end of this chapter to help you assess when video is essential and when it is not. Specifically, read each question and indicate yes or no. If you answer "yes" to two or more of the questions, the camera probably needs to be on.

A Few Words of Support for Telephone Meetings

Please understand that we are not implying that a telephone meeting is never an appropriate choice – only that there are often better choices because of its limitations. A one-on-one conversation, particularly with someone you know well, can work quite effectively. The reason is that you can fill in the visual gaps based on past experience. You know that if you make a joke about a colleague's alma mater getting destroyed on the football field by their archrival, that colleague will likely roll their eyes. You don't need to see that gesture. You know it's happening based upon the umpteen times you've seen it in person. But if you are on a call with a new person on the team, they can't put a name with a face and you are doing them a disservice. They can't fill in the gaps and instead may feel isolated and disconnected. The fact that we often say "so good to connect the face with the name" speaks to humanity's evolutionary desire to see the faces of our fellow human beings (Burke and Sulikowski 2013).

Even Scott Wharton of Logitech, the world's leading vendor of video collaboration tools, is an advocate for holding some meetings over the phone, but he says they serve a different purpose.

"Some meetings, you just need to walk during the day," says Wharton. "My meeting purpose is totally different when I do a phone call. I call them wandering agendas. It almost gives you freedom to meander from topic to topic. When I'm on video, it is purpose-driven. You're looking at someone. You're taking in all the information. You want to convince someone or impart some information. When I'm on a phone call, I deliberately don't have an agenda. I let the conversation go where it goes."

Wandering agendas can breed creativity and solutioning that might not be as forthcoming in a video meeting which, when used to best effect, tend to be targeted toward a goal. However, for getting stuff done, video still provides focus, requires our attention, and holds everyone accountable much more than audio alone.

Conclusion

The rampant spread of video call fatigue is not a reason to retreat from one of the most powerful tools you have in your meeting arsenal, but it does require you to be thoughtful in how you use video to prevent digital exhaustion. That lesson was learned during the pandemic but can certainly be applied in the hybrid world in which we now live. Hybrid by its very nature means that at least some attendees will be joining virtually. This chapter offers some suggestions on when to turn your camera on to establish your presence in a meeting room regardless of your physical location.

Up to this point, we've focused on the dizzying disruption of meeting paradigms since the beginning of 2020 and offered our take on what worked and what did not as we all tried to make sense of the changes. In Part Two, we'll turn our attention to specific strategies that can be used by those who will play a pivotal role in the second major meeting disruption – the leaders of hybrid meetings.

Chapter Takeaways

- Video collaboration platforms have become widely accepted as a primary way of communicating both internally and externally, with Zoom leading the way.

- An overreliance on video meetings coupled with the "meetingization" of our work lives resulted in a phenomenon commonly called "Zoom fatigue."

- A popular article written by a Stanford professor of communication suggested four reasons for the fatigue:

  1. Seeing yourself on screen is exhausting.

  2. Constant close eye contact with fellow attendees is intense.

  3. The cognitive load is higher on a video chat than it is in person.

  4. Video meetings force us to stay in one spot for too long.

- Ways to combat video call fatigue include:

  - Hiding self-view on the screen.
  - Looking at the lens, rather than at yourself, when speaking.
  - Using an external keyboard to allow for proper framing with appropriate distance between you and the camera lens.
  - Evaluating whether a meeting needs to be a meeting at all.
  - Opting for "video-off" time when participation is not expected or required.
  - Designating "camera-on" attendees during large meetings to provide nonverbal feedback to help the speaker adjust their delivery accordingly.

Checklist: Questions to Consider When Deciding Camera On or Off

Ask yourself these questions when choosing whether to use video:	Yes or No
1. Is your relationship new with any of the people on the call?	[ ] Yes [ ] No
2. Does the meeting include important decision making?	[ ] Yes [ ] No
3. Is the meeting smaller than 10 people?	[ ] Yes [ ] No
4. Are you expected to directly participate by presenting information or providing input?	[ ] Yes [ ] No
5. Are external stakeholders invited to the meeting? If so:	[ ] Yes [ ] No
i. Is this the first time you are meeting them?	[ ] Yes [ ] No
ii. Will the meeting involve negotiation?	[ ] Yes [ ] No
iii. Are you trying to make a sale or close a deal?	[ ] Yes [ ] No
6. Is the topic of discussion complicated?	[ ] Yes [ ] No
TOTAL YES	_____

If you answered "yes" to two or more questions, opt to use video.

References

Abrahams, M. 2016. *Speaking Up Without Freaking Out: 50 Techniques for Confident and Compelling Presenting*, third edition. Kendall Hunt.

Bailenson, J. N. 2021. "Nonverbal overload: A theoretical argument for the causes of Zoom fatigue." *Technology, Mind, and Behavior* 2 (1).

Burke, D., and D. Sulikowski. 2013. "The evolution of holistic processing of faces." *Frontiers in Psychology* 4, 11. https://doi.org/10.3389/fpsyg.2013.00011

Brandl, R. 2021. "Video Call Victories: Map reveals the most popular video conferencing platforms worldwide." EmailToolTester.com, March 24. https://www.emailtooltester.com/en/blog/video-conferencing-market-share/

Croes, E. A., M. L. Antheunis, A. P. Schouten, and E. J. Krahmer. 2018. "Social attraction in video-mediated communication: The role of nonverbal affiliative behavior." *Journal of Social and Personal Relationships* 36 (4): 1210–1232. https://doi.org/10.1177/0265407518757382

Fosslien, L., and M. W. Duffy. 2020. "How to combat Zoom fatigue." *Harvard Business Review.* https://hbr.org/2020/04/how-to-combat-zoom-fatigue.

Leary, M. R., and M. R. Kowalski. 1990. "Impression management: A literature review and two-component model." *Psychological Bulletin* 107 (1): 34.

Littlepage, G. E., and H. Silbiger. 1992. "Recognition of expertise in decision-making groups: Effects of group size and participation patterns." *Small Group Research* 23 (3): 344–355.

McKinsey & Company. 2021. "Author Talks: Karin M. Reed on virtual meetings." McKinsey & Company, April 20. https://www.mckinsey.com/featured-insights/mckinsey-on-books/author-talks-karin-m-reed-on-virtual-meetings?cid=other-eml-alt-mip-mck&hdpid=b1799535-ebc6-437f-8372-026cb4146d7f&hctky=9683162&hlkid=f4e2c71b1ac4423980304e0d3cbf9f3b

Ramachandran, V. 2021. "Four causes for 'Zoom fatigue' and their solutions." *Stanford News*, February 23. https://news.stanford.edu/2021/02/23/four-causes-zoom-fatigue-solutions/.

Reed, K. M., and J. A. Allen. 2021. *Suddenly Virtual: Making Remote Meetings Work.* Wiley.

Zoom. 2020. "90-day security plan progress report: April 22." *Zoom* (blog). https://blog.zoom.us/90-day-security-plan-progress-report-april-22/

PART TWO

Leading a Hybrid Meeting

The first part of this book was intended to explain the environment created by the events leading up to the migration to hybrid meetings. We've looked at what has shaped this transition, identified lessons learned from our fully virtual experience, and given suggestions on how to recalibrate the use of video for those who are joining meetings remotely. Now it's time to arm you with information and specific strategies based in science to help you effectively *run* these hybrid meetings, which are unlike any you may have run before.

Our first bit of data intel sheds light on the people who will be attending your meetings and their likely frame of mind. Yes, we may all have been ordered to stay at home, but that experience, while communal, was not universal in its impact or its implications. If you go by the results of the survey shared in the Microsoft 2021 Work Trend Index, the forced work-from-home experiment wasn't so bad . . . that is, if you were a business leader (Microsoft 2021). More than 60% of managers reported that they were "thriving" during the pandemic versus only 38% without decision-making power who reported they were doing well. Given this gap, leaders would be wise to summon all of their empathetic powers to help their employees, who statistically may have been impacted more negatively than they have, to adapt to hybrid work and hybrid meetings.

However, there's another disconnect of note here between leaders and their direct reports regarding the adoption of flexible work schedules. After the collective call for hybrid options, most organizations are incorporating models that allow both in-person and remote work. It's a move that is being celebrated by the rank and file but likely causing angst among many front-line managers and executives who worry about its effect on company culture. After all, managing by walking around will definitely be passé when only a few people are in the office at the same time, unless the walking around also involves driving, flying, or taking the train to track down employees who are working from anywhere.

For many a manager, that's a major source of stress. "They're worried about building and shaping culture because there's never going to be as many in-person meetings," observed Dan Hawkins, founder and CEO of Summit Leadership Partners, a top leadership and organizational effectiveness firm. "There's never going to be all of that face-to-face relationship building." Relationships will have to be built in other ways, with different processes.

For leaders of a hybrid workforce, that culture-building requires new techniques and strategies: a new approach that will be reflected and manifested in the meeting culture that leaders shape. And it's not just a matter of dusting off the corporate mission and values and tweaking them for the post-pandemic world. It means doing things differently and embracing new ideas for regulating and maintaining company culture, vision, and mission within each group or team.

"Leadership behaviors drive culture, not values put on people's business cards," says Dan, whose team has engaged in more discussions around this topic now than ever before. "Leaders need to articulate, 'What behaviors do we need to exhibit every day? What behaviors should we stop? And what other habits do we need to start in the company to support this cultural shift?'"

During much of 2020, leaders didn't have time to be strategic; it was survival mode. According to Dan, "The first year of the pandemic, no one talked about meeting culture. They just said we need to have Zoom calls or video calls all the time. And it's back-to-back-to-back from 7 in the morning until 7 at night. Now, because people are seeing the management fatigue and drain, they're being more intentional about it."

That intentionality led to policy changes like allowing no more than two back-to-back Zoom meetings, or carving out time in a call for purely social conversation where people could talk about and hear what was going on in people's lives outside of work. Management started to recognize that people simply needed and wanted to be seen, heard, understood, and supported.

With the transition to hybrid, meeting policies and procedures will also likely need to be adjusted based on how they play out "in the wild." However, starting with a solid plan can mean the difference between a total overhaul of meeting practices and the need for some simple tweaks. Instead of survival mode, organizations and leaders have a moment to prepare, plan, strategize, and execute hybrid meetings effectively. The next few chapters are intended to provide you with a science-based path forward to allow for planning and implementation in an effective, responsive, and adaptive manner.

In this part, we will delve into the challenges of leading in a complex communication environment (Chapter 5) when a meeting involves a web of networks. A hybrid meeting might include people showing up on the screen from their home offices, folks sitting around the conference room table, and even a few popping up in their individual video boxes from quiet spots in the brick-and-mortar office that they found more appealing or convenient than the physical meeting room. With all of this complexity in mind, we will also give you specific strategies to help you better manage these meetings (Chapter 6) and raise your awareness about some of the potential problems when leading hybrid meetings, along with techniques you can try to avoid them (Chapter 7).

This is designed to be a practical guide, so be sure to grab a pen or pencil. We encourage you to fill out the checklists, from either the book itself or online at www.wiley.com\go\reed-allen\hybrid, provided throughout all three chapters that will empower you to effectively manage your hybrid meetings.

Reference

Microsoft. 2021. *2021 Work Trend Index: Annual Report – The next great disruption is hybrid work – Are we ready?* Microsoft. Retrieved July 13, 2021 from https://www.microsoft.com/en-us/worklab/work-trend-index/hybrid-work

Chapter 5

The Complex Communication Network Environment

When you hear the words "communication network," what comes to mind? Maybe you first think of the technology involved – telephone lines, broadcast signals, or perhaps the internet itself. If you're like Karin, you think about people and how they communicate with each other in an organization. For a meeting scientist like Joe, the immediate thoughts are about the channels, patterns, and flows of communication that we will be discussing in this chapter.

When it comes to hybrid meetings, that communication network can look more like a bowl of spaghetti than a series of straight, orderly lines. This thought is echoed by Jared Spataro, CVP at Microsoft 365, who said, "We've figured out how to get things done when everyone is working from home. Now we need to rethink how to handle that messy middle—when some people are together in person, and others are remote" (Microsoft 2021).

The first step in figuring out how to manage the "messy middle" is gaining a better understanding of the elements that make it so, and how the patterns or networks of communication may impact the effectiveness of a team or group. For those leading hybrid meetings, a functional knowledge of communication networks is both instructive and potentially essential for the success of future working in groups and teams. So that's where we'll begin – with a bit of a primer on the changing communication paradigms. Once you are steeped in the science, we will move from theory to practical advice.

In this chapter, we will explore:

- The nature of communication networks in meetings
- Potential communication breakdowns along fault lines when hybrid
- The evolving nature of participation in meetings
- Assessing meeting participation in your own organization

The Nature of Communication Networks in Workplace Meetings

Over the past 40 years, the channels to communicate have evolved and changed in many ways, making the practice of communicating a different experience altogether. In the 1980s, teleconferencing emerged, but video was not a thing. In the 1990s, videoconferencing started to emerge, but only in special rooms in Fortune 100 companies that could afford the bill for its setup. In the 2000s, with the advent of smartphones, video calls and videoconferencing became possible in the hands of every person who bought a phone. Yet, the adoption of new communication strategies lagged behind the technological capabilities until the COVID-19 pandemic, when videoconferencing became the primary meeting modality and communication pattern. Each emergence of a novel modality introduced new channels of communication, rearranged flows, and impacted patterns of communicating. In other words, communication networks changed in response . . . and it's happening again. Hybrid work and hybrid meetings introduce a complexity to communication and social networks that most have yet to experience.

To understand the organic nature of communication networks in organizations, scientists developed a new method for studying groups and teams called social network analysis (Borgatti, Mehra, Brass, and Labianca 2009). Broadly defined, social network analysis is a set of theories and methodological tools for analyzing and understanding the structure and relationships within social networks. Researchers who employ social network analysis typically analyze data on the number of people and connections or relationships between these people within a network by means of specific software, which also typically produces pictures that display the patterns of connections between the people of a network (e.g. Borgatti 2002; Borgatti, Everett, and Freeman 2002). It is these patterns of connections that help us understand how people communicate, who has influence upon whom, and why some interactions (i.e. meetings) feel more collaborative than others.

Although we could certainly spend the rest of the chapter talking about communication networks in general and the wonderful nuances of the various theories of social network analysis, the focus here is on how these communication networks emerge and how they are experienced in workplace meetings (Sauer, Meinecke, and Kauffeld 2015). In particular, we want to talk about the complexity shift from the traditional face-to-face meeting to the hybrid meeting. We turn our attention to that issue now.

From the Simple Network to the Complex Network

The biggest issue with communication and social networks in meetings is how dynamic they are and the complexity they introduce as you change from medium to medium (i.e. modality to modality). The pre-pandemic go-to form of meeting was face-to-face, which used an all-channel network of equivalent medium. What does that mean? Well, it means that everyone is in the same room and is able to talk to each other, through the medium of soundwaves through the air. For a seven-person group meeting together, it would look something like this:

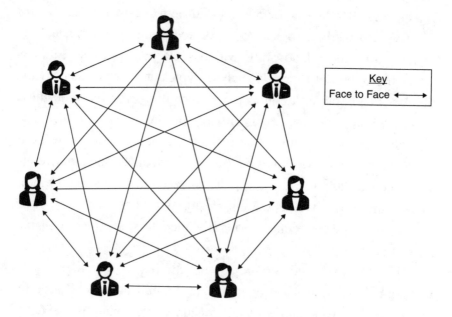

In this case, everyone can see and hear one another in the same room. The modality and method of communicating is the same and so we depict all the lines as equivalent. Now in all actuality, we acknowledge that when doing social network analysis of a given meeting, the results won't look so uniform. Using social network analysis, we'd use thicker lines to indicate more talking from a given person to another person or to the group, along with representations of other nuances. For example, if a social network analysis were used to depict the meeting with Bob, and Bob is going to be talking more than anyone else, his lines to the group would be thicker and potentially more centralized. However, the point here is that in a face-to-face meeting, there's only one modality through which communication occurs across the whole team.

Interestingly, that same picture applies to a situation where everyone is on video or everyone is on telephone. In all of those cases, the communication network contains only one mode of communication and everyone is on a level playing field, as it were, for communicating. For those who are thinking, "But what about the chat function?," we'll get to that. For now, let's just agree that in these three single-modality situations with everyone using the same form of communication, the network is relatively simple.

Now, let's mess with the simple network a bit and talk about introducing multiple modes of communication. That is, what would the communication network look like for a group of seven people meeting if three people were together in a room, two were on video, and two were on teleconference? This example would be a hybrid meeting comprised of a combination of the three modalities we've used in all our data analysis and chapters thus far.

Here's the depiction of this group. The people in front of the laptop are joining via videoconference, the people wearing headsets are on the telephone, and the three people in the middle box are in person in the same room.

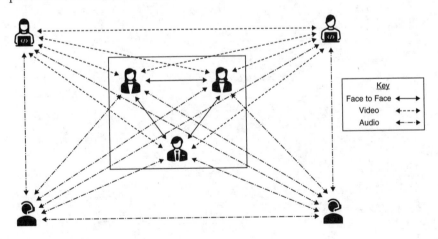

The Complex Communication Network Environment

Notice some differences? First, we depict the face-to-face modality with a solid line, the video with a dashed line, and the audio with a dot-dashed line. Second, you'll notice that depending on who is talking, people are hearing or seeing different things. For example, the video people see the three people in the room sitting at the table while those in the conference room see the video people in individual boxes in the gallery view common to most videoconference platforms. The audio people see no one, but hear everyone. Third, take note of the number of lines here. You might think that there are more of them compared to the diagram on the previous page, but guess what . . . there aren't. There are actually no more lines on this diagram than there are in the single-modality meeting situation (i.e. the previous picture). So the overall number of communication lines is not increasing, just the nature of the communication modality.

Given these observations, it's no surprise that hybrid meetings are more complex in terms of the communication network, and with that complexity come challenges like keeping track of everyone across all of the modalities used within a single meeting. To illustrate further, let's add two more people in the room. Here's what that would look like.

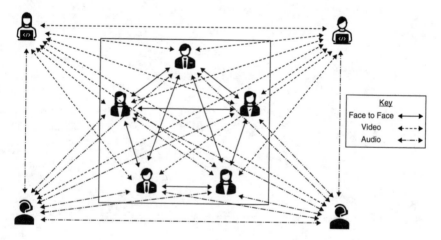

Suddenly Hybrid

Just two more people in the room results in a significant increase in the number of lines of communication. Obviously, the network becomes even more complex, but we show this for another reason as well. The more people who are in the room, the more prone people are to forget those online, particularly those on the phone. The in-person bias is real and all too common. Those whose physical presence is diminished, especially those who are dialing in, become more anonymous and the "out of sight, out of mind" idea becomes more easily enacted. When you have the in-person people seen and the remote people not seen, artificial fault lines emerge in the hybrid meeting, which is our next topic.

The Danger of Fault Lines in a Hybrid Meeting

In a hybrid meeting, one of the biggest pitfalls involves something called "fault lines," which are not unique to hybrid but may take on a greater role. Scientifically speaking, when people break into subgroups within a workplace meeting, we refer to these instances as the emergence of fault lines within the meeting group, which can be characterized as natural or artificial (Straube and Kauffeld 2020). Natural fault lines often break down by subgroups defined by similar individual characteristics such as gender, race, age, and so forth. For example, in a group with three men and two women, a natural fault line that could emerge would be along gender lines. In contrast, artificial fault lines are those that emerge within the meeting due to ideological or technological differences. For the purpose of this discussion, we will focus on the technological fault lines created by communication modality.

Let's use our last picture, the group of nine, as a hypothetical demonstration. The meeting as shown here has two people on video, two on audio, and five in person. This hybrid meeting could easily fracture along the communication modality fault line. What do fault lines do to the communication within a meeting? A number of different possibilities could occur. A common one is the group of five in-person attendees will simply forget about those on audio entirely. (Sadly, even Joe's done this before as a meeting leader. Sure, it's embarrassing when it happens to a meeting leader, but imagine how much more embarrassing it is when the meeting leader is also a meeting scientist, trying to follow his own research-defined best practices.) Another possibility, one you may not have even considered, is that the chat function could blow up with side conversations between those who are on video or audio, at the exclusion of the people in person. In other words, instead of one meeting taking place in the picture, three meetings occur.

If these modality fault lines go unchecked, it can completely derail the meeting. A meeting leader now has essentially three side conversations going on. These conversations may or may not be about the meeting. They may even not be heard (e.g. chat) or accessible to the leader (e.g. they are in-person and not on chat). In this way, the communication flow that should be or had previously been collaborative becomes fragmented. What should have been a meeting where a final decision was to be made becomes a meeting that winds down with little or no decision occurring.

Getting out of these fault-line-created dynamics requires deliberate behaviors on the part of the meeting leader and/or attendees. For example, one could try to rein in the communication by saying something like, "Hey all, we really need to discuss the key issue here together." Such statements reseal the faults and enable collaboration once more. We will talk more about specific strategies to combat the eruption of fault lines and other common hybrid meeting challenges in the next chapter.

For now, though, our goal is to enlighten you to this reality: the complexity of the hybrid meeting communication network introduces new challenges that are simply not present in the single-modality situation. No wonder even seasoned facilitators tend to advise against even attempting the hybrid meeting, suggesting to instead make everyone come into the office or make everyone get on video in their office (or wherever they are).

As you've no doubt gathered, we politely disagree with this advice. Given what we've already shared about the potential for hybrid as shown by early adopters, leaders will want to rise to the challenge of running an effective hybrid meeting, which our data shows can be more inclusive and participatory than other meeting modalities. But where to start? It begins with a shift in mindset on the part of leaders and attendees, but it's the former who can set the tone for all by managing the conversation in a more proactive way.

Responding to the Changing Face of Participation in Hybrid Meetings

As very young children, we learned how to participate in the classroom: raise your hand and the teacher will call on you. The process was simple and overt with little nuance. In a business meeting pre-COVID-19, participation was almost as simple and usually involved speaking up: letting your voice be heard with or without hand-raising, depending on how formal the meeting was. In a hybrid meeting, participation isn't quite as straightforward. It can and should take on new forms as we seek to capitalize on the different ways to provide input, to enter our ideas into the discourse, and to probe with questions that others may have overlooked. For the meeting leader of today, that multifaceted mélange of participation requires proactive facilitation beyond what may have felt necessary or even appropriate before.

Summit Leadership Partners founder Dan Hawkins has seen some executives demonstrate this first-hand: "I've seen some CEOs who are very good at saying, 'Let's hear from those on Zoom first,' or after a decision is made, they'll go around the table and ask, 'Can everyone live with this decision?' and make sure that the people dialing or Zooming in have their voices heard."

That level of awareness of who is in the room, virtually and physically, is a critical component to successful facilitation, and cultivating robust and even participation is imperative for meeting success (Yoerger, Crowe, and Allen 2015). However, a highly participatory meeting has benefits beyond just better meeting satisfaction and effectiveness. In one study, Joe and his team found that participation in meetings actually enhanced employee engagement, a particularly hot topic as businesses struggle especially to keep their remote workers from feeling isolated (Yoerger, Crowe, and Allen 2015). The science is clear: an engaged workforce is a high-performing workforce (Mackay, Allen, and Landis 2017). So if the path to higher employee engagement runs through meetings that involve high levels of participation, then focusing on ways to encourage that seems like a wise use of time and resources.

A Quick Data Dive into Participation across Modalities

But what role does participation play in how attendees feel about the meeting itself, and does it make a difference whether they are showing up on video, by phone, or in person? Joe and his team decided to find out by asking those questions of the same people he has tracked over the past few years (2019–2021), and whose data we started reporting in Chapter 2. He wanted to know how important participation is across modalities for both meeting satisfaction and meeting effectiveness.

What constitutes participation can mean different things to different people, so before we share the data, let's offer a little clarification. Some might consider showing up and leaving the camera on while checking email counts as participation. Others might argue that participation requires saying something or sending a chat to everyone in the meeting.

The science of meetings defines participation as someone speaking up and sharing their ideas, opinions, and thoughts that are relevant to the meeting. Furthermore, this definition breaks participation into two types. The first type is participation that is induced or encouraged by the meeting leader – we call this "meeting participation." The second type is participation that is self-motivated by individual attendees – we refer to this as "individual participation."

In general, all evidence suggests that more participation of both types is good for meetings and helps improve the overall feelings of satisfaction with and effectiveness of the meeting. However, we wanted to know which kind appeared to matter most across the different modalities. To do this, we correlated meeting participation and individual participation with both meeting satisfaction and effectiveness. In this case, we expected them to be positively related across the board. This means that if people engaged in more participation, they would also be happier with the meeting and the meeting would be more effective. These positive correlations are on a scale from 0 to 1, with higher scores indicating a stronger relationship. Here's what we saw:

Participation and Meeting Satisfaction Across Format

Format Style	Correlation of MP with MS	Correlation of IP with MS
Video	.47	.61
Face-to-Face	.47	.50
Hybrid	.22	.56
Telephone	.37	.32

Note: MS = meeting satisfaction, MP = meeting participation, IP = individual participation

Participation and Meeting Effectiveness Across Format

Format Style	Correlation of MP with ME	Correlation of IP with ME
Video	.38	.64
Face-to-Face	.70	.58
Hybrid	.38	.73
Telephone	.68	.63

Note: ME = meeting effectiveness, MP = meeting participation, IP = individual participation

From these correlations, we garnered some fascinating implications concerning participation in meetings, both overall and more specific to hybrid meetings.

Correlation Implication 1: Participation Plays a Huge Role in Meeting Satisfaction and Effectiveness across All Modalities

In all cases, across all formats, how much participation was encouraged by the leader as well as how much an attendee actually did participate were related to both meeting satisfaction and effectiveness. Participation is essential in every format and enables both the feeling of a good meeting (meeting satisfaction) and the logically driven actual good meeting (meeting effectiveness). So, both encourage others to participate and be sure to speak up yourself!

Correlation Implication 2: Individual Participation Is Even More Important in Hybrid Meetings in Terms of Meeting Satisfaction and Effectiveness versus Other Meeting Modalities

Individual participation appears to have a stronger relationship with both meeting satisfaction and effectiveness for hybrid meetings. In other words, self-motivated speaking up has a greater impact than the meeting leader encouraging individuals to speak up. This actually is consistent with the notion that people in hybrid meetings are desperate to be included and to be seen. However, if they are able to make that happen for themselves, it appears to have more meaning for the outcomes of the meeting than if it is induced by their supervisor. Basically, if Joe makes it a point to speak up and share his ideas in the meeting, he's going to be more satisfied and feel the meeting was more effective than if he waited for his boss to call on him.

Correlation Implication 3: The Path to Satisfaction and Effectiveness for a Hybrid Meeting Starts with the Leader But Passes through the Individual Attendees

You may have noticed that in hybrid meetings, there appears to be a pretty small correlation between leader-initiated participation and the key outcomes, but how much an individual participates – their self-motivated efforts to speak up – has a much stronger correlation. Does this mean that the leader should give up because their encouragement doesn't matter to the key outcomes anyway?

Not at all. Looking a little deeper into the data, we uncovered an interesting finding. As leader-initiated meeting participation increases, individual participation increases at a substantial rate. In other words, the pattern suggests that there may be an order in which this takes place in hybrid meetings. An effective hybrid meeting leader will first encourage participation, creating an environment in which attendees feel safe to speak up and do so. The end result? Attendees will believe the meeting was both satisfying and effective. If we were to illustrate this concept, it would look something like this:

The Complex Communication Network Environment

What this shows is that higher individual participation leads to better meeting satisfaction and effectiveness, but the way to get higher individual participation is through the meeting leader, who sets the stage.

In order to achieve a satisfying and effective meeting, the leader must initiate the participation pathway by encouraging participation. The individual attendees reciprocate by participating and the meeting itself becomes more satisfying and more effective. Conversely, if the meeting leader doesn't encourage participation, individuals are left to their own volition to take part in the discussion. The likelihood that they will engage is drastically reduced – and the meeting outcomes themselves will suffer.

Assessing Meeting Participation in Your Own Organization

To help you with evaluating your own meetings, answer the questions in the checklist we provide here (or online at www.wiley.com\go\reed-allen\hybrid) as a way to diagnose if your recent meeting included adequate encouragement and personal participation.

Meeting Participation Checklist

Responsible Target	Criteria	Yes or No
Leader Behavior	There were adequate opportunities for attendees to speak during the meeting discussion.	[ ] Yes [ ] No
Leader Behavior	All meeting attendees were given a chance to participate in the meeting conversation.	[ ] Yes [ ] No

Responsible Target	Criteria	Yes or No
Leader Behavior	Attendees were frequently provided with moments in which they could contribute, if desired.	[ ] Yes [ ] No
Individual Behavior	I contributed to the meeting.	[ ] Yes [ ] No
Individual Behavior	I spoke up during the meeting.	[ ] Yes [ ] No
Individual Behavior	I provided at least one valuable insight in the meeting.	[ ] Yes [ ] No
	TOTAL YES	_____

Now, as you fill this out and reflect on your meeting, don't feel too bad if you do not say "yes" to all of them. In fact, based on our data, meetings that are often rated as "good" usually only have four of these behaviors present. However, the key is that they have both leader and individual attendee behaviors present. So, aim to do all six, but definitely strive to get a mix.

Conclusion

This chapter has been a bit heavy on the science, but that was for good reason because the context should help shape your actions and approach as you navigate the hybrid meeting challenge. Now that you understand the theory, it's time to discuss more specific strategies you can employ to tease out participation from all, regardless of how they attend. Chapter 6 is chock-full of tips and tricks that were culled from those who have had success in the hybrid meeting modality – strategies that you can apply in your own organization.

Chapter Takeaways

- Hybrid meetings introduce new complex communication networks with unique channels, flows, and patterns as people join using different modalities.

- While leading a hybrid meeting can be challenging, learning how to do it well is a worthwhile venture considering the high levels of meeting satisfaction and effectiveness hybrid meetings receive.

- The more people are encouraged to participate and the more attendees actually do directly impacts how satisfied people are with the meeting and how effective they consider the meeting to be.

- If someone in a hybrid meeting speaks up on their own, without being forced to do so, it leads to even better meeting outcomes.

References

Borgatti, S. P., A. Mehra, D. J. Brass, and G. Labianca. 2009. "Network analysis in the social sciences." *Science* 323 (5916): 892–895.

Borgatti, S. P., M. G. Everett, and L. C. Freeman. 2002. UCINET 6 version 6.232: Software for social network analysis. Natick, MA: Analytic Technologies.

Borgatti, E. 2002. FREEMAN: UCINET VI for Windows. Software for Social Network Analysis. User's Guide.

Mackay, M. M., J. A. Allen, and R. S. Landis. 2017. "Investigating the incremental validity of employee engagement in the prediction of employee effectiveness: A meta-analytic path analysis." *Human Resource Management Review* 27 (1): 108–120.

Microsoft. 2021. *2021 Work Trend Index: Annual Report – The next great disruption is hybrid work – are we ready?* Retrieved from https://www.microsoft.com/en-us/worklab/work-trend-index/hybrid-work

Sauer, N. C., A. L. Meinecke, and S. Kauffeld. 2015. "Networks in meetings: How do people connect?" In J. A. Allen, N. Lehmann-Willenbrock, and S. G. Rogelberg (Eds.), *The Cambridge Handbook of Meeting Science*, 357–380. New York: Cambridge University Press.

Straube, J., and S. Kauffeld. 2020. "Faultlines during meeting interactions: The role of intersubgroup communication." In A. L. Meinecke, J. A. Allen, and N. Lehmann-Willenbrock (Eds.), *Managing Meetings in Organizations*, 163–183. Emerald Publishing.

Yoerger, M., J. Crowe, and J. A. Allen. 2015. "Participate or else!: The effect of participation in decision-making in meetings on employee engagement." *Consulting Psychology Journal: Practice and Research* 67 (1): 65.

Chapter 6

Strategies for Running a Hybrid Meeting

It's foolhardy to think, after so many months of flailing through figuring out virtual meetings, that the transition to hybrid will be smooth. No matter how much investment is made in hardware, software, room design, and training, the evolution to a whole new way of meeting is bound to come with some significant speed bumps.

"My concern is people are going to hate it and just give up on it quickly because it's going to be painful," suggests Lisette Sutherland of Collaboration Superpowers. "Unless you have the right things in place, it's just not going to work very well." At least, not from the start.

But what *are* the right things? Unfortunately, the answer may be a moving target. There isn't only one version of a hybrid meeting, and there isn't only one way to make a hybrid meeting work. Techniques will be tried and adjusted over time. However, we can steal plays from the playbooks of those who have already found success in their hybrid meeting methodology and approach. By the end of this chapter, you will have many more strategies/tools for being a leader of hybrid meetings that work.

In this chapter, we will explore:

- The extra emphasis placed on pre-work in advance of a meeting
- Strategies to get people talking or at least chatting
- The importance of early acknowledgment of remote attendees
- How to prevent the "meeting after the meeting"

The Pre-Work Mandate

In academia, there's a teaching methodology that's called a "flipped classroom" (Trach 2020). This blended learning style involves students interacting with new material as homework, say by watching a videotaped lecture on the subject prior to coming to class. Then, the actual classroom time is reserved for discussion of that material and application of it.

The corporate world is beginning to adopt a "flipped classroom" model of its own, with a heavier reliance upon pre-work completed before the meeting. It's one proven strategy to cut down on the number of meetings clogging up the calendar. In this new model, instead of thinking of the meeting as a starting point, it is considered to be either the middle or the end of the journey. The time in the meeting is focused on discussion, rather than on simply sharing information that could easily have been transmitted in an asynchronous way.

It's a solution to a problem that Lisette has seen in her work with clients. "I think people are getting a little bit lazy because we are just setting aside time to talk about something next week, but none of us have done any of the prep work. It's just '2 o'clock on Tuesday next week, let's talk about client X.'"

Pre-work can take many forms. If you plan to discuss the results of a recent report, send it out in advance for attendees to review before the meeting, but do hold people accountable. A pre-read has no value if no one reads it. Lisette suggests hiding "Easter eggs" in the document to identify who has done the work and who has not:

> For instance, I'll say, "I need you to read through this document. If you've read it, sign your name at the bottom so that I know you've read it." Before the meeting even starts, I can go through and see, aha, Joe didn't read it. I can then reach out to Joe before the meeting and say, "Hey, I really need you to read this." *(Of course, this Joe would ALWAYS do his pre-work.)*

Pre-work can also mean soliciting opinions prior to the actual session to save time in the actual meeting. A typical practice in any meeting is to have participants weigh in on a topic in a round-robin sort of way. However, consider this alternative: ask everyone to type a three-to-five-sentence update to be shared before the meeting. Then the meeting itself can be reserved for discussion and collaboration.

For brainstorming sessions, asking participants to do some deep thinking on their own in advance also can lead to a more productive meeting. Rather than just coming to the meeting cold, they've actually devoted some time to pondering the topic at hand, resulting in a more fruitful discussion right from the beginning. Maybe they can even refer to notes they've taken prior to the session that can accelerate the decision-making process and fast-forward to the meaningful exchange of ideas. If you listen to the science, the best group brainstorming sessions happen after individuals spend time doing their *own* brainstorming, generating more creative and innovative ideas than those who didn't begin with pre-work (Paulus and Kenworthy 2019).

How Much Pre-Work Should Be Done?

How much preparation is required of the leader and the attendees is dictated by the kind of meeting to be held. An operational-type meeting, like a weekly stand-up where you are simply going over sales numbers, might require less work in advance, but it does require a clear agenda and the expression of a desired outcome. If it's a strategic meeting, that's when prep work is nonnegotiable, according to Summit Leadership Partners' Dan Hawkins: "There has to be more up-front work planning the agenda, planning the topic, having information disseminated to all key people." That meeting time is precious, so arming people with information and an opportunity to come mentally prepared will help you make the most of it.

Participation Hacks to Pull Out Engagement

The biggest challenge for any hybrid meeting leader is to move the virtual attendees from their default position of passive observer. Up until the widespread adoption of videoconferencing tools, people were conditioned to simply watch screens, not engage through them. When those who are remote log into a meeting, they still may want to adopt that role or do what we alluded to before: "sort of" attend the meeting. Sure, their cameras might be on, but their brains are off . . . or at least off the topics being discussed in the meeting. Even when the camera is on, the seduction of multitasking is ever-present and threatens the effectiveness of the session.

How do you compel people to switch from passive observer to active participant? The following are some specific strategies to employ.

Priming for Participation with the Meeting Invitation

Participation doesn't just happen by accident in a hybrid setting. Usually, it's the result of a level of intentionality that infuses the meeting before it even takes place. Leaders need to inspire input from both the "Zoomies" and "Roomies" – those joining virtually and those joining in-person – and it begins with optimizing the meeting invite as an engagement management tool.

Don't just send a calendar invite with a link to the video collaboration platform of choice. Best-in-class hybrid organizations use the invitation to convey pertinent information for better preparation by attendees. For example, in the title or subject line, identify what kind of meeting is being planned and declare the purpose of the meeting. Some organizations use an "H" for hybrid, an "I" for in-person, and a "V" for a fully virtual meeting. That way, attendees know what to expect when they show up – either on the screen or in the physical room.

In an invitation for a hybrid meeting, let all attendees know what tools will be used. Prepare them to participate by notifying them that you'll be using polls, breakout rooms, and/or chat. If a new tool is being introduced – say, a digital whiteboard that hasn't been used before – send along a link to a video or text tutorial. It removes one barrier to entry and allows everyone in attendance to be able to use it right out of the gate.

Of course, we would encourage you to also express within the invitation the desire that those who are remote turn their cameras on for all the reasons we've already mentioned. Articulating this in the meeting invite underscores its importance and your expectations. Doing so also has the potential to further enhance the communication environment.

Lean into Chat

Speaking up in a virtual meeting can be intimidating, particularly when the group is larger, or one is new to a group. In a hybrid meeting, the fear of speaking up is often compounded when some people are physically in the room and you are not. That's why it's important for meeting leaders to include and value chat as a mechanism for participation. From the beginning, establish that adding comments, questions, and reactions in the chat is a welcome way to provide input.

The use of chat can also augment the verbal discussion while avoiding the challenges of talking over each other. For example, say someone is speaking and offers a really innovative idea that another attendee wants to build upon or even simply endorse. Rather than waiting for a turn to speak, that colleague can add an immediate comment in chat. Socioemotional behavior such as agreements and affirmations are essential for building cohesion and trust, but they are difficult to interject in the flow of a hybrid meeting for remote participants (Lehmann-Willenbrock and Allen 2014). However, this dual-medium collaboration, verbal and chat, can result in a more fluid and inclusive experience beyond one person speaking at a time. Chiming in on chat is efficient and often makes it easier for someone to insert their opinion in a timely fashion without interrupting the flow of the idea being shared.

Chat can also be used to clarify or supplement something that was said previously. Let's say an attendee forgot to add a really key point when asked to argue for or against an initiative. Rather than try to flag down the facilitator to regain the floor, that person can put the additional commentary in chat. Joe likes to do this by inserting some of his favorite scientific articles to back up his argument in the chat. But take note, attendees: sometimes that can come across as a bit snarky. So, tactful chat use is important to keep in mind.

But all of that valuable input will be for naught if no one looks at it and then brings it into the verbal discussion. That's why it is incumbent on the meeting leader to actually attend to that string of text and incorporate it into the conversation. This is no easy task, though. The additional cognitive burden of keeping track of the chat discussion and facilitating the verbal one can be a bit too much for many a meeting leader. That's why we advocate assigning the role of "chat monitor" when possible, delegating the responsibility to someone who can help you weave the written participation into the overall dialogue. In Chapter 9, we'll talk more about the chat monitor and other potential roles to fill in a hybrid meeting.

Remotes Speak First

As a meeting leader, you set the tone and establish the ground rules for everyone, and one way to signal to your team that everyone's voice is equally valued is ensuring that those who are remote speak first. This policy of immediately giving voice to those who are not in the physical room is common practice at organizations that recognize the potential disadvantage experienced by virtual attendees. No matter how well equipped both the meeting room and the home office are to enable hybrid meetings, those who are not within the confines of the conference room can have less "presence" than those who are physically present.

We recommend meeting leaders level the playing field by offering those who are joining virtually the opportunity to speak first. At Envato, the policy has paid dividends, according to Jay Hyett:

> If we were doing a workshop, for example, we would throw a question to the remote people first and get their input before anyone in the physical room. When you ask a question, you may ask it to the people on the screen, knowing that they don't necessarily have to have an answer. But you always want to make sure that they feel included the entire time.

Use Icebreakers

As the pandemic wore on, savvy managers started recognizing the sterilization of their virtual meetings and began to introduce ways to restore humanity to meetings. In a face-to-face meeting, there was natural social lubrication that would happen organically – those moments of informal chitchat that occur as people are settling in around the conference room table. Meeting scientists call this "pre-meeting talk" and although it can include all sorts of topics, the most effective is actually just plain old small talk (e.g. How was your weekend? Did you see the game last night?) (Allen, Lehmann-Willenbrock, and Landowski 2014).

When organizations first went fully virtual, there was a certain abruptness to the start of a meeting that resulted in a loss of that nonbusiness, conversational catching up. While cutting out that chitchat might have seemed like a timesaver at first, there's plenty of research indicating how important that chitchat is for better business outcomes, as well as for fostering team cohesion (Allen, Lehmann-Willenbrock, and Landowski 2014). For these reasons among others, the icebreaker became a common practice for virtual meetings.

In a hybrid situation, icebreakers also have value, and not just for establishing rapport among teammates. Icebreakers also provide voice opportunities early on in the meeting that can prime the pump for greater participation throughout. Research shows that people who speak up once are more likely to speak up many times over. If you go around the meeting room and ask all attendees to speak, whether they are remote or in-person, you can encourage a "speak-up" culture that will hopefully last for the duration of the session. For the introverts in the room, icebreakers can be a way to literally "break the ice" and enable them to have the courage to share their ideas more openly (Lee, Diefendorff, Kim, and Bian 2014).

This does not mean you need to consult a list of icebreaker ideas before every meeting, nor does it mean that the topic has to be non-business-related. Lisette Sutherland of Collaboration Superpowers suggests, "The name connotates playfulness, so you're always thinking like, 'Take a picture of your shoes and show what's on your feet,' or 'What's your favorite drink?' But it can also be, 'What are you hoping to get out of this meeting today?'" By changing it up, you can determine what fits the meeting climate for that moment – do you want to prepare the group to discuss serious matters of business or offer an opportunity for everyone to be silly together? If it's the latter, do know there's good evidence that workplace fun leads employees to be more willing to help each other out, so it's a win-win (Yang and Wang 2020).

Set the Cold-Calling Expectation

Another way to pull out participation from all attendees is setting the expectation that you may not wait for someone to speak up or comment in chat. Let your attendees know that you plan to cold-call, but with good intention. Explain that your motivation is not to put anyone on the spot, but rather you hope to ensure that everyone has had an opportunity to weigh in regardless of how they are joining the meeting. This "remotes speak first" orientation sends a strong signal: everyone's voice is valued and, as a leader, you recognize that those joining virtually may need an extra boost of "presence awareness."

This extra attention, though, may create some anxiety for remote attendees who may be fearful of being called on. You can help them feel safe by giving them a clear out. Here's Lisette again: "One of the things I do at the top of a workshop is I establish that I'm going to call on people. I tell them you can say pass. You don't have to tell me why. I'll just move on to the next person."

Be the Eyes and Ears for All

No matter what videoconferencing technology you are using, or the number of cameras or microphones you have placed within the meeting room, those who are joining virtually may still miss important body language cues that are easier to read in person. The meeting leader can help fill in those gaps by being almost overly communicative for the benefit of those who are remote.

"When you are facilitating, do play-by-play/color commentary," says Matt Abrahams, a lecturer in organizational behavior at the Graduate School of Business at Stanford University. He emphasizes the importance of providing additional context for those joining virtually. "Comment on the nonverbal behavior of the people in the room because some people who are remote might not be able to see that. You could say, 'Joe, I see you leaning in . . . do you have something that you want to say?' You want to paint the picture for those who are remote."

If you listen to podcasts, you may have heard versions of this. For example, let's say a guest gives a sarcastic response to a question. The host might offer context to listeners by saying something like, "If you saw how hard they are rolling their eyes, you'd wonder if they were getting dizzy." The visual conjured up by the podcaster helps to bring listeners into the room, creating a more immersive experience. The same can happen for meetings, if the meeting leader engages in, practices, and develops this skill.

Leaders Leave Last

Anyone who has attended a meeting in person knows what typically happens after a meeting officially adjourns. Often a meeting *after* the meeting begins. When people are both remote and in-person, that becomes a real problem and a source of isolation.

Once the meeting is ended on the video collaboration platform, the virtual attendees are completely left out of those conversations among the in-person attendees, and even if no discussions occur, those who are remote still might feel like they are happening out of their earshot.

The best way to ward off any backchannel discussions is to ensure that you as the leader wait to shut down the virtual meeting link until everyone has left the physical room. You remove the shadow of doubt and let the remote attendees know that they aren't missing any further discussion that might have taken place outside of the official agenda.

Keeping a link open beyond the official adjournment of the meeting also allows for something that occurs naturally after in-person meetings. While the majority of attendees might leave the room, one or two people might want to linger to ask an additional question or get clarification on a comment made during the meeting. Sometimes those questions are directed toward the meeting leader, and sometimes they're for another attendee. Keeping the virtual environment open facilitates these conversations, which can reduce the need for a follow-up phone call or check-in meeting on the already busy calendar. This is particularly important when a meeting goes poorly. One bad meeting creates more bad meetings, but one way to mitigate that is allowing for a natural debrief that can occur between individuals as the majority of the group starts to leave the room (Allen, Rogelberg, and Scott 2006).

Keeping track of all of the strategies mentioned might be a bit cumbersome, so we've included this checklist for quick reference and reflection. While it is designed for meeting leaders, attendees can also use this list to assess how many strategies their meeting leader employed. Consider your last hybrid meeting, and answer the following questions.

Checklist of Success Strategies for Leading a Hybrid Meeting

Ask yourself the following questions:	Yes or No
1. Did you assign pre-work to make the meeting more productive?	[ ] Yes [ ] No
2. Did you leverage the meeting invite to set expectations?	[ ] Yes [ ] No
3. Did you establish the use of chat as a valuable way of participating?	[ ] Yes [ ] No
4. Did you attend to the chat and incorporate written comments into the verbal discussion?	[ ] Yes [ ] No [ ] Yes [ ] No
5. Did you let those who are remote speak first?	
6. Did you use icebreakers?	[ ] Yes [ ] No
7. Did you cold-call with good intention and establish it as a norm?	[ ] Yes [ ] No
8. Did you provide commentary on the nonverbals of the in-person attendees to give context for the remote attendees who may not be able to see them?	[ ] Yes [ ] No
9. Did you wait to close the virtual meeting link until everyone in person had left the room?	[ ] Yes [ ] No
TOTAL YES	_____

How did you or your meeting leader do? Please know that successful hybrid meetings don't have to incorporate all of these techniques; however, if you are dissatisfied with how your meetings have been going so far and you did not check all of the boxes, there's an opportunity to improve that's highlighted for you. Try the strategies that haven't been implemented and see if they can help improve your meeting outcomes.

Conclusion

Leading a hybrid meeting can be challenging, but with a better understanding of the dynamics at play and some specific techniques to apply, it is possible to lead them well. If all of the techniques mentioned are being used and you still haven't found success, the problem might not be what you *aren't* doing but rather what you *are*. In Chapter 7, we will move from the "dos" to the "don'ts" when leading a hybrid meeting.

Chapter Takeaways

- Use the meeting invite to include critical information outlining the kind of meeting it will be (in person, virtual, or hybrid), the tools to be used, and the expectation that remote attendees will have their video on.

- Assign more pre-work to optimize time spent in the meeting for discussion.

- Use and validate participation via chat.

- Allow those who are joining remotely to speak first.

- Use icebreakers to encourage participation throughout.

- Establish that cold-calling will happen, but create psychological safety by encouraging people to pass if they don't have something they'd like to add.

- Provide play-by-play commentary of the nonverbals demonstrated by the in-person attendees for the benefit of the virtual attendees who may miss out on those cues.

- Be the last to leave the meeting and don't close the virtual meeting link until all of the in-person attendees have left the room.

References

Allen, J. A., N. Lehmann-Willenbrock, and N. Landowski. 2014. "Linking pre-meeting communication to meeting effectiveness." *Journal of Managerial Psychology* 29 (8): 1064–1081.

Allen, J. A., S. G. Rogelberg, and J. C. Scott. 2008. "Mind your meetings: Improve your organization's effectiveness one meeting at a time." *Quality Progress* 41: 48.

Lee, G. L., J. M. Diefendorff, T. Y. Kim, and L. Bian. 2014. "Personality and participative climate: Antecedents of distinct voice behaviors." *Human Performance* 27 (1): 25–43.

Lehmann-Willenbrock, N., and J. A. Allen. 2014. "How fun are your meetings? Investigating the relationship between humor patterns in team interactions and team performance." *Journal of Applied Psychology* 99 (6): 1278.

Paulus, P. B., and J. B. Kenworthy. 2019. "Effective brainstorming." *The Oxford Handbook of Group Creativity and Innovation* (P. B. Paulus and B. A. Nijstad, Eds.), 287–386. Oxford University Press.

Trach, E. 2020. "A beginner's guide to flipped classroom." *Schoology* (blog). https://www.schoology.com/blog/flipped-classroom

Yang, G., and L. Wang. 2020. "Workplace fun and voice behavior: The mediating role of psychological safety." *Social Behavior and Personality: An International Journal* 48 (11): 1–8.

Chapter 7

Potential Pitfalls When Leading a Hybrid Meeting

Knowing what to do is just as important as knowing what *not* to do when leading a hybrid meeting. Given the fact that this meeting format is new to the majority of organizations, the likelihood of missteps is high. In this chapter, we aim to highlight some of the typical pitfalls leaders are likely to stumble into unless they are looking for them. The hope is that by raising awareness, we can help leaders steer clear of these pitfalls or course-correct if necessary.

Meeting effectiveness is always a moving target, however, and that's why it is valuable to frequently evaluate how your hybrid meetings measure up. We'll wrap up this chapter with a feedback template that we recommend meeting leaders adopt as either a self- or group reflection exercise.

In this chapter, we will explore:

- The danger of falling back into bad habits
- The memory lapse about what it's like to work remotely
- The communication gaps that could widen based on in-person versus remote attendance

- The overreliance on larger meetings and how that may further isolate remote workers
- The importance of the post-meeting postmortem

The Leader as Tour Guide

If you've ever taken a tour of a museum, historic site, or new locale, you know the impact an excellent tour guide can have on your overall experience. As a meeting leader, you have the opportunity to greatly influence the impact of each session, according to Stanford lecturer in organizational behavior Matt Abrahams: "Your job when you are leading any meeting, whether it's in person, hybrid, or virtual, is to be a good tour guide. And a good tour guide is all about expectation-setting, reviewing where you've been and where you are going so everyone stays on the same page." Just like a bad tour guide can lead to a bad overall experience, a meeting leader who doesn't follow best practices runs the risk of creating a bad meeting experience for all. In a hybrid meeting, a format so new to so many, it's all too easy to make mistakes.

Slipping Back into Bad Habits

While we called this book *Suddenly Hybrid*, the transition to hybrid as a whole has not been all that sudden. In fact, discussion about how to make this work started months, if not a full year, prior to the actual move to this meeting modality. Business leaders, with good intention, sought to rethink their processes, implement new policies, and build up the proper infrastructure to make the return to the office on flexible terms as smooth as possible. With all these changes, though, one thing remains stubbornly the same: the gravitational pull of bad habits is strong (Graybiel and Smith 2014).

One reason for the pull toward long-standing bad habits is all about schemas and human nature (Myers and Smith 2012). All humans develop schemas. "Schemas" are mental concepts or templates that guide human perception and interpretation of their environment (Myers and Smith 2012). In other words, they are schematics for our thinking about our world. They help us organize our thoughts and behavior into easily understood, digestible chunks, allowing for easy transition from situation to situation. Examples of schemas include social roles, stereotypes, worldviews, and cultural celebrations (Michalak 2021). Specifically, if we asked you to think about an eight-year-old's birthday party, you would probably have a pretty good idea of what you'd see and do at the party. For example, you might expect there to be presents, cake and ice cream, a group singing "Happy Birthday" to someone, and perhaps games and other activities. Joe's eight-year-old had all these things with a Harry Potter theme as well, which probably introduces a secondary schema about what one might expect to see and do at a witch-and-wizard-themed birthday party. We have schemas for all sorts of activities we engage in, from sporting events to weddings, from dates to family reunions.

We even have them for meetings, including face-to-face, virtual, and hybrid meetings. Schemas are shortcuts for our brains and provide a lot of value in a complicated world. Having them means you can go to various events and know what to expect, know how to behave, and not really have to think deeply about it. Apply that to meetings and the schema holds on to both the good and the bad routines and rituals of meeting. In other words, the schema defines what is expected and is locked into a person's thought processing. It keeps things consistent for meeting after meeting after meeting.

The downside to schema is that when bad elements are incorporated, getting rid of those bad elements is a challenge, even with interventions, training, and reminders. If you've read *Suddenly*

Virtual, you may remember some of the bad habits that are all too common across all meetings. Some major ones worth special mention are:

- Not starting or ending on time
- Failing to send out an agenda in advance
- Allowing only a few people to monopolize the conversation
- Having too many people in the meeting, undermining its effectiveness
- Not expressing a clear purpose and goal for the meeting
- Complaining during the meeting
- Running off-topic repeatedly

We could go on and on here, but we would direct you to the comprehensive list of counterproductive meeting behaviors that often become habits that we shared in *Suddenly Virtual* in Chapter 3 (see Allen, Yoerger, Lehmann-Willenbrock, and Jones 2015). Joe also has a number of insomnia-curing academic journal articles on the topic that you are welcome to use for your most restless nights. Note, this would be where Karin, the meeting leader, would say that Joe is being sarcastic and rolling his eyes, as he always thinks his research is truly remarkable, meaningful, and should be read by everyone. See, we are trying to follow our best practices even in book form.

The good news is that when there is a major disruption to an environment, new schemas form and old schemas get rocked. This is reason for hope that this time may be different. We all lived through COVID-19, which sent a huge proportion of the workforce home. That collective experience may have rewired us in a way that will allow for those new good habits to stick, and perhaps some of the old bad habits to be broken permanently.

"I do think people who are coming back to the office are likely to revert back to their old habits," says Matt Abrahams of the Graduate School of Business at Stanford, "but I do think all of us had such a powerful experience of being remote that we have a chance of people remembering what that was like." For meeting leaders, being able to harken back to what it felt like to be remote could ward off one of the potential pitfalls of being remote, a tendency to only view the meeting through one's own experience and chosen medium.

Forgetting What It's Like to Be Remote

While there will certainly be exceptions, the majority of managers have returned to the brick-and-mortar office to lead their teams as they did pre-pandemic. In many cases, though, their team has not joined them full-time, five days a week. Even for teams that designate a certain day for fully in-person meetings, unscheduled meetings happen on a fairly regular basis outside of the planned "everyone in the same room" day. Hybrid meetings happen, but when the leader of those meetings is always conducting them from the office, that can create blind spots.

If a manager is working in a more traditional model of being in the office five days a week, there might be a tendency to always host those hybrid meetings as an in-person attendee, gathering in the same room with team members who are also in the office that day. It might seem logical. Why not take advantage of the conference room that has been fully equipped (hopefully) to accommodate hybrid meetings? But here's the rub: if a manager always leads a meeting from an on-site conference room, it may be easy for them to forget what it's like to join virtually.

Why is this a problem? Plenty of research has highlighted how much more taxing it is to attend a meeting virtually than it is to attend in person. The results of a study by Microsoft illustrate this quite well. Researchers found that video calls, especially those without enough breaks, increase stress and brain noise (Microsoft 2021). The study measured the brain impacts of two different meeting styles. In the first meeting style, participants were asked to sit through a two-hour-long video call with no breaks. In the second style, the two-hour meeting was broken up into four half-hour chunks with 10-minute breaks in between. During the long meeting with no breaks, participants showed higher levels of beta waves, which are related to stress, anxiety, and concentration. What's more, the longer the meeting went on, the higher the levels of stress rose. When the two-hour meeting became a series of shorter meetings with breaks in between, the participants' levels of stress decreased significantly and their level of engagement rose.

Why is this observation important within the hybrid construct? Because even though some people will be meeting in the traditional face-to-face way, other attendees will still be joining through video and therefore experience these same challenges. When everyone is joining a meeting via video, that shared experience raises the awareness of the need for breaks. However, if some attendees are in-person, and others are dialing in by phone as well as appearing via video, that level of awareness, especially that of the meeting leader, who is likely in-person too, may be diminished.

How could this play out in a real-world scenario? Let's say a meeting leader (we'll call her Jane) has brought the team together and laid out a rather ambitious agenda. Five people are gathered in the same room with her at the corporate headquarters. Three of her people are working from home today and have chosen to call in via videoconference. The team has a lot of ground to cover, but Jane is excited about the new initiatives they've been assigned. She launches into the agenda full-bore. The conversation is animated and productive. In fact, she's doing a good job of pulling out participation from all team members. About 45 minutes in, she looks at the clock.

They're only a third of the way through the agenda. She considers taking a break and even does a quick gut check. Does *she* feel like she needs a break? Actually, she's feeling just fine and even energized by the progress that the team is making through the line items. She opts to keep plowing through. Meanwhile, her team members who are joining via video are starting to feel their mental focus wane. A 10-minute break would have allowed for a quick stretch, a run to the restroom, or even the opportunity to snag another cup of coffee. Instead, the meeting runs a full two hours before it's officially adjourned. The in-person attendees applaud the effectiveness of that meeting. Look at everything they accomplished! The video attendees are exhausted.

This fictional scenario can easily play out in the real-world if leaders don't make efforts to put themselves in the shoes of all of their attendees, regardless of how they are joining the meeting. It can be difficult to remember what it's like to experience a meeting through videoconferencing, especially if you always facilitate the discussion from the conference room with colocated team members, but there is a solution: rotate the way you show up to lead the meeting.

For some meetings, go ahead and grab your folks, and head to the conference room that you've equipped with cameras, microphones, and monitors to allow for a truly effective hybrid meeting. Kick off that meeting on the video collaboration platform of choice so those who are remote can join you. But then, for some other meetings, lead them through the lens of your webcam by joining virtually instead of in person. To effectively lead a hybrid meeting, you need to understand the perspective and needs of everyone who shows up across all the modalities. Rotating how you join and lead meetings will allow you to have a wide enough view of the meeting experience that will better ensure that you don't have blind spots . . . like a tendency to not take enough breaks!

And speaking of breaks, leaders can leverage some technology tools to remind themselves to insert breaks in meetings. For example, Microsoft created settings in Outlook that allow individuals or organizations to change the default settings to shorten the length of meetings by 5, 10, or 15 minutes when using Microsoft Teams (Microsoft 2021). If an organization so chooses, a 30-minute meeting can become 25 minutes by default. The intentional insertion of those forced breaks can make all the difference, allowing for a mental reboot and a less exhausting experience on either side of the 10-minute-break divide.

Communication Gaps between In-Person and Remote Attendees

When leading a hybrid meeting, it's imperative to ward off potential communication siloes that can occur when participants are both in the office and not. Meeting best practices already call for clear communication before, during, and after a meeting (Mroz et al. 2018). When people are attending meetings using different mediums, this takes on even greater urgency. Stanford's Matt Abrahams urges meeting leaders to be mindful of this: "The way you summarize a meeting becomes really important. Ask people to summarize what they heard to ensure fidelity was high." In other words, make sure the folks who joined remotely understand and have access to the discussion points. Why is this especially important when hybrid? Because those who join virtually are at a disadvantage when it comes to receiving a message. The highest level of communication fidelity is found when in person. While video communication is a close second, there is still a deficit that needs to be taken into account.

Great hybrid teams put extra emphasis on keeping track of action items and who is responsible for them, and then socializing them afterward for accountability. They keep all of this information in a place where it is accessible by everyone to ensure transparency and inclusivity. Sometimes that information is in the form of a text, a Word document, or a PDF, but more and more often, that information is found in the form of recorded video.

Most video collaboration platforms allow meetings to be recorded. Those videos can serve two purposes. Someone who attended the meeting live might want to watch the video to ensure they heard something correctly the first time through. The video can also be viewed by team members who may not have been able to make the meeting live but still need to be up to speed. Some companies choose to record every meeting. Others don't record any meeting. Often, it depends upon the industry and the regulatory environment.

The bottom line is that archiving the meeting information in an accessible way is a best practice for any meeting modality but when meeting hybrid, it is critical.

Defaulting to the Massive Meeting

You may be familiar with the term "All Hands Meeting" – the enterprise-wide type of meeting where executives can relay important information to the entire company. While we may argue that many of these meetings would be better delivered as a recorded message, the popularity and relative simplicity of hosting a large meeting on-site and beaming it to those who are remote might seem all too enticing. It's instantaneous. It's efficient. (It's also the most expensive meeting your organization can hold when you consider the hourly rate of all those who are in attendance.) But it's also not the kind of meeting you want to heavily rely on for better business outcomes.

Those massive meetings may have their place, but it's the smaller meetings that really make the difference in terms of productivity, according to research by McKinsey & Company. Through extensive interviews with executives across the globe, they found that organizations that have been productivity leaders throughout the pandemic relied on small connections between colleagues to move the needle. In fact, two-thirds of productivity leaders said that these "microtransactions" increased during the pandemic (McKinsey & Company 2021). The study authors strongly advocated for that practice to continue to harness the productivity gains when hybrid.

A recent study by Joe and his team supports these findings by McKinsey & Company (Allen et al. 2020). In Joe's study, he wanted to see how effective meetings connect to team task performance. The obvious answer is that better meetings mean better performance. Unsurprisingly, the research indicated that, indeed, better meetings mean better performance, but the interesting part was that the *smaller* the meeting, the better the performance. The sweet spot in number of attendees seems to be between five and seven people. So, to get the most engagement from effective meetings, managers and meeting leaders must keep them small. Size matters!

Those smaller meetings also help to foster relationships when teams are not always colocated. For companies that do hybrid well, it's all about frequent manager/employee check-ins – not as a means to check up, but rather as a way to build ties, something observed by Jay Hyett: "What I've really appreciated at both Envato and Culture Amp is trust is given to you implicitly on the first day you arrive. People know you are there to do a job and do the work. There are really tight feedback loops with genuine connection points with your manager. They know everyone comes with the best intentions to get the job done." Those one-on-one touchpoints need to be prioritized and their cadence increased to ensure that communication is flowing smoothly to all.

The Post-Meeting Postmortem

As this part has demonstrated so far, hybrid meetings are complex communication network environments that require deliberate efforts to foster participation, enable communication, and inspire action by leaders and attendees. However, we also demonstrated how the hybrid meeting environment changes as the makeup of the group, their modality for communicating, and the number of people attending changes. The network changes, and so the effort and approach need to adjust as well. We've given you some specific recommendations that may apply to your meeting, but given the many incarnations of a hybrid meeting, they may not. You need feedback from those who are in your own particular brand of hybrid meetings to ensure that your efforts are working for all. That's why it is so important to add post-meeting postmortems to your standard operating procedures.

We recommend that after a hybrid meeting, individual leaders, or perhaps even the whole group as well, should engage in a post-meeting postmortem. This is a common practice in many organizations that engage in high-intensity, sometimes dangerous activities; they use a post-meeting postmortem so they can continue do their work safely (Allen, Baran, and Scott 2010). How do they do that? They engage in after-action reviews or debriefs to learn from their experiences and do better in the future. While your hybrid meetings may not hold the same gravitas as the work of firefighters, healthcare workers, military patrols, or nuclear power plant operators, you can still derive a ton of value by using a version of their tool to help you engage in continuous improvement efforts (Allen, Reiter-Palmon, Crowe, and Scott 2018).

Building on the actual cue cards firefighters carry and use for their postmortems, we provide here a series of questions that a meeting leader or attendee or even the group can go over together.

During the early stages of the transition to hybrid meetings, these questions should be asked after every hybrid meeting, especially as policies and procedures evolve. As the responses help identify things to try and things to continue to do, the leader, attendee, or group will hopefully find a homeostasis in their meeting behavior that is wonderful and worth continuing. Here's the checklist of questions for your post-meeting postmortem.

Post-Meeting Postmortem Checklist

Question	Notes
1. What was the purpose of our meeting?	
2. What went well?	
3. What could have gone better?	
4. What might we have done differently?	
5. What will we do differently next time?	
6. Whom should we share this with?	

In looking across these questions, you'll notice that we start with something basic. What was the purpose of our meeting? Too often, we leave a meeting wondering if we accomplished anything at all.

Answering that question may be painful at first but is truly diagnostic. The rest of the questions uncover what the group is doing well in their hybrid meetings and what they are not doing well.

If a leader fills out this assessment on their own, it can serve as a valuable exercise. But imagine what they could learn if they used it to gather feedback from their *team*, either through an email request for comments or through a brief conversation with their team at the end of a meeting that just occurred.

Also, notice that these questions are generic enough that a person could use these for any meeting type, not just for hybrid. This was a deliberate choice. We hope that our readers will embrace this continuous improvement idea for all their meetings, with a particular emphasis on their hybrid meetings.

Conclusion

While the meeting leader does set the stage by setting expectations, establishing participation norms, and carefully curating the meeting process itself, all of the responsibility doesn't rest solely on their shoulders. Attendees also need to step up and adjust their behaviors as well, which is where we turn our attention in Part Three.

Chapter Takeaways

- Beware of falling back into bad habits. The hybrid meeting disruption demands a new approach that has been adapted for this new reality and creates an opportunity to develop good new habits.

- Rotate between leading a meeting in person and leading as a virtual attendee to be in tune with the meeting experience from both perspectives.

- Make sure communication before, during, and after a meeting is available and accessible to all, and consider recording meetings for viewing afterward.

- Adopt a regular practice of evaluating meeting effectiveness by holding a post-meeting postmortem.

References

Allen, J. A., B. E. Baran, and C. W. Scott. 2010. "After-action reviews: A venue for the promotion of safety climate." *Accident Analysis & Prevention* 42 (2): 750–757. https://doi.org/10.1016/j.aap.2009.11.004

Allen, J. A., R. Reiter-Palmon, J. Crowe, and C. Scott. 2018. "Debriefs: Teams learning from doing in context." *American Psychologist* 73 (4): 504.

Allen, J. A., J. Tong, and N. Landowski. 2020. "Meeting effectiveness and task performance: Meeting size matters." *Journal of Management Development* 40 (5): 339–351.

Allen, J. A., M. A. Yoerger, N. Lehmann-Willenbrock, and J. Jones. 2015. "Would you please stop that!? The relationship between counterproductive meeting behaviors, employee voice, and trust." *Journal of Management Development* (October).

Graybiel, A. M., and K. S. Smith. 2014. "Good habits, bad habits." *Scientific American* 310 (6): 38–43.

McKinsey & Company. 2021. "What executives are saying about the future of hybrid work." https://www.mckinsey.com/~/media/mckinsey/business%20functions/organization/our%20insights/what%20executives%20are%20saying%20about%20the%20future%20of%20hybrid%20work/what-executives-are-saying-about-the-future-of-hybrid-work.pdf?shouldIndex=false

Michalak, K. 2021. "Schema." *Encyclopaedia Britannica.* https://www.britannica.com/science/schema-cognitive

Microsoft. 2021. "Research proves your brain needs breaks. https://www.microsoft.com/en-us/worklab/work-trend-index/brain-research

Mroz, J. E., J. A. Allen, D. C. Verhoeven, and M. L. Shuffler. 2018. "Do we really need another meeting? The science of workplace meetings." *Current Directions in Psychological Science* 27 (6): 484–491.

Myers, D. G., and S. M. Smith. 2012. *Exploring Social Psychology.* New York: McGraw-Hill.

PART THREE

Participating with Impact – The Attendee's Turn

If you are a meeting leader, you might be feeling overwhelmed at this point. There are so many factors to consider when it comes to effectively facilitating a hybrid session. Even the strategies that we suggested might seem daunting to implement, especially when put within the context of day-in, day-out business metrics to which you are held, not to mention the 8 to 10 meetings you may have every day. So perhaps this next statement will help to at least lighten the weight on your chest: the success of a meeting is a *shared responsibility* of both the meeting leader and the attendees. That's right, it's not all on the meeting leader! Meeting attendees are responsible for their engaged behavior, or the lack thereof.

You can "sort of" attend a meeting quite easily, whether you are in person or remote. You can walk into the conference room totally ill-prepared, find a chair that puts you out of the eye line of the meeting leader, and open up your own laptop, which allows you to weed out your inbox while the meeting is taking place. When remote, you "sort of" attend a meeting when you join virtually but keep your camera off and your microphone on mute. As long as you don't slip up and turn on your video by accident, no one will know you are doing *another* kind of weeding . . . actually pulling stray shoots in your backyard garden.

Making a hybrid meeting work requires engagement by all, and the leader can't do it without the cooperation, support, and participation of attendees. If you don't participate, you not only risk undermining the value of the meeting, but you also risk undermining how *you* are valued within the organization. In other words, as Joe often says, participate or get lost.

It's a danger that is especially acute for remote attendees whose physical presence doesn't loom as large as their in-person coworkers'. "The onus is largely going to be on the remote worker to be more proactive in communication," says Lisette Sutherland of Collaboration Superpowers. "Just insert yourself, because the office is a natural place where people hang together." The meeting environment needs to be conducive for that participation to occur, however, and it requires everyone's buy-in.

In this part, we focus on the attendee's role in creating a hybrid meeting culture that is positive, inclusive, and beneficial for all. In Chapter 8, we will explain how to foster and maintain a "speak-up" culture in hybrid meetings and offer some tips on how attendees can make their presence known. In Chapter 9, we will look at ways to codify that culture by co-creating a team meeting agreement, and we'll offer suggestions on what that should include.

What you will notice is a theme demonstrated throughout this book – hybrid requires a higher level of intentionality, and this section is no different. For attendees, that intention needs to be set on participating as fully as possible, no matter how they are joining the meeting. Perhaps Jay Hyett of Culture Amp puts it best: "Meetings shouldn't be a spectator sport. They should be a team sport. We want everyone contributing. And the spectators? We can give them information later on."

Chapter 8

Being Seen and Heard
in Hybrid Meetings

Nothing is more important to the success of employees and people in organizations than being seen and heard – to have their ideas, opinions, and thoughts listened to, validated, and potentially even followed. And where might someone have the opportunity to be seen and heard? In their meetings.

In our virtual world, being seen and heard became more challenging not only because of the physical distancing from colleagues and customers, but because of the seductive allure of being able to multitask while hiding behind the anonymity of the black box labeled with just our name. We could be officially in attendance, but not really present.

In our ever-changing and complex hybrid world, being just a black box with a name puts remote attendees in real danger. By not turning video on, a remote attendee's "presence" is significantly diminished or perhaps even forgotten.

This happened all too often during what we used to consider hybrid meetings in pre-pandemic days when video was not as readily available or accessible. Consider this story from Eric Taylor, a collaboration technology evangelist whose career has taken him from SAS Institute, to Lenovo, to Logitech: "I remember in the early days of this when we were using the Polycom, the star phone, on the table. You know, we would go 15 or 20 minutes into a meeting before we would remember, 'Oh, somebody was going to dial in.' That person would have been sitting there in limbo for 10 or 15 minutes. They missed all the good stuff." And we (Joe and Karin) would argue further that those who actually were in the meeting the entire time likely missed all of the great input that could have been provided by that remote person as well.

With today's video collaboration platforms, getting into the meeting might be easier (or at least the meeting organizer will be visually notified if someone is in the waiting room), but that is only half of the battle. Being seen and heard will not only require virtual attendees to keep the camera on, but will also call for additional effort from all other attendees and leaders of meetings in order to be aware of who is in the room, and to assist in amplifying voices that might otherwise be lost. This chapter is devoted to explaining how to create a more inclusive meeting culture that will set the stage for everyone to feel comfortable and confident adding their voice to the conversation.

In this chapter, we will explore:

- The importance of and need to maintain a "speak-up" culture in meetings
- How to adopt a psychologically safe meeting environment
- What attendees need to do to be seen and heard in their hybrid meetings
- The need to get over the fear of speaking up

The Speak-Up Meeting Culture

Speak-up culture, in general, refers to a healthy and supportive work environment where employees feel free to share their ideas, concerns, and opinions without worry or fear of retaliation (Finnie 2019). In many cases, this idea of a speak-up culture is associated with something negative, like feeling comfortable enough to call out a toxic company culture and environment, but it is also associated with simply feeling like it's okay to contribute your ideas in a meaningful way. That type of speak-up culture means sharing who you are and feeling that what you bring to the table is important, valued, and even encouraged.

Perhaps it's no surprise, given the topic of the book, that one of the best places to witness a speak-up culture is in workplace meetings. In fact, one could argue that every organization has a certain level of speak-up culture, but it can have both positive and negative connotations. Some value it to the point that it truly enables a participative work-meeting environment. Some fall on the opposite end of the spectrum, where speaking up results in retaliatory or penalizing behavior.

In a meeting, when people feel that they can speak up and share their ideas, we describe that behavior as voice behavior. "Voice behavior" in meetings refers to the degree to which the meeting leader and attendees:

- Encourage each other to speak up during the meeting
- Provide adequate time and space in the meeting to do so
- And then actually engage in that behavior (Allen and Rogelberg 2013)

While voice behavior involves the manager or meeting leader calling on people, it also involves meeting attendees responding to those efforts by both speaking up themselves and encouraging others to do so as well. Speak-up culture and voice behavior in meetings can't be dictated by just the leader. It is a shared responsibility between meeting leaders and attendees.

What the Data Tells Us about Voice Behavior in Hybrid Meetings

In collecting data for this book, we asked about people's voice behavior and learned something rather fascinating concerning participant behavior in hybrid meetings. The questions focused on the degree to which employees felt as though they were encouraged by the meeting leader to voice their ideas, opinions, and thoughts and to what extent they actually did so. Voice behavior was measured on a 7-point scale, with 0 being no voice behavior and 7 being extremely high levels of voice behavior in the meeting. Take a look at the data by meeting modality in the following table.

Voice Behavior in Meetings – June 2021

Format Style	Voice Behavior
Hybrid	5.54
Face-to-Face	5.16
Video	5.16
Telephone	5.03

What does the data tell us? First, our survey respondents are doing a pretty good job of encouraging and engaging in voice behaviors. In fact, they're doing better than what we might have expected, scoring above the mid-point of the scale in all meeting formats. Second, and what we alluded to previously, our early adopters of hybrid are once again setting the stage for success in their meetings by engaging in the highest amount of these behaviors compared to their peers in other meeting modalities. In other words, the meeting leader and attendees are supporting each other and enabling a greater speak-up meeting culture in the hybrid setting than in the other settings.

Combining what we learned from the data about high levels of participation in hybrid meetings in Chapter 2 with our findings regarding voice behaviors, there's a considerable amount of hope generated by these early signs of effectiveness, which should be an impetus for us to all capitalize on the promise they hold.

Psychological Safety Is a Team Sport

Cultivating a speak-up culture in meetings requires the cultivation of a closely associated scientific underpinning of that environment: psychological safety. According to the originator of the term, Dr. Amy Edmondson of the Harvard Business School, "Psychological safety is a belief that one will not be punished or humiliated for speaking up with ideas, questions, concerns, or mistakes" (Impraise 2021; Edmondson 1999). You might be thinking, "Um, Karin and Joe, I don't see much of a difference between this and a speak-up culture." You aren't too far off, but there is indeed a key distinction between the two.

Speak-up culture is a shared value among team members and manifests as behavior. Psychological safety is an individual's belief that it is safe to speak up and allows that behavior to happen. Sure, we use the behavior as an indicator of psychological safety, but that neglects the fact that some people may feel safe to voice their ideas but choose not to do so anyway.

For example, introverts may not offer up their ideas as openly as some of their more extroverted colleagues. They may want to test their ideas, think about them more, see them alive in the world, and then point people to them. That's typical introverted behavior. It doesn't mean that an introvert feels like they are going to get punished for not speaking up – quite the opposite. It often means that they simply prefer to take more time to contemplate their own ideas before sharing them with others. They are less impulsive and more contemplative in their voice behaviors. As this illustrates, seeing voice behaviors and witnessing a speak-up culture does not necessarily equate to a psychologically safe work environment – it is more nuanced than that.

As Dr. Edmondson would argue, psychological safety is a team sport. Although psychological safety is an individual belief, it takes cooperation, collaboration, and intentional behaviors on the part of leaders and peers. For example, for someone to feel psychologically safe, they probably have to see their leader talk about the importance of speaking up, witness them calling on people on their team during a meeting, and see them listen to ideas without dismissing them out of hand. For a person to feel psychologically safe, they probably also need to see their peers support each other as they share ideas, no matter the quality or originality of the ideas raised. To shore up this ethos even more, this openness to new ideas without judgment needs to be seen both inside and outside workplace meetings. Therefore, attendees can help the team develop and maintain psychological safety by engaging in an intentional approach that involves actions taken before, during, and after a meeting. We dive into these behaviors in the next section.

Attendees Being Seen and Heard

If meetings are a team sport, all attendees need to step up their game to be seen and heard. Many of the behaviors we suggest attendees display have value in any meeting, but they become even more necessary, and their absence more glaring, the more remote the meeting and the more complex the communication environment. However, here we will focus on some best practices for attendees to adopt before, during, and after a hybrid meeting.

Attendee Actions Before the Meeting

If a meeting leader has followed best practices, an agenda has been created and socialized to all attendees, but all of that work is pointless if the attendees ignore the information. That agenda allows attendees to prepare for what will be discussed. (Leaders get extra points if they have actually sent out the agenda to attendees well in advance and asked for input on what is or should be included.) While a quick glance at the agenda is perhaps the minimum effort required, attendees may find they need to do one or more of the following:

- Schedule some time to prepare content they will need to present
- Think about ideas they might have on a line item of particular interest
- Develop potential solutions to the problem that is listed as the key discussion point on the agenda

The key here is that unprepared attendees are less able to participate and feel more put on the spot when called upon. The richness of the discussion is lessened by their lack of legwork beforehand, so it is important to take this pre-work seriously.

Attendee Actions During the Meeting

Once the meeting is underway, attendees have significant influence over how much participation takes place and by whom. After all, while the meeting is taking place, speak-up culture, voice behaviors, and psychological safety can all be displayed to promote participation.

Allow us to highlight some specific strategies attendees can use to enhance their own participation as well as enable the participation of others.

- *Use a procedural statement.* You know how sometimes people run off-topic. Perhaps you have a person on your team who is notorious for monologuing about a particular issue that they simply cannot get over. Perhaps your team just has a tendency to go down rabbit holes that are sometimes related and sometimes unrelated to the topic at hand. A procedural statement allows you to simply bring things back to the agenda item, purpose, or topic of the meeting (Lehmann-Willenbrock, Allen, and Kauffeld 2013). For example, you could say, "Those are good points that are related to some degree to [insert agenda topic here]" or "Let's table that topic for the moment and address it later. Right now, we really need your thoughts on [insert agenda item here]." There are many ways to gently wrangle the wayward speaker, but they all have the same purpose: to keep engagement high by keeping the meeting on track. And this is not just a leader behavior – attendees can be empowered by a meeting leader to do this as well.

- *Provide feedback.* Another strategy is to provide feedback on an idea that was proposed by building upon it in a meaningful way. Assuming the sharing environment is one where people feel psychologically safe, the feedback will be open, honest, and true to the knowledge and expertise of the person giving it. Keep in mind that when providing feedback, you should be considerate of the meeting leader or attendees' role and situation to ensure that the information is shared effectively and to some degree with care. That behavior will likely be copied by others, legitimizing the kind of meeting environment that enables both idea generation and development.

- *Share observations.* Often during a meeting, ideas are shared that prompt people to recollect experiences that they have had. Too often, however, we don't share those experiences or stories that help solidify ideas or even augment solutions. Therefore, this strategy is all about being willing to share your observations, experiences, and stories about the topic at hand. Now, you might be thinking, "But Karin and Joe, you just told us *not* to monologue all the time." Yep, we did. To prevent yourself from monologuing, keep your observation directly tied to the topic at hand, and keep it short and sweet. Doing this keeps you individually engaged and demonstrates a behavior that others can imitate. Humans are all about copying successful behavior (Mesoudi 2008), so if you do this right, you'll get others to chime in, making the whole meeting experience better.

- *Invite others to weigh in.* This strategy refers to your role in directly pulling out participation from your fellow attendees by asking them to share their thoughts. It does require situational awareness that allows you to read obvious cues that others wish to participate. For example, the meeting leader may be talking about something. Perhaps they are sharing an idea, a proposed solution, or some key thought. While they are doing that, you might notice that Dave turned on his microphone and leaned forward, behavioral cues that he wants to say something. However, when the leader stops talking, there is only a brief pause before they launch into something else. Dave lost his moment. It is at this point that you have an opportunity to invite Dave to weigh in on the topic. You could say, "Hey, Dave, I noticed you turned on your mic. Did you have

Being Seen and Heard in Hybrid Meetings

something you wanted to share?" Most meeting leaders can't keep track of what they are saying and at the same time monitor all the attendees' nonverbal cues. It's okay to help them out, especially when you are trying to foster a speak-up culture with a psychologically safe environment.

- *Validate other people's input.* If you think someone has a good idea, say so. Praise a colleague. Build upon the good ideas shared by others. Engage in supportive statements following another attendee's participation. Not only does that encourage them to engage in the meetings more fully in the future, it just makes them and everyone else feel good. There is no sense in holding back compliments, encouragement, and gratitude, particularly in a hybrid work environment where physical distance doesn't always allow for the fist-bump or elbow-knock (or whatever we call our enthusiastic greetings in our now handshake-hesitant world).

- *Use chat to demonstrate the value of nonverbal participation.* You've probably noticed that in some virtual meeting and hybrid meeting platforms, the chat draws people's attention pretty quickly. Just recently, Joe was in a meeting and the conversation was intense. It was clear that he was not going to get a word in, with people going back and forth. While enthusiastic participation is a good thing, if not managed well, like in this case, it can quickly become less inclusive of some attendees. What did Joe do? He put his idea in the chat. Suddenly, five or six people looked away from one part of their screen to another, and one of his colleagues engaged in the "invite others to weigh in" strategy. Chat is a tool that has proved its value in a virtual setting, and continues to do so when hybrid. Use it to share your questions, so others see it as a viable option for sharing their own questions. Use it to call out ideas, interject opinions, and even have the occasional side conversation. Nonverbal participation is still participation, and it does impact the overall success of the meeting and the team. However, as a caution, do not allow the chat to create a fault line and divide the meeting up. This can generally be done by simply paying attention to the chat and using procedural communication to bring people back into the conversation. Again, chat can be used well and it can be used poorly.

- *Outline and clarify your own action items as well as those of others.* This suggestion might have you stumped, because you might think, "How does telling people what I'm going to do enable other people's participation?" Don't just tell them what you are going to do – ask for confirmation. Instead of just saying, "Okay, so I'll work on drafting the executive summary for the report," say instead, "Based on what we've discussed, I'll draft the executive summary for the report and pass it along to Dave. Dave, what will be the next step from there?" It's a simple difference, but now Dave is paying attention and probably a couple other people are as well, because a question has been raised and an answer needs to be given. Wait for that answer, and now you've enabled another person. It would feel inappropriate if another attendee answered with a simple "yep" and didn't also say what they would do. You are creating a pattern of participation and inspiring others to follow suit.

Now that you are familiar with some tried-and-true behaviors for enabling participation, it's time to evaluate how well you have displayed them. Think about your last meeting and answer the questions in the following checklist or online at the website (www.wiley.com\go\reed-allen\hybrid).

Checklist of Attendee Behaviors for Enabling Others

Voice and Encouraging Behavior	Yes or No
1. Did an attendee use a procedural statement?	[ ] Yes [ ] No
2. Did an attendee ask for honest feedback from others?	[ ] Yes [ ] No
3. Did an attendee share an observation?	[ ] Yes [ ] No
4. Did an attendee praise a colleague and invite their input?	[ ] Yes [ ] No
5. Did an attendee prompt a colleague to share an idea?	[ ] Yes [ ] No
6. Did an attendee use the chat to ask a question?	[ ] Yes [ ] No
7. Did an attendee build upon another person's idea?	[ ] Yes [ ] No
8. Did an attendee identify their assigned tasks and those of others?	[ ] Yes [ ] No
9. Did an attendee ask a question of other attendees?	[ ] Yes [ ] No
10. Did an attendee use supporting statements following another attendee's participation?	[ ] Yes [ ] No
TOTAL YES	_____

This checklist includes actions that the science of meetings has shown to empower inclusive participation in meetings. You may not have indicated "yes" for all of them for the last meeting you attended or led, but that's okay. The key here is to get you and others thinking about how to ensure that an inclusive environment exists. So, take this checklist as a starting point of known effective behaviors, and then keep adding to it as you discover new ones occurring in your own hybrid meetings.

Attendee Actions After the Meeting

Often the end of a meeting is the beginning of a series of actions that need to be taken by individual attendees. For example, the assigning of to-do's helps to build psychological safety, because it sets clear expectations of what needs to happen next. Good attendees will remember to do the action items assigned to them. The best attendees will also help others remember. In fact, in the case of interdependent tasks, the best attendees will get their work done so others can build upon it. Doing so leads to mutual trust within the group, and people will begin to feel seen, heard, and validated.

Ultimately, building trust among hybrid attendees is critical in the hybrid work environment. The physical disconnect between team members because of the lack of colocation can lead to feeling greater distance psychologically, resulting in overall lower team cohesion. However, when people follow through on assigned tasks, other members of the team notice, and this helps bridge the physical gap when team members see work being done regardless of location. In other words, doing what you say you're going to do to support the success of the team helps the hybrid team even more than one might expect.

Fear of Speaking Up in a Hybrid Meeting

Even if your team has fully embraced a speak-up culture and has made it come alive in a hybrid meeting, there is another barrier that stands in the way of everyone's voice being heard: a fear of public speaking. It doesn't have to be a formal presentation that paralyzes someone. It can simply be saying something in front of any group of people. In fact, research indicates that people fear public speaking more than they fear even death (Burgess 2013).

Meetings are not typically public speaking situations, but they still can strike fear into the hearts of many who would rather do anything other than raise their hand to verbalize their thoughts to add to the discussion. The hybrid or virtual meeting can heighten that anxiety, according to Matt Abrahams, the author of the best-selling *Speaking Up without Freaking Out:* "I do think it's more difficult for people to speak up during virtual or hybrid meetings because we just have fewer specific, nonverbal cues. It's harder to know when to speak, how long to speak, or if people are following along."

Consequently, even with the best of efforts being made by the leader and other attendees to encourage participation by all, some may never feel comfortable sharing their input, which is to their own detriment as well as that of the group. "People might perceive that person who doesn't speak up as nervous, unknowing, or unprepared," says Abrahams. "Fundamentally, we miss out on different ideas and opinions. If diversity and inclusion are the goals, then we need people to feel comfortable speaking up."

Two structural meeting factors can influence how intimidating the environment might seem: size and distance. In this context, "size" means how many people are in the meeting. Often a meeting involving more than 10 people is less collaboration-based and more presentation-oriented, which is likely to feel more like a fear-inducing, public speaking event. The larger a meeting gets, the greater the public speaking fear that can paralyze people from speaking up. The other contributing structural meeting factor, "distance," refers to the relationships existing within the group. It's often harder to speak to a crowd of strangers than to people you know who already value you and your opinions. That gives you a buffer to their immediate reactions. When you are speaking to strangers, it's harder to read how they are responding to you because you don't have a backlog of previous experiences with them. It's also more difficult for them to read you for the same reason.

So, what can be done to ease public speaking anxiety in a hybrid setting? First, we recommend a practice called cognitive reframing or a "shift in mindset" (Besieux, Edmondson, and de Vries 2021). Cognitive reframing is the practice of simply thinking about the situation that's causing stress or fear and considering what is the most likely worst outcome. Typically, you realize that the worst-case scenario is one that you can live with and likely will not happen anyway.

But let's get more specific with respect to meetings. In an article in the *Harvard Business Review* (2021), Tijs Bisieux, Amy Edmondson, and Femke de Vries suggest three shifts in mindset related to speaking up. Allow us to share them in brief:

1. The first shift changes your focus from trying to come up with the solution to being the possible catalyst for the eventual best solution. Instead of thinking, "My idea is incomplete," consider the possibility that, "My idea could be a source for someone else's breakthrough." It takes the pressure off the idea's being perfect when it first comes up in the meeting.

2. The second shift requires going back to the origins of the team you are on and your role in its collective success. Rather than thinking, "It's probably not my place to speak up," consider that silence is not in the best interest of the team. You were placed on the team for a reason. Perhaps it's your expertise in a given area. Perhaps it's because you are a good team player. Whatever the reason, teams that function well collaborate openly and honestly, and filtering ideas that could be useful runs counter to that.

3. The third shift requires a dismissal of the desire to want to sound intelligent, which the *Harvard Business Review* authors suggest is selfish. Sure, no one wants to sound stupid, but

Being Seen and Heard in Hybrid Meetings

wanting to sound intelligent suggests a desire for prestige that could get in the way of contributing to the goals of the team. Instead, shift the mindset to one focused on the collective intelligence of the team – this allows everyone to succeed.

While these cognitive reframing concepts can enable meaningful collaboration in any meeting modality, they can be especially valuable in hybrid or virtual meetings when public speaking anxiety can be magnified. Here are a few additional strategies suggested by Matt Abrahams, an expert in this area:

- Practice, practice, practice. Going into a virtual presentation well-prepared can alleviate much of that stress. Record yourself delivering the presentation and then watch it so you can identify any rough patches and smooth them before the real thing.

- If you are going to be doing presentations on a regular basis, find a mentor who will be in the meetings with you. Ask them to provide you honest feedback so you can grow.

- If you are joining a hybrid meeting as a virtual attendee, talk to someone in advance who will be physically in the meeting room who will advocate for you to be heard. For example, that person may say, "Hey, let's hear from Ann who's remote." In addition, that in-room advocate can make a point to second or validate what you have said so you can feel confident weighing in.

The bottom line is that the best solutions and ideas are often an amalgam of all of the opinions and comments offered by the group. Attendees have a duty to their coworkers to add their points of view to benefit the team as a whole.

Conclusion

Understanding the importance of creating an inclusive meeting environment where everyone's input is valued sometimes doesn't go far enough. Often, it requires a codifying of the practices, processes, and ideals that the team agrees to adhere to in their meetings. In the next chapter, we will walk you through the creation of a team meeting agreement and share the key ingredients that make it actionable.

Chapter Takeaways

- A speak-up culture in a meeting means attendees feel free to share their ideas, comments, and concerns without fear of retribution.

- Data suggests meeting leaders and attendees are supporting each other and enabling a greater speak-up meeting culture in the hybrid setting than in the other meetings that use a singular modality.

- While a speak-up culture is experienced at the group level, psychological safety is an individual's belief that it is safe to speak up and allows speak-up behavior to happen.

- A speak-up culture requires attendees to do their assigned pre-work to allow for optimal participation.

- During a meeting, it is equally as important for attendees to encourage others to speak as well as to speak up themselves.

- Public speaking anxiety can prevent sharing of ideas by all, but strategies such as a change in mindset and seeking out an advocate or mentor within the meeting group can help alleviate that fear.

References

Allen, J. A., and S. G. Rogelberg. 2013. "Manager-led group meetings: A context for promoting employee engagement." *Group & Organization Management* 38 (5): 543–569.

Besieux, T., A. C. Edmondson, and F. de Vries. 2021. "How to overcome your fear of speaking up in meetings." *Harvard Business Review*, June 11. https://hbr.org/2021/06/how-to-overcome-your-fear-of-speaking-up-in-meetings

Burgess, K. 2013. "Speaking in public is worse than death for most." *The Times*, October 30. https://www.thetimes.co.uk/article/speaking-in-public-is-worse-than-death-for-most-5l2bvqlmbnt#:~:text=A%20fear%20of%20public%20speaking,of%20society's%20most%20pervasive%20fears.&text=The%20top%20ranking%2C%20at%206.41,a%205.63%20for%20public%20speaking

Edmondson, A. 1999. "Psychological safety and learning behavior in work teams." *Administrative Science Quarterly* 44 (2): 350–383.

Finnie, T. 2019. "Understanding "speak up" culture and how it can benefit the workplace." LinkedIn. https://www.linkedin.com/pulse/understanding-speak-up-culture-how-can-benefit-workplace-tanya-finnie/

Impraise. 2021. "What is psychological safety and why is it the key to great teamwork?" *Impraise* (blog). https://www.impraise.com/blog/what-is-psychological-safety-and-why-is-it-the-key-to-great-teamwork

Lehmann-Willenbrock, N., J. A. Allen, and S. Kauffeld. 2013. "A sequential analysis of procedural meeting communication: How teams facilitate their meetings." *Journal of Applied Communication Research* 41 (4): 365–388.

Mesoudi, A. 2008. "An experimental simulation of the 'copy-successful-individuals' cultural learning strategy: Adaptive landscapes, producer–scrounger dynamics, and informational access costs." *Evolution and Human Behavior* 29 (5): 350–363.

Chapter 9

Creating Team Meeting Ground Rules

"Gitlab is very prescriptive that we work handbook-first. The GitLab handbook is the operating manual for the company. If it's not in the handbook, it doesn't exist."

These are the words of Darren Murph, the head of remote at GitLab and one of the most passionate remote-work evangelists you are likely to find. The GitLab handbook is an ambitious read at over 2,000 pages of text that are constantly being iterated on by its fully remote workforce. At GitLab, documentation is not just a process – it's a value that everyone adheres to, and one that hybrid workplaces need to adopt, says Darren. "The accessibility to the information must be agnostic. You should not have more access to information if you're remote. You should not have more access to information if you're in an office."

The underlying reason for the documentation orientation is clear: it turns all tacit knowledge into explicit knowledge by making it visible to all. (In fact, anyone can check out the GitLab handbook by going to https://about.gitlab.com/handbook/.) As companies and teams are transitioning to hybrid work and hybrid meetings, it might be wise for them to steal a page or two or 10 from this tome, but we'll start here with the emphasis on documentation, specifically as it relates to hybrid meetings.

In order to make meetings that involve both in-person and remote attendees work, you need to set ground rules for how those meetings are going to be conducted. Meeting scientists have been recommending setting ground rules for any kind of meeting for some time (Allen, Rogelberg, and Scott 2008). These ground rules may answer such questions as: What needs to happen before the meeting? What should happen during the meeting? And most importantly, what should happen after the meeting? The answers to these questions can't be simply "understood" – they need to be co-created by the team, explicitly documented, and then followed by all. Ideally, they are backed by real meeting science, and that's where a team meeting agreement comes into play.

In this chapter, we will explore the different elements of a team meeting agreement including:

- What questions to answer when designing a team meeting agreement
- Expectations for what happens prior to a meeting
- Ground rules for attendee engagement during the meeting
- Expectations for what happens after the meeting
- The assignment of meeting roles

Answering the Right Questions in a Team Meeting Agreement

You may have heard of team agreements. Maybe you are even part of an organization where they are the norm. But at most organizations, the idea of creating a document that spells out expectations for how a team will work together is considered an unnecessary step. Perhaps that may be true if a team is colocated, but when some members of the team are remote, that can be a real problem.

According to Lisette Sutherland, "When we work together in the same place, we can see what people are working on. Behavior is implicit when we can easily observe people and make inferences. When we work remotely, we have to make our behaviors more explicit: leave nothing implied so that there is minimal room for confusion."

With all of the complexity of a hybrid meeting, there is plenty of room for confusion, resulting in ineffectiveness at best and chaos at worst. That's why a team meeting agreement can make all the difference. It provides parameters for making the most of these meetings and helps to mitigate the potential for problems.

If you think a team meeting agreement can be handed down from on high, think again. In order to get buy-in, everyone in the meeting needs to be a part of the creation process. A leader should not just send out an edict, laying down the meeting rules. A team meeting agreement needs to be just that: an agreement between everyone who will be showing up in the meeting room, whether virtually or in person. Taking the time to hammer out the details with input from everyone is key, because the team meeting agreement is of vital importance. It establishes the underpinning for hybrid meeting success, and everyone needs to believe in and adhere to it.

But what needs to be included in a team meeting agreement? In Journalism 101, you learn that every story should answer the five Ws and the H: who, what, where, when, why, and how. Those same questions can be used to craft a solid team meeting agreement that is thorough and multifaceted, identifying what both the meeting leader and attendees pledge to do before, during, and after the session. For each of these periods in the meeting lifecycle, we will identify line items to include in the team meeting agreement, based on the answers to these questions.

First, a quick caveat: by now, you know that the first step in the meeting process is determining if a meeting is even necessary. The team meeting agreement assumes the event does need to take place, and will likely be a meeting designed to be collaborative, dialogue-based, and purpose-driven. Obviously, it's best not to violate this assumption.

Before the Meeting – Answer the Five Ws

As you've learned, a hybrid meeting demands a higher level of work in advance than a meeting that is held in person, where missteps can more easily be rectified on the fly. The margin for error is slimmer for a meeting involving multiple modalities of attendance, so determining what needs to be done prior to the meeting and then holding people accountable for following through takes on even greater significance.

In this section, we will focus on answering the Five Ws: who, what, when, where, and why. The responses to these questions will help inform the first section of your team meeting agreement on actions to be taken *before* the meeting.

Who Will Attend?

For someone to be included on the meeting invite, at least one of the following needs to apply:

- They are leading the meeting.
- Their expertise is required to inform the decision-making.
- They have decision-making authority on the topic being discussed.

You'll notice spectating is not on that list. Those who do not need to have a voice in the meeting need not be in the meeting at all. Extra attendees only add to the complexity of the communication flows and often can bog them down (Allen, Tong, and Landowski 2020). Anyone in the room, whether in person or virtual, needs to be there for a reason and have a direct role in the discussion. That means that the meeting content is relevant to them, and their full participation is not only desired but required.

Team Meeting Agreement Item 1

The only people on the meeting invite are those who need to be there.

What Is the Meeting About?

We can't stress enough how important it is to have an agenda for the meeting – an agenda that is not presented as the meeting begins, but one that is crafted, socialized, and perhaps even iterated on prior to the actual session. It's the number-one recommendation of meeting practitioners and scientists alike, and yet some estimate that fewer than 10% of meetings have an agenda (Cohen, Rogelberg, Allen, and Luong 2011; Meeting Science 2021).

The agenda gets people invested in the meeting itself because they can easily see how it impacts them. If the right people are on the invite, the line items are germane to their jobs and they will prioritize the meeting. The best way to keep people from multitasking is to ensure that each person present has a stake in what's being discussed.

The agenda can be sent as a static document with or without a request for comments or feedback, or as a link to a collaborative document that can be modified. The latter allows attendees to add topics beyond what was initially proposed by the meeting organizer. Rather than having to go back and forth for edits on the static agenda, those additions can be made on the document shared by all meeting attendees. But a word of caution: beware of "agenda creep." Remember, the best hybrid meetings are shorter. If the agenda grows beyond what can reasonably be addressed in the time allotted, see how the list of items can be pared down or even redirected toward asynchronous methods of communication.

Team Meeting Agreement Item 2

All meetings will have an agenda that is sent out in advance of the meeting.*

What Work Needs to Be Done Ahead of Time?

In order to maximize the discussion time, teams should lean into doing as much pre-work as possible so they can start the meeting at a collective level of understanding of the issue at hand (Odermatt, König, and Kleinmann 2015). In addition to a basic agenda, meeting leaders should send out any reports, documents, articles, or spreadsheets necessary for the attendees to review prior to the session. Just like the agenda itself, these pre-reads can be sent in static form like PDFs or as links to the appropriate online content. GitLab believes in providing links to any relevant resources directly on the live agenda doc. (GitLab uses Google Workspace, ergo Google Docs.) Housing the links on the agenda itself saves people the trouble of searching on their own for the pertinent background information.

While the meeting organizer might be the most likely person to pass along resources in advance, a team member who is being asked

---

*Teams should determine how far in advance based upon their workflows.

to present may also have information to share ahead of time. In that case, it is the responsibility of the attendee to ensure that everyone has access to that information, either by passing it along to the meeting leader for distribution or by sending it out themselves.

Team Meeting Agreement Item 3

Pre-work will be assigned to allow attendees to prepare for the meeting.

However, team meeting agreement item 3 means nothing without the attendees taking responsibility for actually *doing* the pre-work. Up to this point, much of the onus has been on the meeting organizer, but here's where the responsibility starts to fall squarely on the shoulders of the attendees. You know that carefully crafted agenda that was sent out? It has absolutely no value if attendees don't do anything with it.

Attendees must pledge to:

- Familiarize themselves with the agenda so they know what is being discussed.
- Read and review the documents and reports sent out prior to the meeting.
- Click on the links that take them to articles that will help inform their view of the topic on the table.
- At a minimum, put in some think-time and even jot down the ideas that came to mind as a result of their own brainstorming efforts.

> **Team Meeting Agreement Item 4**
>
> All attendees will come prepared by reviewing the agenda and accomplishing assigned pre-work.

Where Will the Meeting Take Place?

The location of a hybrid meeting can be both physical and virtual. However, if all of the infrastructure is in place from a technology and room design standpoint, how people choose to join shouldn't matter. Still, it is helpful and also respectful to let the meeting organizer know how you plan to attend. If most people are planning to join from the office, that might dictate a larger conference room is reserved rather than a smaller video-equipped huddle room. In some cases, even the in-office people might decide to just find a quiet spot on the premises and join from their individual boxes on the screen. It's also helpful for the meeting leader to know how many attendees will be joining virtually. Keeping track of total attendees can be a challenge, but knowing how many boxes should be on the screen can simplify that aspect.

> **Team Meeting Agreement Item 5**
>
> Participants will let the organizer know what modality they plan to use to attend, in-person or virtually.

When considering how people attend a meeting, it is imperative that an attendee's contributions are not diminished or enhanced by how they show up. In a truly hybrid environment, location shouldn't matter, according to Darren Murph of GitLab: "Hybrid is not about where you work. It makes no difference where you work in a knowledge-based company. Focusing on where people work is completely missing the point. Focus on how people work and how things are done."

From where you attend a meeting should be a product of what works best for each individual within the guidelines offered by the organization. Remote? In the office? Your location only plays into the logistics of possibly booking a conference room to accommodate the meeting. It should have no impact on how your attendance is perceived or the value that you provide to the meeting itself. As we mentioned previously, leaders can send a strong signal by alternating how they attend their own meetings – alternating between running a meeting in person from the office conference room and leading the meeting as a virtual attendee.

When Will the Meeting Take Place?

As we've mentioned earlier (see Chapter 2), with bulging calendars stuffed with meetings, setting start and end times and sticking to them is crucial to meeting effectiveness and satisfaction (Allen, Lehmann-Willenbrock, and Rogelberg 2018; Lehmann-Willenbrock and Allen 2020). Still, certain organizations consider it a part of their culture to be lax about the clock. For those companies that have a loose relationship with time, employees might consider it completely fine to show up five or even 10 minutes late, but this inevitably results in either wasting precious time catching up the latecomers, or going over because the agenda did not account for a delayed start. In fact, the science of meetings is pretty clear in declaring that meeting lateness is universally problematic around the world (van Eerde et al. 2020). One of Joe's recent academic articles included data from a number of countries and confirmed that even in places notorious for being lax about the clock, starting late annoyed meeting leaders and attendees (Allen et al. 2021).

Being disciplined about starting and ending on time requires full team commitment, which is why it should be included in the team meeting agreement. If one person is perpetually late, it throws off the entire meeting flow. Including it in the agreement may not solve the late-person problem, but it can give you explicit ammunition to force them to course-correct.

Team Meeting Agreement Item 6

Meetings will start and end on time.

Team Meeting Agreement Item 7

All meeting participants will show up on time.

In Chapter 3, we acknowledged the challenges of setting meeting times if your team is worldwide, and offered some tips on managing meetings across multiple time zones. If your team stretches across the globe, it is worthwhile to address how to navigate that in the team meeting agreement. Jay Hyett of Culture Amp explains how they schedule meetings for their team whose members' locations range from Melbourne to San Francisco to London: "They think globally: 'How do we make it work for everyone?' And that means sometimes we do things early and sometimes we do things late." The key here is sharing the burden and not being biased toward one time zone over all others.

> **Team Meeting Agreement Item 8**
>
> Meetings will be scheduled at times that do not favor just one time zone.

Why Will the Meeting Take Place?

The best meetings are purpose-driven, and hybrid meetings are no exception (Mroz, Allen, Verhoeven, and Shuffler 2018). Make sure everyone knows why you are meeting and what the desired outcome is. In fact, having a goal for the session might be even *more* important when so much effort needs to be taken ahead of time to make them effective. Not expressly stating a desired outcome is like setting off on a trip without a destination in mind. That's a perfectly fine approach if you have all the time in the world and simply want to enjoy the ride. However, if you want to get to a particular destination, you need to set that end point and then stay laser-focused on your GPS.

> **Team Meeting Agreement Item 9**
>
> The purpose of the meeting will be explicitly stated.

During the Meeting – Answer the "How"

So far, we've focused on what it takes to set a team up for success prior to the meeting taking place. However, all of that work leading up to the meeting can be worthless unless meeting expectations and norms for behavior *during* a meeting are established. It's time to talk about the "how" from the perspective of meeting leaders and attendees.

How Will Participants Show Up?

Both virtual and hybrid meetings rely on communication networks that are only as strong as the internet service that carries them, and when attendees can work from anywhere, that means the responsibility for the stability of the connection often falls on the individual. Wonky Wi-Fi is not okay if you want remote work to be a viable option for you.

Remember Envato, the Australian company that allows its employees to work from anywhere for up to three months? That perk isn't without parameters. Workers who want to exercise that option need to present a plan to their team that includes a guarantee that they will have a solid internet connection to support their continued contributions. Visions of an afternoon spent Zooming on a beach in Tahiti may not be plausible if you are getting internet speeds under 20 megabits per second.

Adequate bandwidth is a must. While some companies have invested in shoring up home internet for employees, many have not; but either way, it's no longer okay to make others suffer from your bad Wi-Fi. Technology is fickle, so occasional issues are bound to crop up, but regular and frequent internet issues can't be tolerated in a hybrid setting. Frozen screens, audio drops, and cryptic conversational snippets hurt everyone's meeting experience.

Team Meeting Agreement Item 10

All remote participants will have a solid internet connection.

Creating "presence" regardless of whether participants are remote or in the office is one of the great challenges in a hybrid setting. It's a challenge made infinitely worse when remote individuals choose not to show up on camera at all. That's why we strongly endorse creating a camera-on culture and including it in the team meeting agreement. Of course, there will be exceptions to the rule – say someone is eating lunch and doesn't want to gross out fellow attendees, or their normally stable internet connection is having an off day, only allowing enough bandwidth for audio alone. However, exceptions like those should be few and far between.

Team Meeting Agreement Item 11

All participants will attend the meeting with video on.

But just turning the camera on isn't enough, especially when remote. An imbalance in creating "presence" is even more exaggerated when remote workers don't put any thought into how they are showing up on the screen.

For in-office attendees, presumably much of the work will be done for them provided an investment has been made in equipping meeting rooms with high-quality cameras and high-fidelity microphones and speakers. However, remote attendees are in charge of their own personal production values, and here's where many fall short.

How you "show up" in the box on the virtual meeting screen matters – it matters to you, but more importantly, it matters to the people on the call with you. We can make the case for why you should care about looking as professional as possible. (Yes, people will judge you if you are lounging on your bed as if you were chatting with a friend about what you binge-watched last night.) But the argument that holds even more weight is related to respect – respect for your fellow attendees.

When participants join virtually, it is not as easy for others to read their nonverbals. The number of signals they can send is limited by the screen size, so it makes sense that remote attendees would want to maximize what body language they can convey. That's why it is mindboggling to see people show up with their faces entirely in shadow or with parts of their body cut off by the frame. ("I thought Jim had a chin but perhaps he doesn't?")

The job of a remote attendee is to make it as easy as possible for people to receive whatever message they're trying to convey. Not paying attention to how you appear on the screen or how you sound to others in attendance shows a disregard for the needs of your fellow attendees and a level of carelessness that reflects poorly on your commitment to the meeting itself.

During the pandemic, many people discovered how to amplify their virtual presence by adopting best practices for lighting, framing, and backgrounds. Many people, through personal or company funds, invested in external webcams and audio options that provided professional polish. But there are still many people, including some who desire the flexibility of a hybrid schedule, who continue to miss the mark. This is no longer tenable.

If you plan to attend a hybrid meeting as a virtual attendee, here is what you need to focus on to show respect for everyone in your meeting:

- *Make sure your face is well lit.* So much of how we communicate a message is through our facial expressions, so hiding them in shadow greatly reduces our ability to communicate in full. If you want people to be able to read the intent of your message, you need them to be able to read your facial expressions. If you have a window in your space, face it. Natural light is flattering and doesn't require you to plug anything in. No window? Grab a lamp or two to put on either side of your webcam so your face is illuminated evenly.

- *Attend to your audio.* When we are remote, we can't hear how we sound to others, but you can bet your fellow attendees are annoyed when you sound like you are talking from an echo chamber. Laptop microphones might be fine for most business users, but how well they work will depend upon the acoustics in your room. Do you have a lot of hard surfaces in your space? Hardwood or tile floors? High ceilings? Lots of windows with no curtains? These can create a very bouncy environment for sound. In that case, a better option might be a headset, a stand-up microphone, or a clip-on lapel microphone. We'll talk more about hardware in the next section but the bottom line is to not assume you sound fine on the call. Either record yourself on the platform and listen to how it sounds to your own ears when you play it back, or ask a trusted colleague to hop on a call with you to tell you if you sound like you are talking from a tin can.

- *Curate your background.* While virtual backgrounds might be easy to use and cover up a considerable amount of chaos, they have some serious limitations. The artificial intelligence used to generate those backgrounds isn't perfect and can have a hard time distinguishing between where you end and the background should begin. The result? Those watery edges that can be distracting. Instead, opt for staging a space that is simple and neutral. You don't need a lot of room. In fact, positioning yourself toward a corner can add depth to the shot. Consider adding a plant or basic artwork for a bit of visual interest. The key is having a backdrop that is professional but not distracting. A conversation starter on a bookshelf is fine. Ten conversation starters will just appear to be clutter.

> **Team Meeting Agreement Item 12**
>
> All participants will easily be seen and heard without distraction.

How Will the Conversation Flow Be Managed?

In a hybrid meeting, a conversation free-for-all will not work. If everyone is in person, talking over each other may not be a best practice, but it can be managed. When some people are in person and others are joining virtually, talking over each other creates inequities. Those who are virtual will only hear snippets of sentences while in-person attendees will likely only hear themselves talk. That's why it's imperative to establish a turn-taking ritual that everyone abides by.

What that ritual is needs to be established by the team, but there are a variety of options. Maybe it's raising an emoji hand, or if the group is small enough, raising a physical hand and waiting to be called on by the meeting leader. Some teams prefer to have a question or comment put in chat, and then allow the leader to weave it into the group discussion. In that case, the leader can read the chat comment out loud and then call on the author to expand upon it.

Whatever process chosen by the group, it needs to be agreed upon and understood. Including it in the team meeting agreement will help to provide accountability, but it's also wise for the leader to reinforce it with a reminder at the top of each meeting about how to get in the conversation queue.

> **Team Meeting Agreement Item 13**
>
> All attendees will adhere to the turn-taking ritual agreed upon by the team.

How Will We Handle Mute Etiquette?

The mute button is one of the most vexing tools in the virtual and hybrid meeting arsenal. Mute etiquette for virtual meetings is a bit clearer because the rules apply to everyone, but in hybrid, there is no mute button for individuals gathered around the conference room table (as much as some might wish there was). As a meeting organizer, you may appreciate the ability to mute the microphones of all virtual attendees in one fell swoop, especially when a remote employee's dog decides to loudly greet the UPS driver who just left a package at the door. However, muting just the virtual attendees creates the potential for inequality. So, what is the best way to approach muting in a hybrid meeting?

There may be times everyone should be on mute, save for the person speaking. If someone is giving a five-minute presentation, there's no reason for anyone other than the presenter to be off mute. However, in a dynamic discussion, having people off mute allows for a more natural flow, provided that people follow the turn-taking process and don't interrupt, but if the number of attendees is beyond a handful, this becomes unwieldy.

The best advice is to decide as a team on what muting policy makes the most sense. Consider the size of your team, how much back-and-forth dialogue typically occurs, and how likely serious audio interference may occur. Remote collaboration expert Lisette Sutherland offers these insights:

> I personally like when people are not on mute because it feels like more of a conversation. You can hear people laugh at your jokes or when they take an intake of breath before they're about to speak, but that means everyone has to have a quiet background. So, if you don't have a quiet background, you have to be conscientious about muting yourself.

177

Creating Team Meeting Ground Rules

How Often Will We Take Breaks?

We've already established how important it is to take breaks when virtual attendees are present. A meeting is more taxing, mentally and physically, when joining remotely via videoconference. In a hybrid meeting, especially one where the majority of attendees are colocated, it can be easy to forget to take breaks, as we demonstrated in the example from Chapter 6 where the meeting leader decided to press on because as an in-person attendee, she didn't feel the need to stop. That's why it is valuable to have established guidelines around how often breaks are taken.

The general rule is if you are going over an hour, you need to take a full break, with enough time for everyone to stretch, go to the restroom, or simply do a mental reboot. In fact, the science suggests that meetings that go longer than an hour should have refreshments (Cohen, Rogelberg, Allen, and Luong 2011). At about 45 minutes in, remote attendees will likely feel their energy start to flag. A 10-minute break can make a dramatic difference in their ability to focus and continue to contribute in full.

How Will We Record What Happens During the Meeting?

Taking minutes during a meeting is a traditional tactic used to keep track of the discussion highlights, action items, and the people assigned to complete those items. Organizations have different policies relative to taking notes, and some even opt out of doing so. However, most organizations at a minimum record next steps.

In some organizations, recording meetings is a norm by using the built-in feature of their video collaboration platform of choice, and, as mentioned in Chapter 7, this method is gaining in popularity. However, there are legal considerations around using this functionality that vary by industry and corporate culture, so make sure to consult your legal team for guidance.

Team Meeting Agreement Item 16

We will document/record what happens during the meeting according to our team policy.

After the Meeting – Back to the Five Ws

What occurs after the meeting is as important, if not more important, than what happens before and during the meeting. After all, the purpose of a meeting is to move business forward, so everyone in attendance should come away with a sense of accomplishment and a clear vision of what happens next. If it was time well spent, the meeting should be the spark for a series of next steps that have been assigned and need to be acted upon. For guidance in establishing the after-meeting team policies, we turn again to the five Ws, lumping the first three Ws into this next team meeting agreement suggestion.

What Are the Action Items?
Who Is Responsible for Each?
Where and When Will the Information Be Available?

Assigning action items is part of any meeting, no matter the modality. When hybrid, it is important to have a process in place that ensures that everyone knows what those next steps are and who is responsible for them. Conversations in a hallway can't be heard by remote employees, so any minutes, action items, or follow-up discussions related to the meeting need to be documented, not simply verbalized. How they are shared will depend on the collaboration platform of choice. (In Part Four, we will share expert advice on what to look for in a collaboration platform to help you assess what is currently on the market.) However, regardless of the software chosen, the key is making post-meeting information visible to all.

Here is where we take yet another cue from GitLab's Darren Murph:

> The thing you want to avoid is the "song in the shower" problem. Say you're a songwriter and you're standing in the shower, and this lick comes to mind and you think, "That is a billion-dollar song," but you don't hum it into the phone. You don't write it down. You think, "I'll remember it later." You'll never remember it later. That is the problem in an office where you only verbalize and documentation is not a part of your culture.

Team Meeting Agreement Item 17

We will make all information recorded in the meeting available to all attendees on the collaboration platform of choice.

When Will Post-Meeting Information Be Made Available?

The speed of business usually dictates as quick a turnaround as possible for any information gathered during the meeting, so those who are responsible for the action items can get to work right away. If a meeting has been recorded, that video file only takes minutes to be converted, and access to it can be granted immediately. Minutes or a list of to-do's can be circulated quickly as well.

Some organizations opt for note-taking using shared document software, like Google Docs, which allows meeting attendees to view and add content simultaneously for real-time collaboration. In this case, the post-meeting information is being created during the meeting, and there's no lag time for access afterward.

Disseminating information after the meeting is time-sensitive, meaning the longer the wait, the more potential for missteps that run counter to what was decided in the meeting. Don't leave the time for release to chance. Create accountability by explicitly stating how quickly post-meeting information will be available to all stakeholders.

Team Meeting Agreement Item 18

Post-meeting information will be available (within x days/ immediately).

Why Are All of These Line Items Necessary?

Perhaps we should have answered this question first, because often people won't get on board with the "what" until they understand the "why." As we wrap up this step-by-step guide for creating a team meeting agreement, let's discuss why this seemingly ponderous process is worthwhile.

The "why" behind the team meeting agreement stems from the hybrid environment itself. What might seem like granular documentation is a necessity when people are not sharing the same physical space because the potential for communication silos created by the dividing line between in-office and remote teammates is high. Remember how a coworker might remind another of a deadline when passing them in the hall, or simply seeing a person in the office can provide a cue to accomplish a task? Those cues are greatly reduced in a hybrid environment where between-meeting interaction may be limited. A team meeting agreement sets a standard of operation that helps break down those silos and foster inclusion and team cohesion. If you have your doubts, consider what Lisette Sutherland has to say: "Whether you're starting with a fresh team on a new project, or whether you've been working together for a long time, creating a team agreement helps form the glue that binds your team together."

To make it easier for you to create your own team meeting agreement, we've included a checklist at the end of this chapter with a list of all the items we've covered.

Share the Responsibility for Success: Assign Meeting Roles

Making hybrid meetings work will require effort from everyone who will collectively agree to adhere to the policies and procedures outlined in the team meeting agreement, but that will only get you so far. In order to operationalize the agreement, we suggest assigning meeting roles so the burden is shared across the team as a whole. Some of these roles may be familiar to you, but others may be new, especially since some were created as a direct result of the additional complexities inherent in hybrid meetings.

Meeting Moderator

Leading a meeting is challenging even in the best of circumstances, but in a hybrid environment, the complexity of working through an agenda, driving productive dialogue, and monitoring participation can become overwhelming. The cognitive load can be too much for a meeting leader to manage, especially if that meeting leader is also the one who ultimately has to make a decision at the end about the topic at hand. When that is the case, adding a meeting moderator to the mix can be beneficial.

The meeting moderator should be someone who is familiar with what is being discussed but does not have a direct stake in the outcome of the meeting. Their primary job is to track participation to ensure that everyone's voice is heard and no one is forgotten. For example, if a meeting leader is in the office, there is always a risk for in-person bias, so the meeting moderator's role can include reminding the meeting leader to ask for input from those who are remote, and keeping tabs on any virtual hands that might be raised.

The meeting moderator can also take on administrative tasks that can be overly burdensome for meeting leaders. Perhaps someone has already been put in charge of taking notes during a meeting, but if that's not the case, a meeting moderator can take on that duty and log action items as the session progresses. In addition, the meeting moderator can keep an eye on the clock and the agenda, making sure the meeting stays on track and breaks are taken when required.

Ultimately, the meeting moderator shifts some of the administrative tasks away from the meeting leader, allowing them to focus on making the best decision possible by carefully listening to the content being presented without, for example, wondering if they've heard from Jane yet.

Technology Lead

Everyone has experienced a virtual meeting where at least one person has had challenges with the videoconferencing platform. Maybe they can't connect to audio or their camera isn't being recognized. Rather than halting the entire meeting to troubleshoot, consider assigning a technology lead who can handle any challenges that crop up during the meeting. The meeting leader (or moderator) can put the technology lead and the person who is having trouble into a breakout room where they can work on the problem without disrupting the meeting flow.

Not only can the technology lead serve as basic tech support, but they also can help manage any tools that are being used during the meeting. They can launch and display polls, or assign participants to breakout rooms when appropriate. While some meeting leaders are adept at doing these tasks themselves, others will welcome the extra help.

Chat Monitor

Trying to facilitate the verbal conversation flow and following a separate communication flow on the chat channel is challenging and sometimes impossible to do well. Remember the myth-busting we did in Chapter 3 about multitasking? It doesn't work. That's why it can be helpful to assign a chat monitor to keep track of the comments and questions that are coming in through that valuable stream of text.

The chat monitor's job is to be on the lookout for any input that should be incorporated into the verbal discussion. Funny side or off-topic comments can likely just be consumed by those reading the chat, but pertinent questions or salient commentary should be brought to the attention of the meeting leader and woven into the ongoing dialogue.

Even if a meeting leader stops periodically to check the chat, it can be inefficient and ineffective to try to scan through all of the text, especially if it's been an active written conversation flow. A chat monitor can help cut through the noise and elevate what is relevant to the discussion in real-time.

Meeting Buddies

Despite best efforts by the meeting leader or moderator, sometimes it can be difficult for a remote attendee to break into the conversation. In that case, a meeting buddy can make all the difference. A meeting buddy is an in-person attendee who serves as an in-room advocate for a remote attendee. Sometimes raising a virtual hand or putting a comment in chat isn't enough to get the attention of the meeting leader. An in-room voice that is tethered to a remote person can raise awareness that the remote person has something to add. Some teams might prefer that individuals seek out their own meeting buddies, but others might want to formalize the process, notifying teams of the in-person/remote pairings before each meeting.

You might look at this list of roles and think this is overkill. Is this really necessary? It depends on your team culture and processes. What is universal is the fact that hybrid meetings require a more intentional approach to be successful. Expecting a meeting leader to run the meeting, adhere to the agenda, keep track of time, pull out participation from everyone in the physical and virtual room, and make the right decision seems unreasonable. Soliciting some help from attendees themselves seems like a smart move to avoid issues that can legitimately be anticipated.

Conclusion

Hybrid meeting success demands careful planning with inclusivity at its core. Many of the suggestions discussed in this chapter focus on shifting the mindset of those who will be taking part in the meetings and codifying practices that manifest that mindset. However, hybrid meetings can't happen without the proper technological underpinning that this modality requires. The wheels of innovation continue to turn rapidly as the hardware and software industries respond to the call for hybrid meeting solutions. In Part Four, we will offer you some expert advice on what to look for when assessing your options.

Team Meeting Agreement Items

As a team, we agree to the following meeting practices:	Yes or No
1. The only people on the meeting invite are those who need to be there.	[ ] Yes [ ] No
2. All meetings will have an agenda that is sent out in advance of the meeting.	[ ] Yes [ ] No
3. Pre-work will be assigned to allow attendees to prepare for the meeting.	[ ] Yes [ ] No
4. All attendees will come prepared by reviewing the agenda and accomplishing assigned prework.	[ ] Yes [ ] No
5. Participants will let the organizer know what modality they plan to use to attend, in-person or virtual.	[ ] Yes [ ] No
6. Meetings will start and end on time.	[ ] Yes [ ] No
7. All meeting participants will show up on time.	[ ] Yes [ ] No
8. Meetings will be scheduled at times that do not favor just one time zone.	[ ] Yes [ ] No
9. The purpose of the meeting will be explicitly stated.	[ ] Yes [ ] No

As a team, we agree to the following meeting practices:	Yes or No
10. All remote participants will have a solid internet connection.	[ ] Yes [ ] No
11. All participants will attend the meeting with video on.	[ ] Yes [ ] No
12. All participants will be easily seen and heard without distraction.	[ ] Yes [ ] No
13. All attendees will adhere to the turn-taking ritual agreed upon by the team.	[ ] Yes [ ] No
14. All attendees will follow the agreed-upon mute policy.	[ ] Yes [ ] No
15. We will take breaks every 45 minutes during meetings scheduled to be longer than an hour.	[ ] Yes [ ] No
16. We will document/record what happens during the meeting according to our team policy.	[ ] Yes [ ] No
17. We will make all information recorded in the meeting available to all attendees on the collaboration platform of choice.	[ ] Yes [ ] No
18. Post-meeting information will be available (within x days/immediately).	[ ] Yes [ ] No
TOTAL YES	_____

Meeting Roles	Names
Meeting Moderator	_____
Technology Lead	_____
Chat Monitor	_____
Meeting Buddies	_____

Chapter Takeaways

- A team meeting agreement can establish guidelines and remove uncertainty around processes and procedures before, during, and after a meeting.

- The agreement dictates actions required of both the meeting leader and attendees to set the meeting up for success.

- The agreement sets standards for participation, etiquette, and documentation during the meeting.

- The agreement spells out what needs to happen after a meeting by creating a level of accountability for sharing post-meeting information.

- Teams should consider assigning meeting roles to help share the burden of meeting effectiveness among attendees as well as the leader.

References

Allen, J. A., N. Lehmann-Willenbrock, A Meinecke, N. Landowski, S. Rogelberg, L. Lucianetti, S. J. Tong, and H. P. Madrid. 2021. "The ubiquity of meeting lateness!: A cross-cultural investigation of the small to moderate effects of workplace meeting lateness." *Cross-Cultural Research (June)*. doi:10.1177/10693971211024193.

Allen, J. A., N. Lehmann-Willenbrock, and S. G. Rogelberg. 2018. "Let's get this meeting started: Meeting lateness and actual meeting outcomes." *Journal of Organizational Behavior* 39 (8): 1008–1021.

Allen, J. A., S. G. Rogelberg, and J. C. Scott. 2008. "Mind your meetings: Improve your organization's effectiveness one meeting at a time." *Quality Progress* 41: 48.

Allen, J. A., J. Tong, and N. Landowski. 2020. "Meeting effectiveness and task performance: Meeting size matters." *Journal of Management Development* 40 (5): 339–351.

Cohen, M. A., S. G. Rogelberg, J. A. Allen, and A. Luong. 2011. "Meeting design characteristics and attendee perceptions of staff/team meeting quality." *Group Dynamics: Theory, Research, and Practice* 15 (1): 90.

Lehmann-Willenbrock, N., and J. A. Allen. 2020. "Well, now what do we do? Wait . . .: A group process analysis of meeting lateness." *International Journal of Business Communication* 57 (3): 302–326.

Meeting Science. 2021. "100k meetings later . . . How to achieve peak meeting performance." *Meeting Science.* https://meetingscience.io/blog/

Mroz, J. E., J. A. Allen, D. C. Verhoeven, and M. L. Shuffler. 2018. "Do we really need another meeting? The science of workplace meetings." *Current Directions in Psychological Science* 27 (6): 484–491.

Odermatt, I., C. J. König, and M. Kleinmann. 2015. "Meeting preparation and design characteristics." In J. A. Allen, N. Lehmann-Willenbrock, and S. G. Rogelberg (Eds.), *The Cambridge Handbook of Meeting Science*, 49–68. Cambridge University Press.

van Eerde, W., and S. Azar. 2020. "Too late? What do you mean? Cultural norms regarding lateness for meetings and appointments." *Cross-Cultural Research* 54 (2–3): 111–129.

Creating Team Meeting Ground Rules

PART FOUR

Power Up – Tools to Bridge the Physical and Virtual Workplaces

Woe to the poor chief technology officer (CTO) in the age of COVID-19. When the world was quite abruptly thrown into a remote reality, CTOs and all their adjacent teams were tasked with a sizeable job: figure out a way to keep the company connected without anyone being physically in the same location, and do so within a secure environment with as little friction as possible. Oh, and let's throw a webcam shortage on top of that, just for kicks. Nowadays, those same people are being asked to equip their companies to connect in a more flexible way than ever before – building the infrastructure that allows for collaboration when employees have the choice to be either in the office or remote. When in this hybrid environment, the tools chosen need to enable workers no matter where they are located.

At Pearson, the world's leading learning company with 24,000 employees across 70 countries worldwide, the crux of their "return to office" plan is based on each individual and their level of comfort. If you're not comfortable coming into the office, there's no mandate to do so. "You're going to be productive where you're most comfortable. If you make sure that your employees are starting from a position of comfort and safety, you're going to get the best work out of them," says Steve Santana, the CTO of virtual learning, one of the largest divisions at Pearson. He and his team are in charge of the technology that bridges the gap between the physical and virtual workspaces, and at the core of all their planning are the needs of those who will be using the technology. He adds, "You're going to have to figure out how to be flexible and how you're going to become a people person *before* you're a technologist."

The technology sector has responded rapidly to the changes in the way we work, and the speed at which that has occurred has been mind-blowing for those who have been seeking solutions during these unprecedented times. That's something not lost by those like Steve: "The work that Microsoft and Google, Cisco, and Zoom have done on improving their product, improving the security and accessibility, has been amazing. I don't think people appreciate the speed of innovation that has been going on there. It is truly impressive. So when something goes wrong, and somebody whines about something, I tell them that you've got to consider the scale of what is going right here. You have no idea what is happening on the back end for these companies to make their networks, their data centers, and all this other kind of stuff work the way they do. So as a CTO, I appreciate that side of it tremendously."

It's through that lens that Steve is also viewing how Pearson selects their tools to make hybrid meetings work. New products are constantly coming onto the market. However, it is important to be discerning. That shiny, new thing might be woefully outdated a short time later, or as Steve says: "There are landfills chock-full of all sorts of failed 'turnkey' solutions because they were a good idea for a moment in time. Pick an ecosystem, start simple, and grow organically."

For the next part, we took those words to heart and decided to apply them to our discussion of technology to enable hybrid meetings. You won't find specific product endorsements. You won't find a list of items to order from Amazon. What you *will* find are some insights into what to look for when considering the products currently on the market at the time of this writing. We will focus on two key areas when it comes to making hybrid meetings work: creating presence (Chapter 10) and enabling collaboration (Chapter 11) for all attendees, regardless of location.

Technology has to serve both constituencies, the in-office and the remote employees. Focusing more on one over the other is a recipe for disaster, or, in the words of Steve Santana, "I think CTOs that are just kind of building it for one or the other are going to be 'Suddenly Dinosaurs.'"

Chapter 10

Creating Presence for All

Pre-pandemic, not a whole lot of thought was given to how effectively a remote worker could take part in a meeting. Heck, it was often considered a win if someone could even connect to a meeting at all. Suffice it to say, the bar has been dramatically raised with the exponential adoption of video collaboration platforms, which will continue to provide the underpinning for hybrid meetings going forward.

"The expectation has completely changed," says Eric Taylor, an IT and hardware collaboration expert. "There is an expectation if you're going to meet with someone remotely, that there's going to be video. It's going to be high-quality video and the audio will be good."

That's a far cry from where most people were back in March 2020, when "suddenly remote" workers were pretty much left to their own devices (literally their own webcams, if they even had one) and their own bank accounts to figure out how to be "present" in meetings. "The beginning of the pandemic, the funding strategy was . . . whatever you can steal from your office before it closed, or figure it out on Amazon," according to Scott Wharton, the head of Logitech's Video Collaboration Division. Over time, some companies changed their policies and started to pay to equip their remote workers with

195

webcams, and maybe even headsets, a trend that continues to this day. Says Scott, "Now we are seeing a much more structured stipend. I think at first the stipend started small, and then it started to get bigger because they realized it wasn't big enough."

But gearing up employees to appear on the small screens of others isn't enough anymore. Now, companies need to consider how to create "presence" for all when some meeting attendees are virtual and some meeting attendees are back in the corporate conference room. Most meeting rooms prior to COVID-19 were not video-equipped, and business leaders now recognize that situation isn't going to fly in a hybrid environment.

It's a concern being voiced regularly by Logitech customers who are looking for solutions . . . fast. Scott explains, "There's an 'oh shit' moment happening all over the world when people realize they're going to come back. They've gotten used to using video, and they know they can't have their people walk into a meeting room with just a speakerphone."

It's a tricky proposition to create presence for all in a hybrid meeting environment, and yes, the success of those efforts is largely reliant upon the participants themselves. However, even the prodigious facilitation skills of the meeting leader and the good intentions of the attendees can't make up for technology that doesn't put the virtual attendee on an as close to equal footing as possible with those who are physically in the same room. What it requires is a dual focus – equipping the individual and outfitting the meeting space.

In this chapter, we will explore:

- Rethinking the meeting room
- What to consider when evaluating equipment
- Investing in a remote worker's meeting setup

Equipping the Modern Meeting Room for the Hybrid Workforce

Think about the typical conference room in your office, pre-COVID-19. Maybe it held a basic long table surrounded by swivel chairs with a monitor on one end of the room. Maybe it was a fancier version with a management console that allowed you to turn the lights on, draw down the shades, and boot up the projector with the touch of a button. What was less likely to be in a typical room was a video camera.

"This is a new animal for some," says Eric Taylor, who has helped customers develop in-room collaboration systems for both Lenovo and Logitech. "A lot of customers I talked to have meeting rooms, but they were just sort of a place to just come in and talk in person – a place for all of us to get together so we didn't have to loiter in someone's office. Technology was never really a consideration. It was sort of an afterthought."

With the transition to hybrid, that afterthought became top of mind as IT and facilities departments worked to create a modern meeting room capable of supporting meetings with video at their core. For some, the fact that the pandemic dragged on actually provided for a more thoughtful and methodical process, allowing teams to investigate the best solutions for their own unique needs. "They had a lot of time to look at every solution on the market," says Eric. "They didn't just have to buy something and do it. They had a year to evaluate the heck out of everything and ask question after question that they would never have thought to ask before."

So what questions *did* they ask? No matter where you are on the hybrid work journey, it's always valuable to learn how others approached the same problem. Allow us to shed some light on what factors came into play for those who were charged with making their meeting rooms work for hybrid meetings.

Can Everyone Be Seen and Heard?

You may be familiar with the most common incarnation of the video-equipped meeting room. You know, the one that features the "bowling alley view," where one camera is mounted at the front of the room, usually below a monitor. That basic in-room setup was accepted as the norm prior to the pandemic but served no one especially well. What those joining the meeting virtually saw on their screens was the static view offered by the single camera of their colleagues seated around the conference room table . . . or at least that was the plan. In reality, people often were hidden from view if they hadn't adjusted their positions relative to the lens. The problem was compounded when, for example, someone walked over to the whiteboard, which was out of frame.

For the in-room attendees, the single monitor was usually the bigger issue than the virtual attendees' cameras. Provided that the image quality was high enough, perhaps they could make out their virtual colleagues' faces, but that was greatly dependent on the size of the screen. Viewing virtual colleagues quickly went from bad to worse when a slide deck was involved. Eric Taylor remembers those days well: "In the instance with a single display, if someone shared content, like a PowerPoint slide, all of that video was put off to the side. So those remote folks were marginalized."

To combat the issue of "unseen" colleagues, many organizations consider two key components: increasing the size of their displays and leveling up the quality of their cameras.

Meeting Room Monitors

At Pearson, they had the advantage of already being further along the video meeting room continuum than most because of a preexisting culture of video collaboration, according to CTO Steve Santana. He says, "Because we're pretty video-centric, we've always had people who are in the room and not in the room. In fact, usually we have multiple rooms connected. So that would be the Boston room, the London room, the Durham room, the San Francisco room."

Not surprisingly, they also place a premium on maximizing the screen size available to them, so everyone can have as large a presence as the technology will allow. "We have minimum 50-inch displays in our rooms. Most of our large conference rooms are 75-inch. And then in a couple of our large conference rooms, we have a large projector. We did all that, though, pre-pandemic," said Steve, who is based out of the Durham, North Carolina, office. "But what has happened is that because of the pandemic, our office is the template where they're testing out all the cabling, all the equipment, the display sizes, and aspect ratios relative to the size of the room. Big monitors everywhere is key for a true one-to-one experience."

Did you notice that he said "monitors," not "monitor"? A conference room with just one LCD display or ceiling-mounted screen puts everyone at a disadvantage when any content is being shared, as Eric Taylor alluded to earlier. He adds, "We're starting to see a lot of interest in the dual display, where you have video on one display and content on another. That way it keeps the people on video engaged, and people realize that there are folks on the other end."

The chance for the remote workers to disappear from the in-office attendees' minds during a meeting is a real threat if there is no adequate visual representation of them in the room, something Eric saw repeatedly when he observed how people used the meeting room technology. When remote attendees joined with audio alone, they were often forgotten until they made their presence known, sometimes taking their fellow attendees by surprise. "I would see everybody talking in the room and then that remote person would chime in. People would be startled because they'd forgotten that someone was on the line. They would do this thing where they'd look up at the ceiling because the voice was coming from the speaker in the ceiling. They'd look up at the ceiling to talk to them – just this headless voice," recalled Eric with a chuckle. "But you start to see the behaviors change when the video is engaged because now they'll turn and actually look at the monitor. They'll look at the person on the screen to talk to them."

With that in mind, where you place the monitors is also worth extra consideration. Placing the screens behind someone else's head or in a distant corner will diminish the role of the remote attendees. The monitors on which their faces appear should be situated in a way that emulates their place at the table, so they are as easy to see as the faces of those in the physical room.

Take a look at the following photo. Leave it to Google to come up with room design ideas that are on the leading edge. "Campfire" meeting rooms have people sitting in a circle, interspersed between large monitors on which their remote colleagues appear (Wakabayashi and Clifford 2021). Both in-person and remote participants are on the same level – eye level, that is.

Source: Cayce Clifford/*The New York Times*/Redux

What is driving innovation in this area is what we have been harping on throughout the book – being seen and heard is critical to hybrid meeting success, and for remote attendees, that can be a bigger hurdle. The tech industry is constantly seeking to solve this problem by coming up with new products designed to put people on equal footing, whether they are physically or virtually present. As you evaluate what is on the market, use that quest for equality as your guiding principle – choose the products that will provide it best.

Cameras in the Conference Room

Now that we've addressed the screen setup in the meeting space, let's discuss the equipment used to beam the in-person attendees to their remote colleagues. If your idea of a video-enabled conference room is sticking a laptop at the end of the table and using the built-in webcam to capture the scene, your efforts at holding an inclusive hybrid meeting will fail. The goal of an in-room video system is to ensure the remote attendees feel like they are an equal part of the meeting, and offering them a grainy shot of the conference room is sending the wrong signal.

The makers of video collaboration hardware responded quickly to the increased demand of the fully remote work world and accelerated the innovation around it, a rate of change that has not slowed down. With that in mind, rather than focusing on specific products, allow us to share some features that should factor into your evaluation of what is currently on the market.

- *Video Quality* – Remember, the goal is to make the virtual experience as close to the face-to-face interaction as possible. For remote workers, a highly detailed image cuts down on video fatigue because no one needs to squint to make out facial expressions. In-room cameras have come a long way in terms of the image they capture and transmit. Crisp lines and vivid color are all table-stakes. High-quality video is readily available and worth investigating if you have a network bandwidth capable of carrying it. 4K video resolution is no longer something that only the pickiest technologists crave, but 1080p HD video is where most products land. A word of caution: beware of the fish-eye lens, which allows for an ultra-wide angle. While a wider field of view can help ensure that everyone is seen, the distortion along the edges can make the final image distracting.

- *Camera Controls* – We've already mentioned some of the challenges of a static shot. People can often be hidden or drop out of view, and the drawbacks directly impact equal participation by all.

   Imagine this common scenario. One of the in-person attendees has something really important to say but unfortunately is sitting at the end of the conference table, the furthest point away from the camera. The in-room attendees nod in agreement, but the virtual attendees can't weigh in at all. The speaker is so far away that they can barely tell who is even speaking, much less make out what they are saying.

   A way to combat this is to invest in video equipment that goes beyond the static shot. Features like pan, tilt, and zoom can shrink the room and highlight individuals throughout the space, making them appear larger in the frame and increasing their ability to communicate in full through the screen. While some systems allow for manual adjustments to be made, others do it for you automatically, comfortably framing the speakers in a way that fits the conversation flow with auto-zoom, auto-focus, and auto-face detection. Some conference cams are even designed to sit in the middle of the table and revolve

360 degrees, swiveling around to settle on the face of the person who is speaking.

Our advice is to think about what makes the most sense in your space with an emphasis on emulating an in-person experience. Even when we are all in the same room, we focus our attention on one person when they're speaking. Cameras can be optimized for a close approximation of that as well, provided there are ways to control the shot that is being captured. Opting for the single wide view puts the remote people at a deficit by diminishing their window into the in-office action.

From a meeting science perspective, the overarching aim is to help remote participants feel like they are present. That is, we need to get the cameras to make it feel as close to a face-to-face environment as is possible. You might think, "Why would we want to do that when the data you shared suggests hybrid is better?" The data demonstrates success when a hybrid meeting has enabled adequate presence for everyone.

In a face-to-face meeting, it is not typically an issue for participants to be seen or heard, aside from the occasional soft-spoken person who doesn't speak loudly enough. For the most part, it's assumed that a person is present and accounted for simply by being in the room. Sure, sitting at the back of the room or in a corner can diminish one's presence, but a good meeting leader can pull people into the meeting effectively no matter where they sit in the room.

With virtual and hybrid, presence cannot be taken for granted; it must be built through the use of proper tools – ideally, tools that work so well that the attendees forget who's on camera and who's in person. The best technology enables collaboration so effectively that everyone can just meet and create together.

- *Camera placement* – If you are retrofitting a room that previously didn't have a camera, you may be stymied by something that may not have been considered in its previous life: lighting. Perhaps you have a bank of windows that provides beautiful campus views but could potentially put people in silhouette if the camera is capturing people sitting in front of them.

  Some organizations may have the budget to hire a lighting designer who will optimize the available natural light and supplement it with artificial light sources. However, most companies can get away with simply ensuring that no one is in shadow. Avoid pointing the camera at the bank of windows. As a general rule, backlighting is bad.

Meeting Audio Fidelity

While having high-quality video is essential, you could argue that having excellent audio quality is even more so. After all, you could still have a meeting without video. A meeting with no audio is an exercise in miming.

Most conference cams include some sort of integrated microphone and speaker, with some of the better systems offering HD audio in addition to HD video. However, there are some conference cams that produce beautiful images but provide really crappy audio quality. Read reviews to determine whether the product you are considering is deficient in this area. If it is, move on.

Follow the guidelines offered by the manufacturer about the size of the room each conference cam is appropriate for. Pay attention to the microphone pickup range in the specs. For larger rooms, you may need multiple microphones to pick up everyone's voice no matter where they are seated. Think about where there might be audio holes that need to be filled. Some solutions have the ability to daisy-chain microphone pods that can be placed strategically based upon your room configuration.

Ease of Use

Despite all of the changes wrought for meeting rooms as a result of COVID-19, one thing has remained constant: a desire for the room to be easy to use. A system that has so many bells and whistles that no one knows how to even operate it has no value and will collect dust.

Prior to the pandemic, Karin recalls being shown a video-enabled conference room by one of her clients who was excited to show it off. When asked how often it is used, her client responded, "Never, no one knows how to turn it on. The person who originally set it up no longer works here."

Take it from Eric Taylor, who has guided countless clients through the selection process: "It needs to be quick and easy, and fairly immutable. The value of a meeting room is a ubiquitous user interface. So, when you walk into the room, you see the same user interface anywhere in the world." The call for simplicity is being heard by industry. One-touch solutions and all-in-one systems continue to come to market, promising a streamlined process for connecting everyone in the hybrid meeting room.

Leave Room for Improvement in Your Meeting Room Setup

Figuring out what setup works best for a hybrid meeting is a journey, not a destination. Even with the most careful consideration, what you thought might work in theory may not work when put into practice. "It's not a one-and-done. You don't just buy the hardware and set up the room and walk away. You've got to watch it and make sure it works," says Eric Taylor. "Whole rooms will start to evolve, just like our home offices evolved with better furniture, better backgrounds, better lighting, better video and audio. I think we'll start to see that shift in the rooms as well, because they'll say, 'Oh, we're going to start doing a lot of video in here. Maybe our room should have windows, or maybe we should have better lighting. And we're going to have to situate the cameras and the monitors to accommodate this new sort of model.'"

CTO Steve Santana agrees. While Pearson had already put an emphasis on video-enabled rooms pre-pandemic, Steve anticipates that the choices they made then may not be right ones for today's needs. According to Steve, "There's going to be tweaking of the audio. We have little mic pucks that I think we're going to be constantly playing with. Some of the cameras were set up where an architect put it in place, and we didn't really think of putting it on the right wall. Maybe there's a lot of windows that screw up the brightness and contrast. No one likes to chat with someone who looks like they're in the witness protection program. There are things that maybe we haven't spent as much time on that have become much more important."

If you were hoping for specific product suggestions, this is not the right resource for you. Technology companies are spinning out new features, functionalities, and tools on a daily basis. Anything we'd recommend today could be outdone tomorrow as innovation drives new capabilities for cameras, audio equipment, and room setups. Our advice is simple: do your research and ask for feedback from the end users. Just because something is new doesn't guarantee it will lead to a better experience. The key is to be sure to stay at the forefront of these developments, remain flexible, and gravitate toward the tools that truly enable better hybrid meetings and don't just offer features with little to no real benefit.

In-Office But Not in the Meeting Room

Don't be surprised if your in-office employees don't all gravitate to the newly (and perhaps expensively) decked-out meeting room. Remember, workers spent a significant amount of time joining meetings through their own screens and may want to still do that, at least periodically, out of convenience. In fact, in a study released in August 2021 by research firm Metrigy, 35% of the 476 global companies surveyed expect in-office employees to stay at their desks to attend meetings remotely (Lazar 2021). We are already seeing that playing out.

Jay Hyett of Culture Amp holds a daily standup with his team of software engineers, many of whom are back in the office. Jay says that prior to the pandemic, his team members who were physically on-site would typically all gather in the conference room for that daily meeting, but the fully remote experience changed that:

> "I'm seeing that we are all popping up from different corners of the office on the screen . . . not going into a room but popping up. We have our conversation for 15 or 20 minutes and then we close it down and people get on with their day. Whereas traditionally, people would all have stood around a physical whiteboard in the conference room. Now the transparency is all still there, but it's just popping up from wherever."

As this example illustrates, rethinking the meeting room experience is only half of the equation that sets a team up for hybrid meeting success. Those who are joining virtually need to be empowered with the right tools to ensure their presence is known and felt, which is where we now turn our attention.

Equipping the Remote Worker When Hybrid

Let's be clear. Equipping the remote worker doesn't mean equipping only a certain subset of employees at an organization. If you are truly hybrid, investing in high-quality equipment for the remote worker means investing in high-quality equipment for *all* workers. The idea of working hybrid means that any individual could be joining any meeting from the office *or* virtually on any given day, depending on the flexible work option they have arranged. If everyone's participation is valued, everyone needs to be empowered to participate from anywhere, so shoring up the home office setup is an important piece of the hybrid puzzle.

The good news is that many organizations already accomplished this during the days of fully remote work. They subsidized purchases of webcams, ring lights, and external audio options like headsets. But the willingness to pay for enhancements to at-home setups was not universal. Research conducted for Microsoft's 2021 Work Trend Index found that only 46% of workers were reimbursed by their employer for remote work expenses (Microsoft 2021). Additionally, 1 in 10 reported that they didn't have adequate internet connection to do their job, a troubling statistic when inclusive meetings are an imperative.

"If you can't hear them and they can't hear you, people can't contribute," says Dr. Sean Rintel, a Microsoft principal researcher who focuses on meetings. If there is no standardization on at-home equipment, organizations run the risk of creating yet another tiered system, with the top tier being remote workers who show up with excellent visual and audio presence and the lower tier consisting of remote workers whose presence is lacking due to inferior image quality and audio drops. This is especially true if employers do not provide resources to their employees to outfit their home office. Depending on each individual's financial situation, they will purchase the camera and headset of their choosing, creating a truly nonstandard hodgepodge of audio and video quality. Therefore, standardization requires both specifying the camera and headset, and providing the resources to obtain them.

With the realization that virtual meetings aren't going away, organizations are starting to shift their thinking about outfitting home offices, according to Summit Leadership Partners' Dan Hawkins. He says that what used to be considered a perk is now just the cost of doing business: "Prior to COVID, the C-level might have had a fully paid home office with all of their equipment. Now, it's almost like giving someone their employee badge."

If you are among the organizations that already equipped your remote workers when the world was fully virtual, congratulations! You will continue to get a substantial return on your investment with hybrid meetings becoming the norm. However, if you've been holding off, now is definitely the time to do so. We will offer you some basic guidance here, but if you would like additional recommendations, we suggest you check out our previous book, *Suddenly Virtual*, which offers a much more in-depth look at how to empower your virtual meeting participants.

What Equipment Is Essential for the Remote Participants in Hybrid Meetings?

If you are looking for a place to start, sit at your desk when working from home and look straight ahead. If you're not staring at an external monitor, then heed these words from Logitech's Scott Wharton: "Step number one is you need a screen, because a laptop just isn't good enough to work all day from home. Once you make that decision, you need to accessorize everything around it. So, you're talking screen plus webcam, speaker, headset, mouse, keyboard."

The nonnegotiables? An HD webcam and a solid audio option. As we mentioned in Chapter 9, what is built-in to most laptops will not provide the same level of quality as an external camera and microphone (a headset, a standup microphone, or even a speaker-phone pod). Sending out a work-from-home kit that includes a webcam and an external microphone option sends a clear message: We want to make it easy as possible for you to exude presence in the hybrid room by helping you participate in full. We are sending you this equipment because we want to be able to see and hear you as clearly as possible. Your participation matters.

A word of warning: putting the right equipment in the hands of your workers removes one of the major barriers to their ability to participate effectively, but one thing that can't be controlled is how well individuals use the tools, unless a concerted effort is made to train people to do just that. Even if they figure out how to plug in the webcam, they could still end up making all sorts of missteps. They can still situate themselves oddly in the frame, cutting off the top of their head or their chin. They can choose to plop themselves down in front of cluttered shelves of collectibles that distract and detract from their message. The way to address these issues is through training, which we will discuss in full in Chapter 12.

Equipping for Meetings with External Stakeholders

During a hybrid meeting, you want those attending virtually to have the infrastructure to connect effectively with their teammates, but investing in a solid at-home setup also pays dividends for those employees who are customer- or client-facing. Hybrid meetings with external stakeholders are happening as well, often replacing traditional face-to-face meetings.

Many sales professionals are desperate to get back to the handshake model of doing business in person but are finding themselves spending more time on their webcams than they'd like. Research conducted by McKinsey & Company found that only about 20% of business-to-business (B2B) buyers hope to return to in-person sales (Bages-Amat, Harrison, Spillecke, and Stanley 2020). That includes industries where field-sales models have held a strong foothold, like pharma and medical products. In other words, sellers might want to be meeting face-to-face, but many of their customers may not want that.

Dave Egloff is a sales strategy and operations leader at Gartner who has seen this first-hand:

> Most sellers are clamoring to travel even when it's unnecessary. This makes sense since this is how they have found success previously. This is their playbook that they want to resurrect. The challenge is that many buyers don't need or even want to see sellers like they once did. Buyers are changing – therefore, sellers and sales execution must change.

Part of that change? Empowering people with the best equipment to help them land that sale through a virtual meeting.

Think about this real-world scenario. A sales team has a meeting with a client prospect who requested to meet virtually, not in person. Two of the sales professionals join from a conference room in their corporate office. A third colleague joins virtually. The two who are in the office know their video and audio will be top-notch because the conference room has been fully equipped and designed with hybrid meetings in mind, but the way the virtual attendee appears is a wild card. Imagine what would happen if they show up with subpar video that freezes and scratchy audio. What impression would that give the potential client? The way everyone shows up for that meeting is a reflection of the corporate brand. Ensuring that everyone is using high-quality equipment, both in the office and outside of it, provides professional polish that might be a differentiator.

Conclusion

In a complex communication environment like a hybrid meeting, it should be a corporate imperative to provide presence for all, but making sure everyone can see and hear each other clearly is only the beginning. Collaboration among the remote and in-room attendees needs to be supported as well, and, once again, technology can help, as we will discuss in Chapter 11.

Chapter Takeaways

- When equipping a meeting room for hybrid, the focus needs to be on creating presence for both the remote and the in-room attendees.

- Make sure virtual attendees are visually represented enough to provide parity with the in-person attendees.

- Increase the size and number of your monitors, and enhance the quality and features of your conference room cams to go beyond the "bowling alley view."

- Pay attention to the microphone ranges to ensure that everyone's voice in the room will be clearly heard.

- Keep it simple. The latest and greatest may be quickly outdated and underappreciated when ease of use is the top priority.

- Expect your meeting room setup to evolve over time as you observe how it is used during meetings. Be open to tweaking.

- If you did not do so when you went fully remote, consider standardizing the equipment for remote attendees with high-quality webcams and audio options.

References

Bages-Amat, A., L. Harrison, D. Spillecke, and J. Stanley. 2020. "These eight charts show how Covid-19 has CHANGED B2B sales forever." McKinsey & Company, October 23. https://www.mckinsey.com/business-functions/marketing-and-sales/our-insights/these-eight-charts-show-how-covid-19-has-changed-b2b-sales-forever

Lazar, I. 2021. "Weighing personal video conferencing endpoints for hybrid work." TechTarget.com. Retrieved August 30, 2021 from https://searchunified communications.techtarget.com/tip/Weighing-personal-video-conferencing-endpoints-for-hybrid-work?utm_campaign=20210830_Zoom+introduces+new+sharing+features&utm_medium=EM&utm_source=NLN&track=NL-1817&ad=940057&asrc=EM_NLN_177947418

Microsoft. 2021. *2021 Work Trend Index: Annual Report – The next great disruption is hybrid work – Are we ready?* https://ms-worklab.azureedge.net/files/reports/hybridWork/pdf/2021_Microsoft_WTI_Report_March.pdf

Wakabayashi, D., and C. Clifford. 2021. "Google's plan for the future of work: Privacy robots and balloon walls." *New York Times*, April 30. https://www.nytimes.com/2021/04/30/technology/google-back-to-office-workers.html

Chapter 11

Enabling Collaboration for All

The forecasts were dire. Take this headline from an October 2020 article in *Forbes*: "Work from Home Fallout: Productivity Up, Innovation Down" (McKendrick 2020). The article cited the results of a Microsoft survey of some 9,000 managers and employees across Europe that found 82% reporting productivity levels that were holding steady or increasing. That was juxtaposed with a concerning statistic: of those surveyed, only 40% considered their companies to be innovative, a 16-point drop from the year before.

Over the course of the time spent fully remote, many a manager and senior leader lamented the loss of face-to-face time, which they considered to be at the heart of developing new products and insights. But the anecdotal evidence runs to the contrary. Innovation actually accelerated across a wide spectrum of industries. Not only did some organizations come up with new ways of moving the needle by reconfiguring and creating new work flows that fit with their virtual reality (think healthcare and the availability of telehealth, for example), but they also figured out how to innovate and even launch new products and lines of business.

Allow us to share one such example from Pearson:

"We've been wildly successful," says CTO Steve Santana, who oversaw the development of Pearson+, which revolutionized how college students consume textbooks through a subscription model. The idea was hatched about nine months into the pandemic in December 2020, recalls Steve: "I was in the parking lot at a Best Buy buying Christmas presents where I was going over my budget numbers for Pearson+ on a Microsoft Teams call, everyone with 'video on' to establish trust."

Work on the app began in earnest in February 2021 with input from people all over globe. Team members from the UK, Ukraine, India, and both coasts of the United States worked within their own time zones, with even the primary customer research done virtually. As they approached the product launch in late July, hybrid meetings came back into play. Steve continues: "Toward the end, we had some groups of testers that were in conference rooms, and it became more like the way we were before the pandemic, where you have a bunch of people online and you have a room or a couple of rooms all meeting at once." What was most remarkable, though, was the end result. "This product has been delivered with our best quality and with the least amount of noise," Steve says with pride.

Innovation may not be defined by where it happens, but will be seriously limited if organizations don't empower collaboration with the right tools that it requires regardless of location. When hybrid, the way to do that is often reliant on technology that allows information to be put forth, played with, and stored in an inclusive way.

In this chapter, we will explore tools to:

- Enhance collaboration equity during a meeting
- Support the meeting continuum of collaboration
- Promote communication equity

Building Collaboration Equity During a Meeting

"If hybrid meetings are not productive and successful, with a high degree of inclusivity for all participants, then hybrid work itself is at risk," says Mike Fasciani of Gartner, who coined the term "collaboration equity" in an article for *TechTarget* (Irei 2021), where he sounded the alarm for companies that don't retool for the new way of working.

When meeting attendees are both in-person and remote, their ability to participate and influence decisions can be out of balance. Maybe the in-person attendees can dominate the discussion by not giving their remote colleagues an opportunity to cut in. Perhaps the remote attendees can more easily analyze the documents being shared on the videoconferencing platform because they can see them more clearly on their own individual screens. With so many businesses counting on and investing in hybrid, overlooking the potential inequities jeopardizes those plans for flexible work. Collaboration equity in a meeting means creating a level playing field for all attendees, allowing them to be on equal footing with colleagues in how they contribute and interact with each other. It means that meeting leaders, whether part of the in-person group or online, have to work to enable equal contribution in these collaboration environments.

Keep Using the Tools from Our Fully Remote Work Life

Step one in creating collaboration equity is to look to the past. When practically everyone migrated to video collaboration platforms as a result of the pandemic, not only did people learn to embrace video as a way to communicate, they also learned how to use some of the additional functionalities the platforms provided that filled in some of the communication gaps, like using chat to make an announcement to the entire group ("Going off video to answer the doorbell"). As we transition to hybrid meetings, organizations have an opportunity to leverage some of those practices born in the pandemic by continuing to use the tools that helped to create those new communication patterns.

One way to do that when hybrid is to have everyone still join the meeting from their own individual devices, even if they are in a conference room beside some of their colleagues. That's not to say that these colocated teammates are all using their own laptop cameras and built-in microphones and speakers. There's too much risk in audio feedback. Instead, the in-office cohort is represented on the screen by the meeting room camera (or cameras) and using the audio setup in the meeting room itself. You may be wondering, "What's the point of that?"

The point is this: having everyone join from their own laptops or other personal devices allows everyone to use the other platform features that they relied on when fully virtual. We're talking about the tools like chat, emoji reactions, polls, and other functionalities that helped people communicate better when they were all remote. When a meeting is made up of people who are in the same room and people who are virtual, these tools can still help to provide equal opportunity for everyone regardless of location. After all, we learned quite a bit during our "suddenly virtual" experience, and there's no need to throw away these learnings when they could unlock better collaboration and more communication parity. If you are in a meeting where at least some of the attendees are remote, consider the continued use of:

- *Chat* – As we've discussed in previous chapters, chat is a valuable way for participants to express opinions, ask questions, or make comments outside of the verbal discussion. A skilled meeting leader will weave all of that into the meeting dialogue, so input provided via text is given the same level of respect as input provided verbally. This is especially important when hybrid, because using chat helps ward off any potential in-room bias if the remote attendees are having a hard time breaking into the conversation.

- *Emojis* – Since the 2010s, most of us have learned a new language: emojis. Those graphic representations of moods or feelings now number over 1,800, and allow for text to have tone, even though it may not always be interpreted as intended (Nowak 2019). In all-virtual meetings, emojis served a variety of purposes. If you wanted to ask a question or make a comment, you could do so by raising your cartoonish hand. If an initiative required a "yes or no" vote, you could give an emoji thumbs-up or thumbs-down. If someone was presenting, you could applaud their efforts silently on screen so you wouldn't create audio disturbances for the entire audience. Emojis provide shorthand for emotions – something that can take on even greater import, especially if the remote employees might not be able to see the facial expressions of their in-office colleagues as well if they're appearing on one wide-angle view.

- *Polls* – If a meeting is larger than a couple of people, polls can be an effective way of reading the room. Within seconds, you can get a sense of where people stand on an issue, which can help drive the wider discussion. Polls also require all attendees to *do* something and serve as a way to reengage participants who may have tuned out. Being asked to respond to a poll may snap them back to attention.

Rid Your Meeting Space of Disconnected Tools

For organizations looking to retrofit their workspaces to allow for hybrid meetings, certain violations of meeting equity may be easy to identify because there will be tangible representations of an office-only orientation.

"Your company is either remote-first or office-first, and you can tell by walking into a hybrid office. If there is a physical whiteboard that is not connected to the internet, you are office-first. Rip the thing down," says Darren Murph, head of remote at GitLab.

Darren strongly endorses looking at all workflows, processes, and technology through the eyes of the remote worker who will be part of the hybrid equation. He stresses, "You have to remove all vestiges of nonconnected work if you ever hope that this is going to work. Replace the whiteboard with an LCD that streams photos and Slack messages from people outside of the office that serve as a constant reminder that your world is bigger than where you are currently standing."

Ripping things *down*, figuratively and literally, does require you to stand other things *up*, but what kinds of tools should you prioritize to empower collaboration during hybrid meetings? Once again, technology is changing faster than any static book can account for, so we will talk more about what *kinds* of tools are needed, rather than specific products that might be leaders today but laggards by tomorrow.

The Rise of the Digital Whiteboard

As much as an organization might love color-coded sticky notes and the smell of dry-erase markers, anything that requires in-person presence will sideline the remote attendees. Businesses are responding to that paradigm shift by investing in virtual whiteboard technology at a rate not seen before. According to Irwin Lazar of Metrigy, more than 40% of companies are looking at deploying them (Finnell 2021). Unlike physical whiteboards whose content can be erased, digital whiteboarding applications allow for everyone to draw or write on it regardless of location without concerns that what is created will be threatened by the cleaning crew. Virtual whiteboards allow for equitable participation during live brainstorming sessions, and equitable access to the information afterward by storing what was co-created online. Additionally, both in-office and remote team members can continue to build upon it over time because it's a living document.

Co-Authoring During a Meeting

Sometimes collaboration needs to occur around a document or report that does not lend itself to the whiteboarding process. If a team needs to create, revise, or edit a written document, sharing that document on the screen is essential so that everyone can stay on the same digital page. Real-time revisions in something like a Google Doc can be seen by all and added to by anyone who has been given editing authority. In a hybrid meeting, one person can share the document for all to see, but then everyone can manipulate it according to the level of privilege they've been assigned, whether it's as an editor, a commenter, or a viewer.

Consider the alternative: someone shares a static document on a video call and plenty of people want to make edits. The suggestions for new wording come in from all sides and the poor person who is sharing the document is doing their best to keep up. The process for revising that *one* document is clunky and time-consuming, and the majority of the burden is on the shoulders of the person who originally shared it.

With something like a Google Doc, multiple people can tweak the content simultaneously and the revisions are saved as you go along. Co-authoring becomes a truly collaborative experience in both the execution and the final product.

Tools to Promote Participation Equity

For all the reasons we mentioned in earlier chapters, achieving equitable participation for all hybrid meeting attendees can be a challenge. Strategies like inviting a moderator to monitor and prod for input from everyone or having an in-room buddy are part of the potential solution, but sometimes it can still be difficult for people to get into the conversation queue. The technology of today can assist you with this important task.

For example, Microsoft Teams has a feature called "raise hands" that is designed to reduce the cognitive burden for the meeting leader by adding automation to the participation process. When people click to raise their virtual hands, Teams sorts participants in order of whose hand was raised first, taking the guesswork out of it for the meeting leader. This is a great start, but there is a growing body of innovation that seeks to go beyond that and actually monitor participation in a data-based way.

Shiraz Cupala, director of product for Microsoft Teams, offers this prediction: "Over time, you'll start to see us make it easier for people to understand who hasn't had a chance to speak and to engage in more ways to make sure you've heard everyone's voice that needs to be and wants to be heard. So, you'll start to see tools to help you make your meetings more inclusive."

Joe and Karin's wish list for new innovations includes tools that could alert the meeting leader when they or others have spoken for a long time. Maybe a light could flash to let an attendee know that their comment has been longer than a specified time? Perhaps it could incorporate features that would indicate if the meeting was mostly presentation-based or discussion-based, and would identify who the primary presenter will be to allow them to speak beyond the typical limit. The idea would be to establish guardrails on participation to ensure equity in an automated way, similar to the systems used for political debates (even though many a politician has seemed to ignore those flashing lights indicating "time's up").

Tools to Support the Meeting Continuum of Collaboration

Even if you have managed to establish collaboration equity during the live meeting, what happens before and after a meeting are possible danger zones. That's why you need to leverage tools that consider the entire meeting continuum of collaboration. After all, meetings aren't just real-time events. It's a matter of considering the entire meeting lifecycle, according to Microsoft's Shiraz Cupala:

> What does it mean for a meeting to be effective? It's not about the meeting. It's about the work we're trying to get done together. It's about communicating with each other. Oftentimes, that happens before the meeting even starts. Obviously, during the meeting, we want to get together to have a real-time conversation, to work through a problem or to brainstorm and ideate. Then we want to take all that value that's in the meeting and make sure we capture it, so we can follow up and continue collaborating after the meeting.

The need to capture the pre-meeting and the post-meeting communication is consistent with meeting science. One of Joe's earlier studies focused on the kinds of conversations that occurred as people gathered for the meeting (Allen, Lehmann-Willenbrock, and Landowski 2014). What he found is that people talked about all sorts of things, some work-related and some not, but the science showed that pre-meeting conversations that focused on smalltalk, like last night's game, the latest show they streamed, or their kids, actually made the meeting better overall. Specifically, the smalltalk served as the social lubrication to get individuals who may initially be quiet to contribute later on in the meeting. All of that pre-meeting and post-meeting conversation not only serves to educate and inform meeting attendees but it also enables a sense of team cohesion (pre-meeting) while fostering action after the official meeting (post-meeting).

Prior to the pandemic, most corporate communication before and after a meeting was almost exclusively via email. Now, much of that communication is being done through channels created on collaboration platforms like Slack, Microsoft Teams, or Google Workspace, which link all of the various collaboration tools together.

This is music to the ears of Phil Simon, a recognized collaboration and technology expert, and author of the award-winning book *Reimagining Collaboration: Slack, Microsoft Teams, Zoom and the Post-COVID World of Work*. In 2021, Phil used his book to introduce what he calls the "Hub-Spoke Model of Collaboration." He writes that Slack, Microsoft Teams, and other internal collaboration hubs can stitch together previously fragmented tools and communication mediums.

The Hub-Spoke Model of Collaboration

So, what is the Hub-Spoke Model? Let's allow Phil to explain:

> A hub is a general-use application for all communication and collaboration. Say that I want to send you a file, or do a video call, or send you a message. Everything takes place in the hub. By contrast, a spoke is a piece of software that serves a specific purpose. Examples include DocuSign for signing documents, Workday for ERP, and Salesforce for CRM. Leaders need to stop thinking about all of these applications and systems as disjointed components. Rather, they should start viewing their technology as part of a single, holistic gestalt. The Hub-Spoke Model of

Collaboration stitches together all of the important applications and keeps everything in one place. It lets organizations build and maintain a shared and central knowledge repository.

So, what should you look for in a collaboration hub? Here are some top considerations:

- *Cost* – You may already have a collaboration hub that is bundled with other tools you currently use. In that case, paying for another one may not make sense. If not, many collaboration hubs allow you to take them out for a test drive at minimal or no cost. To get the full benefit of the platform, you will need to pay, but often it's per user, per month. This minimizes the initial start-up costs.
- *Compliance* – Different industries need to follow different regulatory environments. Choose one that meets those requirements and then ensure that people use it. Having people go rogue and use their own tools can introduce significant risk.
- *Culture* – The tools organizations use reflect their corporate personality. When choosing a collaboration hub, consider the company's culture. Identify what style of tool your people gravitate toward and find a collaboration hub that reflects it.

These collaboration hubs hold files in a wide variety of forms well beyond just text. Uploading a video file of a recorded meeting for those who missed the session, as we mentioned in Chapter 7, is just the start. This reorientation beyond the written word creates a whole new opportunity for collaboration outside of the meeting that makes the time spent in the session worthwhile.

Joe often talks about how the first type of meeting people should delete from their calendar is the information-sharing meeting. If all that is going to happen in a meeting is someone spouting information at people, then that can be done in a number of other, less time-consuming ways. We already mentioned email and other asynchronous text-based options. But, if you're like us, one more email just might blow up your inbox forever. That's a whole other issue that others have lamented for years: the ever-growing, ever-annoying inbox of emails to process. Therefore, let's consider other options, including asynchronous video and audio messages.

The Value of Asynchronous Video

With the rise of video call fatigue and the overall digital exhaustion due to the influx of information across a variety of channels, many organizations have turned to recorded video to disseminate information to both internal and external stakeholders. Video allows for the message to be delivered with greater nuance, accuracy, and richness, and also offers flexibility for the end user. Both PC and Mac laptops have this recording capability baked in, so it's only a matter of uploading the file to the collaboration platform of choice. Additionally, there are now a bevy of software companies that make this process even easier and more robust.

During the pandemic, enterprise video companies experienced tremendous growth. When people were forced to speak through a camera, they eventually began to embrace it more. Vidyard, a leading video platform for businesses, reported 250% growth from 2020 to 2021, driven largely by customers in sales and marketing who were hoping to better engage their customers and prospects (Duckett 2021). However, the use of recorded video internally has risen dramatically as well, and continues to play a large role in how organizations communicate – whether they're updating colleagues on a project or speaking to the enterprise as a C-level executive.

It's a common practice at Culture Amp, according to Jay Hyett: "I'm really encouraged by all of the asynchronous work being done at all levels. Our CEO, for example, will put out an update on a recorded message on a Slack channel so we can all watch it at our own time. It's not like you are going to miss what was said because he said it during a meeting in Melbourne and you live in San Francisco."

Jim Szafranski, CEO of Prezi, a communications software company, offers these suggestions for integrating asynchronous video into the corporate communications workflow (Kalita 2021):

- Record kickoff meetings for projects, so if someone new joins the team, they can watch the video and get quickly up to speed.

- Rather than shooting over an email, consider sending video messages back and forth to colleagues. Often, it's more efficient and easier to digest than a dense block of text.

- If you need to present information, consider recording yourself narrating the slide deck or spreadsheets and send it out to the key stakeholders. That video may mean one less meeting and a chunk of calendar space that is freed up for other work.

The Rise of Asynchronous Audio

Even though we are advocates for video, we do recognize that there are times we just aren't camera ready but still want to send a message with nuance, personality, and tone. There's another medium that is rising in popularity – asynchronous audio. Like video, you can say a lot in a little bit of time – and if you didn't like what you said the first time through, you can easily go back and re-record before you hit Send.

"Voice is high bandwidth. It's high resolution. You can get out a lot more information with voice than you can by typing," says Justin

Mitchell, CEO of Yac, a voice collaboration platform that allows users to record themselves and send out audio snippets to teammates. Need to update a colleague about an interaction you had with a sales target? Rather than sending over a calendar invite for a video call, you can send a voice message with searchable transcription. Have a status report you need to share with your project team? Rather than sending a 400-word email with a screenshot attached, record yourself voicing over a screen share to deliver it in a richer way.

Having audio files that you can listen to at a time that's right for you reflects the prioritization of flexible work. It allows you to stay on task and choose when to interrupt your own work flow, something that is not lost on Yac's CEO, who appreciates that you can consume the information passively: "One of my favorite things to do throughout the day is to let my recorded team updates pile up for a little bit," says Justin. "I will go for a walk and hit my 'Play all' button in Yac, It's just like a miniature podcast. It's a great way to understand what my team is working on without having to be strapped to my desk and staring at a video call."

The use of richer media to convey messages efficiently and powerfully is a positive step, but many companies are also incorporating another tool that allows for even more inclusive collaboration: captioning.

Tools to Promote Communication Equity

Making all communication visible for all is a key component of hybrid meeting success, but if you are deaf or hard of hearing, a video without captions loses most if not all of its value. The problem is compounded when you are dealing with a multinational team that doesn't all speak the same language. This is the very scenario that prompted the birth of CaptionHub, a software company that specializes in amazingly accurate captioning with multilingual translation.

CEO Tom Bridges recalls the business problem they were asked to solve by a global tech company:

> The head of the retail division was giving a weekly talk to her team as an internal communications exercise, but her team speaks 26 different languages. Traditionally, it would take a week to localize this five-minute video into 26 different languages. So, it instantly made second-class citizens out of all of those people who don't speak English. This company, quite rightly in my opinion, said, "That's not acceptable. We need perfection, but we need to accelerate it. We need you to turn it around in a day." And so that's where CaptionHub was born.
>
> Captioning and subtitling will break down barriers, but it's not just the ability to communicate. It's how you can communicate and how fast you can communicate. That time to market is a really key part of what we're doing.

In a virtual and hybrid workplace always at risk of information silos, any tools that help break down walls to clear and inclusive communication is not just a "nice to have," it's a "need to have." CaptionHub experienced tremendous growth during the pandemic as companies recognized the need, and interest has not waned with the transition to hybrid. With video usage proliferating across the corporate landscape, captions unlock access to information that might otherwise be untouchable for some.

"A really key part of what we're doing is we're making video searchable . . . it's text that has a timecode," says Tom, who considers captions to be a critical part of any company's video strategy. "A big part of what we're doing is enabling that information to be shared in a more digestible, searchable form."

Given the burgeoning science related to the benefits of diversity, equity, and inclusion, tools like these may hold the key to enabling greater creativity in organizations. Accessible information for all leads to greater diversity of thought, unleashing both higher levels of performance and innovation.

CaptionHub has also proved the skeptics wrong who thought innovation would be hampered or even halted if people weren't colocated. They recently launched live products with real-time transcription and translation – products that were launched with their team dispersed across continents.

"To say that you can't innovate without being in the same room . . . I don't buy that," says Tom. "I think we just need a different approach. I do genuinely believe that modern tools are working really well."

Conclusion

Over the past two chapters, we've discussed ways to set yourself up for hybrid meeting success from an equipment and technology standpoint. Creating presence and enabling collaboration for everyone, whether they are joining in person or remote, are two key pillars for an effective hybrid meeting environment. At the end of this chapter, you'll find a checklist of hybrid meeting technology considerations based on what we presented in both chapters.

However, just having the tools does not mean people will use them well . . . or even use them at all. In Part Five, we will talk about training, arguably the biggest factor in the success or failure of your hybrid meetings, and we'll offer you a framework for evaluating your transition to this modern meeting modality.

Chapter Takeaways

- Collaboration equity in a meeting allows all attendees to be on equal footing in how they contribute and interact with each other.

- Build upon the habits from our fully remote world by using the collaboration tools found in videoconferencing platforms, even when in person.

- Remove any disconnected tech from meeting rooms that may marginalize the remote attendees.

- Lighten the cognitive burden of tracking participation by using some of the automated tools already available.

- Make sure all information relevant to the meeting is available and accessible to all. Collaboration hubs such as Slack, Microsoft Teams, and Google Workspace create knowledge repositories that can be used to keep all related materials in one place.

- Embrace trends that go beyond text. Lean into asynchronous video and audio.

- Captioning is imperative for creating an inclusive collaboration environment.

Hybrid Meeting Technology Considerations

How are we creating "Presence for All"?	Yes or No
1. We have equipped our meeting rooms with large monitors.	[ ] Yes [ ] No
2. We have positioned the monitors in our meeting rooms to simulate a natural conversation configuration.	[ ] Yes [ ] No
3. We have invested in high-quality cameras in our meeting rooms.	[ ] Yes [ ] No

(Continued)

Enabling Collaboration for All

How are we creating "Presence for All"?	Yes or No
4. Our in-room audio systems allow everyone to be heard clearly.	[ ] Yes [ ] No
5. We have equipped anyone who may join virtually with high-quality cameras and audio devices.	[ ] Yes [ ] No
6. We have equipped remote workers with external monitors to cut down on fatigue.	[ ] Yes [ ] No

TOTAL YES _____

How are we enabling "Collaboration for All"?	
1. We continue to use collaboration tools on meeting platforms even when hybrid.	[ ] Yes [ ] No
2. We have switched from physical whiteboards to digital whiteboards.	[ ] Yes [ ] No
3. We use documents that allow coauthoring in real time by multiple people.	[ ] Yes [ ] No
4. We use tools on the meeting platform to help with participation parity.	[ ] Yes [ ] No
5. We house all of the information assets from a meeting in one place that is accessible to all attendees.	[ ] Yes [ ] No
6. We use a variety of media to communicate messages related to the meeting.	[ ] Yes [ ] No
7. We use captioning software to make collaboration more inclusive.	[ ] Yes [ ] No

TOTAL YES _____

References

Allen, J. A., N. Lehmann-Willenbrock, and N. Landowski. 2014. "Linking pre-meeting communication to meeting effectiveness." *Journal of Managerial Psychology* 29 (8): 1064–1081.

Duckett, S. 2021. "Vidyard reports record-breaking growth as video becomes essential for digital-first sales and marketing." *Vidyard*, June 10. https://www.vidyard.com/press-releases/video-essential-for-digital-first-selling/

Finnell, K. 2021. "Hybrid workplace model starts with meeting rooms, video." *TechTarget*, March 17. https://searchunifiedcommunications.techtarget.com/feature/Hybrid-workplace-model-starts-with-meeting-rooms-video

Irei, A. 2021. "5 hybrid video conferencing tips for collaboration equity." *Tech Target*, August 2. https://searchunifiedcommunications.techtarget.com/feature/5-hybrid-video-conferencing-tips-for-collaboration-equity

Kalita, S. M. 2021. "How to run a meeting – rather than have meetings running us." *Fortune*, June 2. https://fortune.com/2021/06/02/how-to-run-a-meeting-rather-than-have-meetings-running-us/

McKendrick, J. 2020. "Work from home fallout: Productivity up, innovation down." *Forbes*, October 20. https://www.forbes.com/sites/joemckendrick/2020/10/18/work-from-home-fallout-productivity-up-innovation-down/?sh=374f13a8668d

Nowak, C. 2019. "Why do we use emojis anyway? A fascinating history of emoticons." *Reader's Digest*, May 15. https://www.rd.com/article/history-of-emoji/

PART FIVE

Setting Expectations

People are resistant to change, and hybrid meetings demand a lot of it. They require new tools, new approaches, a new mindset. It's not realistic to expect everyone to get on board – expect some pushback and even noncompliance. However, there is a method that many organizations are leaning heavily into right now that can drive user adoption: training.

In a 2021 survey of human resource leaders conducted by Gartner, 68% say they are prioritizing building critical skills and competencies. This is for good reason, because that same survey indicated that nearly three-quarters of respondents reported that more than 40% of their workforce has had to use new skills as a result of COVID-19 (Gartner 2021). For employees fresh off adapting to the new workflows developed while fully remote, the idea of having to learn a whole new way of working when hybrid may sound exhausting. Organizations that both recognize the need for change and also offer sufficient training and support to help their employees adjust and adopt will find success. We find one such illustration of a business embracing the hybrid environment in what some might consider an unlikely place: the financial services sector.

"I don't know that there's much of an older business than banking. The interaction where you go in and you see a teller – that really hasn't changed much in the last 100 years," says Rick Sems, executive vice president at First Bank, one of the largest privately held, family-owned banks in the country, based out of St. Louis, Missouri. First Bank has been streamlining their processes for several years now, but COVID-19 accelerated that and pushed them in new directions. "It really changed to a point where our clients were no longer standing right in front of us. It turned to more virtual meetings."

For First Bank, that opened up an opportunity for the introduction of new ways to connect with their customers. They introduced virtual bankers, real people who help customers conduct teller transactions through videoconferencing. The tellers appear on screen at special ATMs called ITMs (interactive teller machines), and guide customers through their immediate banking needs, whether that's depositing a check or checking their balance.

"We wanted professionalism. We wanted a smile, and we want the smile to come through the screen," said Rick. But this was uncharted territory for First Bank, and they knew they needed help in honing the on-camera presence and engagement of their virtual bankers. What did they do? They brought in an outside expert to train them, knowing how important that first impression to customers is. Rick explains, "That's why it has been so important for us to do that training, because you don't want people to have a bad experience. Customers will remember that, but especially early on, if you can deliver a good experience with the technology, that can make a big difference in how they accept it."

So far, the results have been very positive, with client satisfaction reports and customer experience metrics like Net Promoter Scores

(NPS) for the ITMs better than they anticipated. That's prompted a move toward using video in other areas as well, with plans to introduce it for other customer support services that might have traditionally been done over the phone and will soon be done through videoconferencing.

The use of video communication also allows for an easier transition to a hybrid approach in the branches themselves. Instead of just face-to-face interactions, each branch will have a combination of concierge bankers who will be available in person to handle things like opening an account, along with the tellers who will be available virtually through the ITMs to handle transactions. Rick says it's an evolution: "We're changing every branch. We're taking out space. We're taking out walls. We're putting in a little bit more technology so you can get your answers quickly. You can pick your path, your journey. You can stay as short or as long as you want in a branch."

Hybrid work is all about giving employees choices in how and where they work, but customers are also asking for choices in how they engage as well. First Bank recognized that shift, and is seeking to meet customers where they want to be met. However, no matter the modality, First Bank wants to ensure that the customer comes away with a positive impression. Training their people in how to achieve that is key, says Rick: "At the end, it's about how do you make that client comfortable? How do you make them feel good about the interaction? That training of what we expect was just critical."

At the heart of the transition to hybrid is an all-encompassing change management process with many moving parts – a process that will not be successful if organizations do not set expectations and then invest in the training that will empower their people to meet them. In this final part, we will discuss the importance of building a training program around hybrid meetings. We'll look at the components of an effective training plan in general, and then translate it to a specific training program for hybrid meeting success (Chapter 12). How do you know if you are on the right path? In Chapter 13, we'll give you a framework for evaluating your efforts thus far, as well as presenting potential next steps.

Reference

Gartner. 2021. *Top 5 Priorities for HR Leaders in 2021*. Report by Gartner for HR. Retrieved August 16, 2021 from https://www.gartner.com/ngw/globalassets/en/human-resources/documents/trends/top-priorities-for-hr-leaders-2021.pdf

Chapter 12

Skill Up for Hybrid Collaboration Success

Applause . . . rolling, rousing applause. Not something most IT people are used to hearing from their fellow employees, but that's indeed what kept happening to Eric Taylor.

As an IT specialist at a leading business analytics company, he was in charge of teaching people how to move from an old Avaya phone system to Skype, which required them to use their computers to make their calls. The initial announcement generated some passionate responses, Eric recalls: "There was literally one gentleman on Yammer who said, 'You can have my phone when you pry it from my cold dead hands.'"

That might have made some IT people do an immediate about-face, but Eric and his team pressed on with a strategy that ended up not only driving user adoption but also creating fans. They did a series of town hall training sessions for departments across the enterprise. Eric explains, "The way we drove adoption was literally me getting up on stage or in front of a conference room with 40 or 50 people at a time and showing them on the screen: 'Look, first you click here. Then you do this and then you click here.'" That step-by-step live tutorial was just what his fellow workers needed to build their confidence. They could master that new way of communicating because Eric showed them how.

He also took the opportunity to explain the reasoning behind the move, something that he recommends to any IT department rolling out new tools. "I am the biggest proponent of explaining 'The Why.' Don't just do something. Tell them why you're doing it because then they can kind of conceptualize it." In the case of the move to Skype, Eric explained how much more robust the system was and the improved functionality that allowed them to carry it with them anywhere in the world. He even told them about the app that they could install on their phones, and suddenly, the naysayers became the proponents. Eric recalls, "Then that guy who said, 'You can have my phone when you pry it from my cold dead hands,' starts to say, 'That's awesome. How do I get it?' The conversation totally changes, but you have to train folks."

The role of trainer is not one that most IT people envisioned they would be asked to fill, but with technology being such a core part of the move to hybrid, it's a role that is necessary and surprisingly rewarding. Eric relates, "It was bizarre to be an IT guy teaching people how to use an IT solution, but at the end, they would literally applaud you like you had just starred in a movie. So, training is key. And it can be rough at first, but it pays dividends."

But the payoff will only be partial if you focus solely on training on the tech. You also need to train people on the processes required to make hybrid work. In this chapter, we will discuss why organizations need to do both as part of their transition to hybrid meetings, and how to craft a training process that, in the words of Eric Taylor, "pays dividends."

In this chapter, we will explore:

- The potential performance drop due to the hybrid meeting learning curve and how to avoid it
- The components of effective training programs

- What needs to be in every hybrid meeting and collaboration training
- How, with a little training, the future could be very collaborative

Avoiding the Performance Drop

The overwhelming concern when everyone was sent home, besides the virus (as if that wasn't enough), was whether we all would be able to work effectively while remote. Would the great remote-work experiment work for the majority of knowledge workers across many different industries? As we've already explored in previous chapters, the surprising answer was yes! In fact, some organizations that took care of their workers, providing them with resources and tools to make their remote workstation effective, saw performance gains. That was definitely not what many people had predicted, although social scientists who study work–family balance and alternative work schedules thought it might happen this way. Most of their research supported the notion that people who were granted alternative work schedules or even remote work *before* the pandemic were just as or *more* productive than their colocated colleagues in the office (Bolino, Kelemen, and Matthews 2021).

Now with the relaxation of pandemic restrictions, we have a new set of questions:

- Will hybrid work create a performance drop?
- Will bringing people back to the office while allowing others to remain remote, either some or part of the time, cause unforeseen problems?
- Will people be able to collaborate effectively in their meetings when there are three people in a room and three people on camera?

The answer to these questions is the most common response from academics across the organizational sciences: it depends!

Anecdotally, we often consider anything that requires a lot of effort to master as having a steep learning curve. What do we mean by that? Well, essentially the learning curve is a graphical representation of the proficiency of a person at performing a task over time (Epple, Argote, and Devadas 1991). Figure 12.1 shows an example.

In other words, for the majority of tasks, people tend to get better at doing things the longer they do them. You probably noticed this with virtual meetings, as the number of "Hey, you're on mute!" statements actually started to decline for teams that started engaging in the best practices previously identified. Basically, we got better at using the tools and remembering where and when to find the mute button.

Like our virtual meeting experience, hybrid meetings and the collaboration before, during, and after them will have a learning curve. It will take time and persistence to get better at them, and a

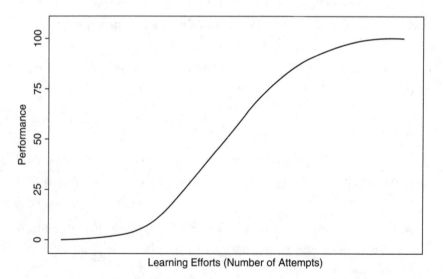

Figure 12.1 The Learning Curve

performance drop is to be expected. However, the questions leaders and individuals need to consider are:

- How much of a performance falloff is okay to them?
- What are they willing to do to mitigate one?

There are three things you must do to avoid a performance drop when it comes to hybrid meetings and collaboration:

1. Have the right tools and equipment
2. Have the right training on the tools and equipment
3. Level up the skills needed to run hybrid meetings effectively

Training on the Tools

With respect to our first two points – having the right tools and equipment, and having the right training – IT leaders in organizations are suddenly thrust into the reluctant superhero role, and if they play it well, they may earn the applause of their coworkers just like Eric Taylor did. It will be well warranted. After all, they have had to be at the forefront of the software and hardware solutions hitting the market in response to the transition to hybrid, and they've had to make decisions about which of those tools to put in the hands or at the fingertips of employees.

When virtual, organizations and their people were in emergency mode. They weren't looking for what worked best. They were looking for what worked – period. Sometimes that meant using software that wasn't the official company option, but that has changed. Gone are the early days of everyone just using whatever videoconferencing platform they wanted. Now IT organizations are standardizing on one, maybe two platforms that serve distinct purposes, perhaps one for internal meetings and another for meetings with external stakeholders.

But simply having the tools available does not guarantee they are used. Karin saw this first-hand during the pandemic when she trained countless people how to communicate through a webcam. Part of the coaching process involved helping people to spruce up their personal production value – making sure their video, audio, lighting, and background were as polished as possible. When a client would show up for an individual coaching session with a pixelated or fuzzy image on the screen, Karin would ask what kind of camera they were using. Often, they would say it was their laptop webcam, but then they would add, "Yeah, we were sent webcams by corporate but mine's still in the box." Karin would ask them to grab that box from the closet, and then walk them through the process of setting it up. Without exception, every person was amazed by the difference in video quality that the external webcam produced, but until Karin insisted, they didn't consider it a priority to take it out of the box.

In order to keep tools from gathering dust, figuratively and literally, IT personnel will need to be able to advocate for the right tools for employees and also be willing to provide group and individual instruction on how they work. Leaving people to figure it out on their own is putting too much faith in both their ability to do so and their willingness or availability to set aside time to train themselves. By designating certain days or even hours to train people on a new piece of software or the new meeting room setup, it demonstrates to employees that what they are learning truly matters. It is important enough to warrant taking them away from their day-to-day duties so they can learn how to use new tools that are pivotal to hybrid meeting success. Think about the signal that sends.

When it comes down to it, it's also in the best interest of the IT department. A few group training sessions to roll out new software or hardware could save them from countless tech support calls from people who are likely to ask the same questions over and over again, which can be a bit mind-numbing for the IT folks.

Within every enterprise, there's a wide array of technical skill. Assuming everyone will be able to adopt and adapt to new technology is a fool's errand. Take the time to train your people on the tech you have spent so much time and money implementing. When you lower the barrier to entry by helping employees understand how to use it, you will get a much higher return on your investment.

Having the right equipment is simply the ticket to play, but if you stop there, you've missed the third leg of our three-legged stool. Training your people on how to manage their team or themselves during a hybrid meeting is also essential, and most people new to hybrid won't understand what that requires. So, let's first review what a good training program requires.

The Six Components of Effective Training Programs

As an organizational scientist, Joe has both taught the topic of training to graduate students as well as developed and implemented training programs within organizations. Following the best practices endorsed by the Society for Industrial and Organizational Psychology (SIOP 2021), there are six components to effective training programs. We will address each of the six components here in general and then apply them to a representative knowledge worker organization in the next section.

1. ***Pretraining environment.*** The pretraining environment refers to the situational characteristics within the organization that will enable or constrain the training. This includes the individual differences among the learners, the support for the training from the organization and its leaders, and the level at which the training is communicated, from basic to advanced. Depending on the nature of these characteristics, the training will need to vary in its depth, breadth, and components.

2. ***Needs assessment.*** The needs assessment refers to the process of uncovering what the training needs to accomplish. What are the goals of the organization and the overall tasks that need to be completed? Additionally, what is the status of people's knowledge level relative to the training topic? Depending on the organization and the nature of the training, different levels of the training may be needed to aid novices all the way to experts in a given area. The needs assessment should help identify these differences and help determine the scope of training that may be required.

3. ***Training design.*** Once the needs assessment is done, the training can then be designed to deliver the content. What topics will be covered? Where will the training be held and in what format? For example, will the training be onsite, offsite, or hosted virtually or hybrid? That decision has a huge impact on how the instructor will go about delivering the content and is a good first question to ask once the needs assessment is completed.

4. ***Training implementation.*** Training implementation is all about the execution of it, but it also includes how an organization ensures everyone who needs the training is able to receive it. Some organizations may mandate the trainings. Some are even required by various federal or state laws, such as training mandated by Title 9. Regardless, implementation is all about carrying out the planned training and being flexible to adjust the approach as needed for the learner.

5. ***Training transfer.*** Training transfer refers to the degree to which the training is used at three levels:

   - First, do they start using the training materials, the newly learned skills, and the behaviors taught to them while on the job?

- Second, do they persist in using these new skills and behaviors over time?
- Third, do they adapt the skills and behaviors as the job changes or new tools are introduced?

In other words, does the training stick, or does it go in one ear and out the other? Joe often jokes that he thinks there's a delete button on the back of some students' heads. It seems like when they leave the classroom, they tap the button, and all the learning that just happened is erased. What it more likely represents is a lack of training transfer, which requires some motivation on the part of the learner. Self-motivated individuals may not have a problem with training transfer, but less motivated people might, and that's where the pretraining environment becomes evident as the key to the success of a training initiative. How much external motivation is given to learners by their managers or the organization as a whole to get trained and use the new skills? If the managers or the organization do not exhibit buy-in to the importance of the training, it is unlikely that training transfer will occur.

6. *Training evaluation.* This refers to the process of assessing whether the training did what it was supposed to do. Typically, this is done on four levels, following the most studied and used training evaluation model by Donald Kirkpatrick (2009).

   - *Level 1 is the reaction level.* At this level we simply ask what participants thought of the training. Did they like it? Was it engaging? Was it relevant?
   - *Level 2 is the learning level.* In this one, we ask about the knowledge and skills that they were expected to acquire. This might take the form of a test in some cases.
   - *Level 3 is behavior.* We want to know the degree to which the learners apply what they learned once they are

back on the job. We mentioned training transfer earlier. This level is where we measure it.

- **_Level 4 is results._** This is commonly known as training evaluation. That is, did we get the outcomes we wanted from the training? Outcomes from most trainings include performance gains as a result of the application of the new skills to the job.

Think about your last training experience on the job. Did you witness all six components occurring? It is unfortunately uncommon for organizations or the consulting firms they hire to incorporate every step discussed here. Of particular neglect are levels three and four: the transfer of training and the training evaluation components. Why? Because if it doesn't work, do the people who championed it in the organization really want to know that? It's likely the consulting firm that delivered the training doesn't want to know, either. If it didn't work, then that makes both those groups look bad, so there's an inherent social bias against the last two steps to a good training. Ideally, clear metrics will be established in advance of the training initiative and used as a way to measure success. If the training falls short of its goals, don't simply give up. Usually a refresher session or a more narrowly focused training that addresses a particular skills gap will enhance the integrity of the original skill-building work and make the key learnings stick.

Applying the Six Components to Hybrid Meeting and Collaboration Training

With the six components defined generally, let's help you construct the best plan for training your people to handle a hybrid meeting. Since the six components follow a chronological order, we'll consider each one. Take note that this plan is outlined for organizations in general. You may need to tailor it for your own unique needs.

1. ***Pretraining environment.*** For a hybrid meeting and collaboration training, the pretraining environment is going to vary widely based on how hybrid an organization is. Is everyone on a flexible work arrangement, or only certain teams or individual contributors? When that question has been answered, the first thing a training organizer needs to consider is who and how many need the training. Other questions to consider include:

   - Is it likely that the entire enterprise will be engaging in hybrid meetings, or will only certain departments?
   - Do you observe skills gaps that exist from our fully virtual work life, and do those need to be addressed first?
   - Have most been using virtual meetings without much difficulty, or are there still folks who need help figuring that out?

   You might be surprised by what you learn as you dig into the pre-training environment.

2. ***Needs assessment.*** The needs assessment is all about identifying where the gaps are. For meeting leaders, we need to find out their knowledge concerning meeting facilitation, their use of technology in meetings, their situational awareness levels, and their comfort with leading and directing behavior in meetings. For meeting attendees, we need to find out how much they engage in multitasking in meetings, how willing they are to participate with and without prompting, and how comfortable they are with using the tools provided to them. We recommend this approach: repurpose the checklists in the book and use them as an assessment guide to find out how often

people are following best practices. In a large organization, this may be done in the form of a survey. In a smaller organization, a short set of questions relative to these topics could be asked of each individual to get a feel for what the need is.

3. ***Training design.*** For this component, the person who will be building the training should use the information gathered in the needs assessment to decide how much breadth and depth is required across the topic areas. For example, let's say we learn that very few people have had facilitation training or even have seen a meeting facilitated by a professional. That means we'd want to spend a good amount of time on facilitation basics, such as how to ensure that everyone participates in a discussion, or how to enable idea generation by both remote and in-person participants. Design also pertains to how the training will be delivered. Will it be conducted in person, virtual, or hybrid? Will it be in the form of a pre-recorded webinar with or without live Q&A, or a high-touch workshop with interaction throughout? Our advice would be to do it hybrid so that you can literally demonstrate the desired behaviors in the training itself. This would allow for role-playing activities, which takes the training from factual to practical.

4. ***Training implementation.*** Now it's time to do the training. Assuming that you've been able to figure out a way to do it live and hybrid, you would want to make sure to emulate as many of the best practices from this book as possible. After all, it's much more impactful when in a training, the instructor can say, "Just as I started this training on time, all of your hybrid meetings should begin on time as well." And it bears

repeating that the training is in fact a meeting, and so be sure to demonstrate effective meeting practices when doing the training. This is particularly important if the training is to be recorded and shared with others, as they will be looking and attending to any errors relevant to effective hybrid collaboration. By doing the training well once, it then could be standardized and shared throughout the organization. No matter what format you land on, we do recommend making it as interactive as possible with plenty of opportunity to answer questions, dive into deeper discussions on certain topics of greater interest, and share real-world examples among participants.

5. ***Training transfer.*** The majority of the training transfer will take place outside of the actual hybrid meeting training itself. We will see it demonstrated in the office or within the meetings we participate in after the training. For example, many organizations are reworking their conference rooms to accommodate hybrid meetings. Training transfer would be observed if we see these rooms being used more for that meeting modality, and if the trend toward hybrid continues. We'd also hope to see better participation in hybrid meetings, with leaders and attendees working together to include everyone in the conversation. The good news is, it won't be hard to find case studies. With the meetingization of our work lives, you will have plenty of opportunities to observe whether the techniques taught are being used with greater frequency in organizations' own meetings.

6. ***Training evaluation.*** The best way to evaluate the success of a training is to refer back to the needs assessment. Have we seen the changes in knowledge, skills, and other characteristics

that we hoped to see improve? In addition to that, we recommend targeting each of the four levels we discussed earlier. Find out how participants liked the training. See if they remember the information taught. Have them self-report on whether they or their peers are doing the expected behaviors. And, perhaps most importantly, find out if their hybrid meetings are just as good as or better than the virtual or face-to-face meetings they have been more acquainted with. After all, we are looking to get immediate results, such as good meetings, as well as more distant results, such as sustained employee engagement and overall performance. These latter outcomes require more sustained effort in embracing and using the best practices from the training, both individually as an attendee and also as a leader of hybrid meetings.

To help you begin building the training plan for your organization, we've provided a table of the questions we recommend asking and considering. This is by no means exhaustive, because every organization is different, and therefore, the needs and challenges will be different. But this list will help you get started with the process and hopefully allow you to carry it forward to fruition.

Questions to Consider in Preparing a Hybrid Meeting Training Using the Six Components

Component	Questions to Consider
1. Pretraining environment	• How supportive is the organization of remote work and hybrid collaboration?
	• What are the plans/policies related to hybrid or remote work?
	• What is the adoption rate among employees of virtual meeting tools that will be used when hybrid?

Component	Questions to Consider
2. Needs assessment	• What are the skills we want people to have? • Do we have a survey tool that we can program to ask about the skills needed for effective hybrid meetings? • How long should the survey or list of questions be? • Who will compile the results for consideration in designing the appropriate training?
3. Training design	• How will the training be delivered? • Based on the needs assessment, how deep and broad do you need to go in each of the key topics/skill areas? • Who will deliver the training? • Can the training be done hybrid, thereby allowing for demonstration and role-play?
4. Training implementation	• When will the training be delivered? • How will we incorporate best practices for hybrid meetings into the logistics of the training (i.e. practice what we preach)? • What other logistical needs do we need to address prior to the training?
5. Training transfer	• Are the newly refurbished conference rooms being used with greater frequency for hybrid meetings? • Do we see more of the participation and inclusion behaviors occurring in meetings? • Several months after the training, is the software and hardware being used in all the ways trained? • Several months after the training, do we still see the best practices for hybrid meetings happening with regularity?

(Continued)

Component	Questions to Consider
6. Training evaluation	• What are the immediate outcomes we want from the training (e.g. more satisfying/effective hybrid meetings)?
	• What are the longer-term outcomes we want from the training (e.g. increased employee engagement and performance)?
	• To what degree are the learners engaging in the behaviors taught during the training?
	• How sustained are the efforts (i.e. consistent behaviors) made by the learners as they get further from the training?

Training That Scales and Sticks

If you happen to be a learning and development professional in a large organization, you may be struggling with how to scale your training. Not only is there a seemingly endless list of new skills that need to be taught, but also they often need to be taught to a wide swath of the enterprise. With hybrid meeting environments, practically everyone should be at least exposed to best practices for making hybrid meetings effective. The larger challenge might be making sure the training sticks.

"The big thing I worry about is: How do we quality-control across the masses?" says Kerry Troester, director of North America training and development at Lenovo. For now, she and her team are concentrating on the sales force, which is 900 people strong, helping them continue to hone their video communication and engagement skills. That means ensuring that people look and sound their best whether they are in person or virtual, so the first impression they make is a good one.

"When you are a sales rep, for example, that is how you're retaining your customer or making and closing deals. You have to have a whole higher level of performance," Kerry continues. "Across the board, we're trying to just upskill everyone and set some standards for how people interact. Every customer interaction makes an impression, and there's a new standard, I think, in how people expect to have a meeting."

Those expectations are a moving target as we proceed further along the hybrid meeting transition journey, which means that just when your team seems to have mastered one thing, they may need to learn another. All the while, training departments are fighting the gravitational pull of old behaviors. People tend to regress back to what they are used to, what they know, or what they did in the past. Therefore, we have a final recommendation relative to training people for better hybrid meetings: consider creating an abbreviated "booster shot" training. Just as a booster shot for a vaccine resurges the antibodies in the human body, booster shot training reenergizes the learner to keep going, keep doing the good work, and keep flexing those hybrid meeting skills. This training should be brief, hit the high points of the initial training, and help inspire maintaining the good behaviors originally taught. With any training, you are fighting the forgetting curve, the memory model that shows how information we learn fades over time (Ebbinghaus 1885). Without a refresher, the forgetting curve wins. That initial training investment is lost because people will revert back to what worked before – even if what worked before was not the best solution for the current hybrid workforce.

Hybrid meetings are a whole new animal for most organizations, and you may see employees try to opt out of having them and go back to all virtual or all in-person meetings. However, we believe firmly that if individuals and organizations skill up a bit, the hybrid meeting could be better than all the other modalities. Why? Because it can ensure inclusion. No other form of meetings allows for multimodal participation, which creates more opportunity for people to be able to attend. With hybrid, if the tools are in place, everyone can engage from anywhere they are, regardless of the circumstances. All voices that should be heard can be heard, resulting in a richer meeting where the sum is greater than the parts. Therefore, hybrid meetings that use all the best practices contained in this book have the potential to be both effective and inclusive.

Conclusion

Bringing the tools and training together is the key to a bright hybrid future. When people know what the best practices are for hybrid meetings, then it's in their hands to make them work. Conversely, if they don't even know what to do with those tools or how to use them well, there's no chance for success. Let's ensure that people have the hardware, software, and what we will call "skillware" to be successful in the new hybrid work and meeting environment. Once we do that, we have the potential to avoid the dreaded performance drop-off, and instead, greatly accelerate people up the learning curve. By doing these things, and those discussed throughout this book, we anticipate seeing a healthy transition to hybrid meetings and collaboration for many individuals and organizations. It is to this healthy transition we now turn in our final chapter.

Chapter Takeaways

- Without training people on how to use the new technology for hybrid meetings, people will likely not use it to best effect, or possibly not use it at all.

- Don't leave people on their own to figure out the new technology. Set up a series of training sessions to help them gain the competence and confidence to use them.

- Training people how to manage their teams and themselves during hybrid meetings is equally as important as training them on the tech itself.

- There are six components of an effective training program:

  1. Pretraining environment

  2. Needs assessment

  3. Training design

  4. Training implementation

  5. Training transfer

  6. Training evaluation

- Create your hybrid meeting training plan by including the six components just listed.

- Don't stop with just one initial training. Design a "booster shot" training to give at a later date to stop bad habits from reappearing.

References

Bolino, M. C., T. K. Kelemen, and S. H. Matthews. 2021. "Working 9-to-5? A review of research on nonstandard work schedules." *Journal of Organizational Behavior* 42 (2): 188–211.

Ebbinghaus, H. 1885. *Über das gedächtnis: untersuchungen zur experimentellen psychologie*. Duncker & Humblot.

Epple, D., L. Argote, and R. Devadas. 1991. "Organizational learning curves: A method for investigating intra-plant transfer of knowledge acquired through learning by doing." *Organization Science* 2 (1): 58–70.

Kirkpatrick, J., & Kirkpatrick, W. (2009, November). "The Kirkpatrick model: Past, present, and future." *Chief Learning Officer, 8* (11), 20–24.

Society for Industrial and Organizational Psychology (SIOP). 2021. *An Instructor's Guide for Introducing Industrial-Organizational Psychology*. https://www.siop.org/Events-Education/Educators/I-O-Resources-for-Teachers/I-O-Psychology-Content

Chapter 13

Signs of a Healthy Hybrid Transition

Within a hybrid environment, meetings and collaboration are challenging and require effort to ensure success, but it's effort that pays off and can directly impact the bottom line. By allowing employees and their leaders to work from the location that suits them best, organizations are banking on the concept that a happy workforce is a productive one. That being said, even a meeting scientist like Joe is still learning how to make it work.

In a recent hybrid meeting, Joe was asked about halfway through the session to lead a discussion of key issues affecting the reconstitution of in-person work with flexibility for remote workers. In other words, it was a discussion of hybrid work. Unfortunately, what was designed to be a strategy session was a glowing example of what not to do in hybrid meetings, because up to the point where Joe jumped in, the meeting leader had not done a good job of involving online and remote participants.

Joe started off with a best practice that we mentioned: he addressed the remote attendees first. He informed them that he would love to have their participation, and that he'd give them a minute to turn on their cameras and would ask for their input throughout the conversation. In fact, Joe was proud to lead by example by drawing attention to the virtual attendees – in essence, reminding everyone of *all* the people in the meeting room, physically and remotely. Joe then proceeded to discuss the challenges and opportunities that reconstituting in-person work would bring.

Joe might have continued to feel quite proud of himself had he not taken a look at the screen a couple of minutes later. Only one of the remote attendees had decided to turn on their camera. The rest remained black squares, even after the overt request to join in. He invited the one visible person to provide their input. During that person's responses and thoughts, another remote person's camera came on. Joe encouraged that person to share their ideas next, and then asked the in-person attendees for comments. None of the other 15 online participants turned on their camera or tried to chime in, even after yet another invitation.

Any guesses what went wrong? Well, first, it was the lack of setting expectations early that the meeting would involve participation from everyone, including online participants. The other meeting leader did not establish that ground rule, so Joe was in essence forced to try to change the rules in the middle of the game. Second, the online participants may not have even heard the invitation to participate, even though Joe asked multiple times. Why? They were likely multitasking with their cameras off. Third, and most importantly, no one in the room besides Joe had ever been trained on how to participate in a hybrid meeting where collaboration is expected. If you've made it to this point in the book, you know that virtual participants have a responsibility to help by trying to engage. But if they don't know they are supposed to do that, then why would they?

Hybrid meeting success isn't an endpoint but rather a journey. It's measured in milestones rather than ultimate goals. Therefore, in this final chapter, we want to give individuals and organizations an opportunity to consider what a good transition to a hybrid meeting environment might look like. In doing so, we'll also introduce our favorite reflection approach that any individual attendee or leader of hybrid meetings can use to help themselves and others decide what to do next.

In this chapter, we will explore:

- The signs of a healthy hybrid transition for organizations
- What individuals need to consider, both as leaders and attendees
- The adaptive improvement model
- What the future of meetings may look like

The Signs of a Healthy Hybrid Transition for Organizations

The first step in identifying whether you are transitioning well to hybrid work and hybrid meetings is to determine just how "hybrid" you want to be. It's not just a matter of figuring out the math problem of who comes in when and uses what desk. It's actually a philosophical question that should be pondered from the start. Take it from Lisette Sutherland, who offers this advice:

> If companies want to really make it work, they have to be really intentional about how they equip their employees and design their processes. The future of work is choice for the individual, but also choice for the company of where you want to be on the remote maturity scale. If you want to just do work from home for a couple days a week, that's very different systems and processes than if you were completely distributed, fully remote. I think companies need to determine where they want to be on the spectrum and then really focus on how do we make that work, because what we know is that we aren't all going to be going back to the office again.

Not only is it important to know where an organization wants to land on the hybrid spectrum, it's also imperative to assess where they are starting from. Moving a company to a hybrid model that traditionally links job performance to hours spent at a desk in the office will be more challenging than moving a company with a pre-existing policy that at least allowed for some flexible work. Whatever choice is made, any decision about adding hybrid options will likely require a whole new way of looking at how the organization does business.

"I think a values audit is a nonnegotiable part of the remote transition, because your values have to work without the crunch of an office," says Darren Murph, head of remote at Gitlab. If your values don't work outside of the office space, then they need be changed.

Once the values are gut-checked for the hybrid model, take a look at your workflows. Do they make sense now that work can be done in a variety of settings? Take this as an opportunity to question the use of procedures and even equipment that no longer fits into the hybrid reality. In the words of Darren Murph: "Use this as a permission slip to ask yourself, 'Why are we still using the fax machine?' Whatever the fax machine is in all of your different workflows, it's time to ask."

With so many facets of hybrid work that need to be addressed, placing someone in charge of overseeing the transition with a watchful eye on inclusivity for remote workers makes sense. The idea of creating a head-of-remote role has been gaining steam as companies seek to implement new processes and procedures that integrate with SOPs of old. And the transition won't happen overnight. In fact, it needs to be a multiyear plan, warns Darren: "This is a fundamental rearchitecting of what people assume and think about work and its integration with life. This is a fundamental rearchitecting of integration with digital tools. It's going to require someone's full attention if you want it to go well."

Indicators of a Healthy Transition

What does a healthy hybrid meeting and work transition look like for organizations? Well, there are quite a few potential indicators. We list some of them here with a few ideas on how you might measure them.

1. ***Overall Performance Is Maintained.*** One of the most important indicators of a successful transition is in the overall performance of employees, leaders, and their organization. Is it remaining the same or even increasing? If the answer is yes, then the transition to a hybrid work and meeting environment is going well. We'd advise organizations to use their internal assessment tools to benchmark key performance indicators (KPIs) before, during, and after a transition to see how things are going, and perhaps be an indicator of when more needs to be done to help people work well. Overall performance could be assessed at the individual, team, and organizational level. Possible interventions might mean assessing or adding new hardware and software, or providing more "skillware," deploying additional training to help people adapt.

2. ***Innovation in Collaboration.*** Another important indicator of a healthy transition would be seeing people meet differently than ever before, but also in a way that is inclusive and collaborative. We know that people will need to try new techniques, new tools, and new ways of meeting. This primes them for a more innovative interaction environment and could foster a more creative and innovative work situation. Organizations could assess this by looking at adoption rates of the new resources and tools provided for hybrid collaboration and meetings, as well as the increase in the generation of new ideas and creative solutions to ongoing challenges.

3. *Employee Engagement Is Maintained or Increased.* A final important indicator of a healthy transition would be a maintenance or increase in employee engagement. There are two reasons this might happen. First, effectively run meetings are known to facilitate increases in employee engagement (Allen and Rogelberg 2013). If organizations, their leaders, and employees embrace the best practices defined in this book, they should have better meetings and enjoy a precipitous increase in employee engagement. Second, effective hybrid meetings will be inclusive and allow people to be who they are personally and professionally, which is essential to employee engagement. In fact, the original theory of engagement came from William Kahn (1990), who asserted that engagement is all about bringing one's whole self into the task. Virtual meetings started to enable that by giving a window into people's homes, and that view of the employee as a full person, beyond just a role or title, became an input to innovation and performance on the job. Hybrid meetings may be able to maintain that and even unlock it further by providing the flexibility to be present no matter where you are. We'd advise organizations to check out their engagement surveys for the past few years and track them against the surveys generated during the transition to hybrid. Allow those measures to show you how the "suddenly virtual" environment and the eventual hybrid workplace impacted people.

If you are reading this book, we are assuming that you are at least curious about, if not an enthusiast for, hybrid work. However, we know this is not a universal feeling, and that is perhaps the biggest barrier to a smooth transition to hybrid. Your organization may have committed overall to include flexible work options, but there may be leaders within the organization who are not on board – leaders who may be unable or unwilling to let go of control over their employees' work location. Some CEOs in mid-2021 began demanding that employees plan on returning to the office, despite the data from pulse surveys indicating that a majority of employees were not ready to come back full-time to the brick-and-mortar building. In fact, in June 2021, articles began to pop up about the "Great Resignation" (Hsu 2021). People started to protest these demands to return to work in person by walking away from their jobs, declaring "I quit," and finding work elsewhere that allows for hybrid or even fully remote.

Thus, probably another barrier to a healthy transition is a lack of recognition of the reality of the transition. Sure, some employees won't be prepared to leave their jobs over it, but plenty are prepared to and indeed have left. The organizations who embrace flexible work schedules will likely attract those who have both the desire for control and autonomy as well as the ability to be self-motivated to get their work done. We call those folks "top performers" or "top talent," and they can find a job in any market, because they are good – *really* good – at what they do. There's a real danger in losing this type of employee. After all, no organization wants to be one that fails to attract and keep top performers simply by being unable to embrace the inevitability of hybrid work.

Individual Considerations for Leaders and Attendees

Beyond the somewhat backward mindset we just discussed among some CEOs and other leaders, there are other individual considerations that introduce challenges to the healthy hybrid meetings and collaboration transition. We'll discuss three of those here.

Challenge 1: Individuals Who Serve as Roadblocks

Across any organization, you'll find a variety of personalities that either help or hinder a transition. You may have seen evidence of this in the abrupt switch to virtual. Some employees adapted quickly to the change with a can-do attitude. Others were paralyzed by this very nontraditional way of working that was foisted on them. Individual demographic differences may make the transition to hybrid harder or easier, just like they made the transition to virtual harder or easier.

We are seeing a degree of self-selection occur where workers who do not want to learn how to thrive in the hybrid model are finding organizations that are choosing to stay in the traditional Monday-through-Friday, in-office model. We are also seeing people take early retirement instead of joining in on the collective challenge of learning a new way of working. Ultimately, a transition is easier when everyone is working toward a mutual goal, so this attrition occurring may actually be a help rather than a hindrance.

Challenge 2: Individual Unwillingness to Participate

Individuals will differ in their desire to put forth effort in hybrid meetings and in the new collaborative environments. Our biggest learning from the data shared and the experiences reported in this book is that a healthy transition to effective hybrid meetings is a team sport. That is, it requires both leaders and attendees engaging in the right behaviors to set the stage for and enable good meetings and inclusive collaboration. The leader cannot do it alone. Individual attendees are not without a responsibility for the success of their meetings. It takes everyone pulling together to get this cart over the next rise.

Challenge 3: Individual Inability to Adapt

For a successful transition to hybrid, there is a profound need for people to adjust to new and different circumstances and situations within the environment. At the individual level, we call it openness to experience. At the group level, we call it flexibility. At the organizational level, we call it agility and adaptation. The future of a hybrid workforce will be bright for those who build a trusting, cohesive, and inclusive collaborative environment that enables openness to new experiences, flexibility, and adaptation.

With the transition to hybrid, sometimes it may come down to tech savviness or at least a willingness to become better at it. For example, when Joe has a problem with his phone, he hands it to his 15-year-old daughter, who fixes it immediately for him. Sure, Joe could have figured it out eventually, but it takes his daughter a fraction of the time to make it right. Familiarity with technology and a willingness to learn new tools will enable or constrain the transition. Don't make the mistake of equating this to age. That's a stereotype that has not held up well during the pandemic, when many people's grandmas figured out how to video call with such expert fashion we wondered if the "old dogs can't learn new tricks" phrase is actually passé. However, there may be some people within an organization who simply aren't willing or wired to adapt or adjust as new things develop beyond the initial hybrid shift.

Resilience is needed now, and it will surely be needed in the future. A successful transition to hybrid creates a blueprint for a successful transition to whatever else comes next. There will continue to be disruptions. The question is: Will organizations institutionalize ways to cope and manage the disruptions, or will the disruptions eventually kill the organization? To guide you and your organization, we want to offer a tool you can use to better ensure you fall into the former category – a reflective exercise that can help you identify next steps wherever you are in the transition.

Looking in the Mirror: The Adaptive Improvement Model (AIM) Framework

Equipped with the knowledge that a healthy transition is achievable though barriers remain, we call your attention back to all those checklists from earlier in the book. If you completed them at that time, you've begun the process of looking in the mirror and reflecting on your own experiences and opportunities in your hybrid meetings. If you have not yet completed them, take a moment to turn back to those chapters, and proceed to reflect on your meeting experiences.

Armed with your reflections, you are now prepared to consider the adaptive improvement model (AIM). The adaptive improvement model is known by many other names in business, including continuous improvement and total quality management. However, AIM is meant to be applicable across all levels – meaning that individuals, teams, managers, and organizations could essentially use the same approach in a collaborative way. AIM requires the consideration of three key ideas: things to continue doing, things to stop doing, and things to start doing. For ease in describing AIM, we focus on the individual level, but one could just as easily replace "I/you" with "we/us" or even "our organization."

1. *Continue.* In the AIM framework, "continue" refers to those things that are happening or being done that you should keep doing. In essence, an individual should ask, "What am I doing in relation to my hybrid meetings that I need to continue doing?" Answers could include turning on the camera when remote, inviting others to participate, setting up a professional background, helping create team meeting ground rules, and

so on. The key idea here is that most individuals, teams, and organizations are doing some good and appropriate things that optimize their hybrid meetings and collaborative work environment. We mustn't abandon what is working, and perhaps we should even celebrate our efforts a bit. It's too easy to get down on ourselves when it comes to yet another thing to do, another challenge, and another transition. Thus, we start with a pat on the back. You're doing great! Keep it up!

2. **Stop.** In AIM, "stop" refers to those things that are being done that should not be done or should be stopped immediately to mitigate or remove hybrid meeting behaviors, processes, and procedures that are hampering effectiveness and even augmenting overall meeting fatigue and burnout. For example, an individual should ask, "What am I doing in relation to my hybrid meetings that I need to stop doing?" Answers might include:

- Stop ignoring the remote attendees
- Stop multitasking
- Stop hindering other's participation

The key idea here is that sometimes we engage in survival tactics when we are dealing with a challenging situation like back-to-back meetings with no recovery time, and our go-to tactics, which may include disengaging in the meeting and cleaning out the email inbox, are not helpful to the long-term function of the individual, team, or organization.

3. **Start.** "Start" in AIM refers to those things that individuals, teams, managers, and organizations need to start doing to further optimize their hybrid meetings. For example, an individual should ask, "What should I start doing to help improve my hybrid meeting experiences?" Answers may include a variety of the things contained in Chapters 5 through 11 but are likely unique to each individual, team, manager, and organization.

Signs of a Healthy Hybrid Transition

Building on the reflection checklists you just completed, you should identify things to start doing, consider the resources needed to make those solutions a reality, and ultimately plan ways to make all your meetings just a bit better. Trying to do too much at once sets you up for failure. Incremental change should be the cadence toward the ultimate goal.

Given these three sections of AIM, and having hopefully just completed some serious reflection on the provided checklists and your current situation, you are prepared (and perhaps your team with you) to complete the AIM worksheet provided here. Again, the goal is to complete each of the boxes, celebrate the things that you are doing well (*continue*), identify the things that need to end (*stop*), and commit to the things that need to begin (*start*). As you do this, consider the various opportunities and barriers to success. Doing so will ensure that foreseen barriers and opportunities for success are accounted for and integrated into the plan.

AIM WORKSHEET

CONTINUE

STOP

START

271

Signs of a Healthy Hybrid Transition

The Future of Meetings – Looking into the Crystal Ball

In our previous book, *Suddenly Virtual,* we predicted that hybrid meetings and hybrid work would become the future of our work lives. That might not seem so impressive now given hindsight, but at the time of our writing of that book, it was no easier back then than it is now to see what the future holds. Regardless, we believe the future really gravitates toward a few broad ideas, and we are confident that these will be helpful as you continue to navigate the hybrid meeting and working environment.

Prediction 1: How We Work and How We Meet Will Be Driven by Choice

We believe that remote work, hybrid work, and face-to-face work will continue; however, the breakdown of these work situations will probably never return to 2019 levels, because employees will continue to demand flexibility and organizations will accommodate this, at least in many cases. We also believe that meetings will be more diverse in terms of modality than ever before. We started to see that in June 2021, and, with time, we expect to see the number of hybrid meetings continue to increase.

Prediction 2: Organizations Will Prioritize Equipping and Skilling Up Employees for Better Meetings

Pre-pandemic, there were certain assumptions about meetings – there were too many of them, they were bad, and there was nothing anyone was going to do about them. The COVID-19 pandemic caused an equilibrium shift, and thus, the demand for tips, tools, tricks, and training on how to make meetings better has never been so high. We expect that in the near term, organizations will look for ways to provide hardware, software, and skillware for their employees to make the most of any kind of meeting. Karin's clients will continue to need coaching about being on camera and getting business done through a webcam. Meetings have always been at the heart of moving business forward, but little has been done to make them better. Organizations spend billions of dollars on meetings every year when you factor in the costs associated with salary/hourly wages, meeting space, technology, and opportunity cost (i.e. they could be doing something other than meeting) (Allen, Rogelberg, and Scott 2006). We believe the meeting disruptions that we've experienced have crystallized the need for quality improvement, and thus, organizations will focus on getting a better return on their investment.

Prediction 3: The Way We Communicate Before, During, and After a Meeting Will Be Multimodal and Continue to Evolve

Face-to-face meetings aren't going away. Virtual meetings aren't going away. Hybrid meetings linking the two are also here to stay. Organizations that aren't equipped to navigate all of them will find themselves at a competitive disadvantage. The pandemic reshaped how people communicate, personally and professionally, and created an expectation that there will always be choices in how to do so. Leading organizations will not fight that shift but embrace it for the opportunities it presents. Communication and collaboration without geographic boundaries mean a wider net can be cast in hiring employees, prospecting for new clients, and cultivating current customers. However, in order to harness all of the meeting channels, organizations will need to constantly assess what is working and what is not. Discard the technology or the process that isn't a good fit and find the right technology that supports and enhances the process that works. The AIM framework is designed for continuous improvement. We suggest putting the emphasis on *continuous*.

Conclusion

The transition to a hybrid meeting model may not be linear. In fact, it may resemble what we've seen in graphs representing the growth of the Dow Jones Industrial Average – a series of peaks and valleys, but over time, a general rise. As you and your organization move toward this hybrid meeting option that reflects flexible work, anticipate that there will be some backsliding that will likely require at least some tweaking, if not some revamping, of your plans. Look at the best practices and select a few to try to implement in your own sphere of influence. Remember to give them some time to prove themselves. Anything new demands an adjustment period. If you find they are not paying off, try another technique or process included in this book. Our sincere hope is you do not simply give up; rather, we expect you and your organization to thrive as you embrace hybrid meetings and make your organization more inclusive than ever before.

Chapter Takeaways

- The first step in the transition to hybrid meetings is for an organization to determine how hybrid they want to be so processes can properly reflect that.

- Consider a values audit to ensure processes can be made actionable both in the office and remotely.

- Look for indicators of a healthy transition by establishing metrics to measure it.

- Beware of internal obstacles to the transition that may undermine efforts.

- Use the checklists throughout this book as well as the AIM framework to assess the current state of your transition and to guide next steps.

- We predict the future of meetings will be:
  - Driven by choice
  - Focused on investment in training and technology more than ever before
  - Empowered by multimodal communication, which will allow for greater inclusivity

References

Allen, J. A., and S. G. Rogelberg. 2013. "Manager-led group meetings: A context for promoting employee engagement." *Group & Organization Management* 38 (5): 543–569.

Allen, J. A., S. G. Rogelberg, and J. C. Scott. 2008. "Mind your meetings: Improve your organization's effectiveness one meeting at a time." *Quality Progress* 41: 48.

Hsu, A. 2021. "As the pandemic recedes, millions of workers are saying 'I quit.'" NPR, June 24. https://www.npr.org/2021/06/24/1007914455/as-the-pandemic-recedes-millions-of-workers-are-saying-i-quit

Kahn, W. A. 1990. "Psychological conditions of personal engagement and disengagement at work." *Academy of Management Journal* 33(4): 692–724.

Conclusion: What to Focus on When the Future Still Seems Blurry

In so many ways, this book is still being written. Despite the name, the second major meeting disruption is not a sudden event, but rather a journey with a path that resembles switchbacks rather than straight lines.

As of this writing, countless companies have laid out their plans for a return to the office, often with flexible work options baked in, only to have those plans delayed by the COVID-19 pandemic's fits and starts. Policies and processes have been hammered out, only to be scrapped a short time later. Article upon article of what to try and what to avoid when transitioning to hybrid are populating news feeds on a daily basis – advice that is sometimes even contradictory. All the while, technology continues to evolve to support the future of work in whatever form that may be. Innovation at a somewhat frenzied pace is driving new software, new hardware, and new designs of physical spaces where teams can gather and connect. The perpetual state of change is dizzying for all who have felt like they've been shape-shifting since March 2020.

If you are looking for some solid ground amid all this uncertainty, we suggest this: focus on your people and tightening up team cohesion. By concentrating on the people in the hybrid meeting equation, you will be able to weather whatever the "next normal" is. The environment surrounding hybrid meetings may always – or at least certainly for years to come as organizations figure out what works and what doesn't – be in a state of flux, but one thing remains the same: teams that feel the most connected do their best work.

Meeting and team science supports this idea through a concept called "entitativity," which refers to how strongly people feel they are part of a team or group (McBride, Blanchard, and Allen 2020). In the hybrid workplace and in hybrid meetings, the higher the level of entitativity, the more positive outcomes you will find in metrics such as meeting satisfaction, effectiveness, and participation, as well as team cohesion. In fact, you could see each of these increase by about 25% if you were able to make improvements to enhance entitativity. That means that if you focus on your people, take care of them, make sure they feel included, and help them feel like they're part of the team, good things happen.

How do you make them feel like they're part of the team and create those connections that will better prepare and enable them for hybrid meetings? You do this in a hybrid way, of course, through experiences both remote as well as in person.

Remember the company Envato that has been hybrid from its inception? They prioritize in-person events called "Back to Base" meetings. Each quarter, employees spread all over the world come back to corporate headquarters in Melbourne for a week of team-building and socializing. Perhaps there is some shoptalk, but mostly it's not about work; instead, it's about fostering relationships in person that may largely have been built virtually.

Jay Hyett remembers those events well: "It was just the simplicity of going to grab a cup of coffee with a colleague you see on the screen all the time, or sharing some food or an experience of some sort. It was always great to see people going off to play mini-golf, having a laugh, and being human. There's only so many Zoom happy hours that you can go to."

Prior to our fully virtual world, companies may have hosted these kinds of in-person events off-site at a resort or corporate retreat.

They were designed to encourage employees to bond through shared experiences and social interactions.

While the purpose of these team-building retreats may remain the same, their setting in our post-pandemic world may change. The "Back to Base" version is one that we may see happening more and more often – an off-site that is actually on-site, where employees are brought together to soak in the culture from a corporate campus that typically doesn't host everyone at once.

"It may not be the most productive week," Jay explains. "But at the center of it was human connection – face-to-face opportunities to connect and collaborate with people you may see on the screen but not in person on a day-to-day basis."

But these opportunities to tighten team ties don't have to be reserved for quarterly or even yearly in-person events. When hybrid, focusing on team cohesion can become part of the regular routine of a company where experiences can be shared regardless of team-mate location.

At CaptionHub, they have adopted the Swedish tradition of *fika*, a designated time for employees to stop work and take a collective timeout to drink coffee, snack on sweets, and chat. In Sweden, what is often a mandatory coffee klatch can happen once or even several times a day, and is ingrained into its culture. In fact, a headline from the BBC explaining this practice pondered this question: "Is This the Sweet Secret to Swedish Success?" (Hotson 2016).

It may not be the secret to CaptionHub's success, but CEO Tom Bridges says it's certainly a way for their now-dispersed team to stay connected and avoid burnout at the same time: "The rule is: you take a break. You have some cake and you talk about anything apart from work. This is designed to replace those casual office interactions that I think all of us have missed to a greater or lesser extent."

Injecting humanity into the workday helps to combat feelings of isolation that can creep into the experience of those who are remote.

The videoconferencing platform provides a portal into the personal lives of our coworkers, a dynamic that continues to shape our professional relationships. Tom Bridges has found that experiences like the biweekly fikas have created a closeness even with members of his team whom he hasn't met in person yet. "I know the names of their children, and what they enjoy doing, because of things like these ad hoc interactions that I think make people feel part of the team. Humans are social creatures, and I think sometimes people forget that."

Perhaps that is one of the most important lessons learned during our "suddenly virtual" world that should be applied to our "suddenly hybrid" world. No matter how we meet, we as humans *need* to connect. We need to feel valued. We need to feel seen and heard. Hybrid meetings hold the promise to link the lives of all coworkers without borders. They can accommodate both those employees who love the hum of the office on a daily basis and those who strongly desire the flexibility of working at least partially remote. By keeping people and their well-being at the center of your hybrid meeting strategy, you are honoring that call, and that's a best practice that will not change.

As for the authors of this book, Joe and Karin hope one thing *will* change – the experience of actually seeing each other in person rather than through Zoom. That's right. After writing two books together, timing, travel restrictions, and virus variants have still kept these two tight colleagues from actually being in the same physical place at the same time. Just like so many organizations, Joe and Karin are eagerly awaiting the opportunity to incorporate face-to-face interactions into what has been a fully virtual relationship fostered over more than two years. But here's the good news – their ability to collaborate has not been hampered by the more than 2,000 miles that separate them. However, they look forward to their version of hybrid work where they can, as Lisette Sutherland would suggest, share a plate of nachos while celebrating their role in helping others find hybrid meeting success.

References

Hotson, E. 2016. "Is this the sweet secret to Swedish success?" *BBC Worklife.* Retrieved August 19, 2021 from https://www.bbc.com/worklife/article/20160112-in-sweden-you-have-to-stop-work-to-chat

McBride, A., A. Blanchard, and J. A. Allen. 2020. "Are we a group?: Entitativity matters in workplace meetings." Research accepted for the Interdisciplinary Network for Group Research's (INGRoup) 15th Annual Conference, July 30–August 1, 2020, Seattle, WA.

About the Authors

Karin M. Reed is the CEO and chief confidence creator of Speaker Dynamics, a corporate communications training firm, featured in *Forbes*. While speaking through a webcam might be new to much of the world, Karin has been teaching business professionals how to be effective communicators, both on camera and off, for nearly a decade, translating her experience as an Emmy-award-winning broadcast journalist into a methodology based on the *MVPs of On-Camera Success*. She has been quoted as a thought leader by various prestigious publications, including *Business Insider, Inc., Fast Company*, and The World Economic Forum and was featured by McKinsey & Company in their "Author Talks" series.

Her first book, *On-Camera Coach: Tools and Techniques for Business Professionals in a Video-Driven World,* was a #1 Hot New Release in Business Communications on Amazon in 2017. Her second book, *Suddenly Virtual: Making Remote Meetings Work,* written with Dr. Joseph Allen, was named one of the Best New Leadership Books of 2021 by Simon Leadership Alliance. It was adopted into the curriculum of the Graduate School of Business at Stanford.

Karin and her team have been the chosen training partner for some of the world's most recognized companies from Lenovo to Eli Lilly. To learn more about Karin and her team, go to www.SpeakerDynamics.com.

Joseph A. Allen, PhD, is a professor of industrial and organizational (I/O) psychology at the University of Utah. Before he completed his doctorate in organizational science at the University of North Carolina at Charlotte (UNCC) in 2010, he received his Master of Arts degree in I/O psychology at the UNCC in 2008 and his Bachelor of Science degree in psychology from Brigham Young University in 2005. His research focuses on three major areas of inquiry, including the study of workplace meetings, organizational community engagement, and occupational safety and health. He has more than 200 publications in academic outlets, another 20 under review, and many works in progress for a number of journals. He has presented over 300 papers/posters at regional and national conferences and given more than 100 invited presentations on his research. His previous academic outlets include *Human Relations, Human Performance, Journal of Applied Psychology, Journal of Occupational and Organizational Psychology, Journal of Organizational Behavior, Journal of Business Psychology, American Psychologist, Accident Analysis and Prevention, Group and Organization Management*, and others. He serves as a reviewer for various journals, including the *Journal of Organizational Behavior, Organizational Behavior and Human Decision Processes, Journal of Creative Behavior*, and *Academy of Management Journal*. He is an editorial board member for the *Journal of Business and Psychology, Group and Organization Management,* and the *European Journal of Work and Organizational Psychology*. He directs the Center for Meeting Effectiveness housed in the Rocky Mountain Center for Occupational and Environmental Health. Dr. Allen has consulted for more than 400 nonprofit and for-profit organizations, including animal welfare organizations, human services organizations, large corporations, government entities, and emergency safety and intelligence agencies, as well as retail conglomerates and external talent management firms. His research has attracted internal and external grant funding of more than $6.5 million since 2010. Dr. Allen's recent work can be found at www.joeallen.org and he can be reached at joseph.a.allen@utah.edu.

About the Authors

About the Website

Thank you for purchasing this book.

You may access the following additional complementary resources provided for your use by visiting: www.wiley.com\go\reed-allen\hybrid.

(Password: Hybrid123).

- Checklist 1 (Chapter 4): Questions to Consider When Deciding Camera On or Off

    With the explosion of meetings, many of them video meetings, video call fatigue has become a significant problem in the modern workplace. While using video when fully remote or joining as a virtual attendee is valuable, there are times when keeping the camera on has diminishing returns. This checklist is designed to help you identify when it is imperative to turn video on and when it is not in a virtual or hybrid meeting.

- Checklist 2 (Chapter 5): Meeting Participation

    Meeting participation is one of the most powerful factors in determining meeting satisfaction and effectiveness. In a virtual and hybrid meeting, participation equality can be harder to manage. This checklist allows you to assess meeting participation from a leader as well as attendee perspective.

- Checklist 3 (Chapter 6): Success Strategies for Leading a Hybrid Meeting

    Leading a hybrid meeting requires facilitation of a session with multiple communication channels and modalities. It can be a daunting task, but this checklist provides best practices for a meeting leader to follow to better ensure meeting success.

- Worksheet 1 (Chapter 7): Post-Meeting Postmortem

    This worksheet borrows from a process used by organizations that regularly engage in high-intensity activities that can be dangerous. (Think firefighters, military personnel, or nuclear power plant operators.) In order to move forward effectively, you need to look back to see what went right as well as what went wrong. This worksheet offers a framework for continuous meeting improvement that can be filled out as an individual or as a group.

- Checklist 4 (Chapter 8): Attendee Behaviors for Enabling Others to Participate

    While a meeting leader plays a pivotal role, attendees themselves also have a big stake in determining how effective a meeting can be. This checklist highlights behaviors attendees can exhibit to enable and encourage colleagues to participate fully.

- Checklist 5 (Chapter 9): Team Meeting Agreement

    Establishing ground rules for team meetings helps set expectations and codify best practices to which all pledge and choose to adhere. A team meeting agreement is designed to be co-created in a collaborative fashion with input from all stakeholders. This checklist offers some standardization for the process and serves as a discussion guide for teams as they develop policies that work best for them.

- Checklist 6 (Chapter 11): Hybrid Meeting Technology Considerations

  Hybrid meetings allow participants to attend using multiple modalities. In order for this to happen in an inclusive way, organizations need to have the infrastructure in place to enable presence for all and collaboration for all. This checklist includes general technology must-haves for a hybrid meeting that provide participation parity regardless of location. While it doesn't make product recommendations, it does focus on the most desirable features that you can look for in whatever is currently on the market.

- Checklist 7 (Chapter 12): Questions to Consider in Preparing a Hybrid Meeting Training

  Hybrid meetings require a complete rearchitecting of the way people prepare for, take part in, and follow up on their meetings. The new skills required are not innate but can and should be taught to avoid a potential performance drop. This tool lays out the six components of an effective training program for hybrid meetings with suggestions on what questions to consider during its creation.

- Worksheet 2 (Chapter 13): AIM Worksheet

  The Adaptive Improvement Model (AIM) is known by many other names in business, including continuous improvement and total quality management. However, AIM is meant to be applicable across all levels and requires the consideration of three key ideas: things to continue doing, things to stop doing, and things to start doing. This worksheet allows readers to bring them all together – identifying what they are doing well, what they should not be doing, and what they should do next.

Index